Japanese Women Artists

1600–1900

Japanese Women Artists
1600-1900

Patricia Fister

with a guest essay by Fumiko Y. Yamamoto

Spencer Museum of Art
University of Kansas, Lawrence

Cover: Noguchi Shōhin, *Women Practicing Arts in a Garden* (detail)

The exhibition and catalogue were made possible by generous grants from the National Endowment for the Arts and the Japan-United States Friendship Commission.

Exhibition schedule:

Spencer Museum of Art	April 2-May 22, 1988
Honolulu Academy of Arts	September 21-October 23, 1988

Designed by Janet Moore
Managing Editor Carol Shankel
Assistant Editors Don Dinwiddie and Karen Gerhart
Published by the Spencer Museum of Art
University of Kansas
Lawrence, Kansas 66045

Table of Contents

Notes to the Reader:

Throughout this catalogue, ages are given in Japanese count (adding about one year to the Western). In the text and bibliographical citations, we have adhered to traditional Japanese and Chinese usage by writing the surname first, except where a Japanese author has published in a Western language and adopted Western usage. In premodern Japan, the names of Japanese women were frequently followed by the Chinese character meaning woman, which is usually romanized *jo* or *me*. *Joshi*, the equivalent of Miss or Mrs., was also common. The character *ni* (nun) was often attached to the names of Buddhist nuns. To clarify that these feminine suffixes were not part of their given names, a space or hyphen has been inserted before them. For the romanization of Japanese words, we have used the system employed by Kenkyūsha's *New Japanese-English Dictionary*; for Chinese words, the Wade-Giles system. In captions, height precedes width. All dimensions exclude mountings.

Acknowledgements

The idea for an exhibition focusing on Japanese women artists was born many years ago, following several research trips to Japan during which I had been exposed to some of their work. Since then I have made further trips to Japan as well as to collections in the United States, and I am deeply indebted to the museums, temples, collectors, and dealers who made artworks available for me to study. The pleasures and rewards of seeing this project through from start to completion have been boundless. Among the greatest pleasures were the chances to explore new areas of Japan, the opportunities to share my thoughts with friends and colleagues, and the warm support which I received everywhere.

The exhibition and catalogue would not have been possible without the generous funding from the National Endowment for the Arts and the Japan-United States Friendship Commission, and I gratefully acknowledge their financial support. Additional support was received from the Mary Livingston Griggs and Mary Griggs Burke Foundation. My research has been supported by summer stipends from the National Endowment for the Humanities and the University of Kansas Research Allocation Fund, as well as travel grants from the Kress Foundation Department of Art History, the Hall Center for the Humanities at the University of Kansas, and the Northeast Asia Council.

I extend my deepest gratitude to those museums and individuals who agreed to lend to the exhibition. My debt to them is enormous. Stephen Addiss has been an enthusiastic supporter at all stages of the project, and I wish to thank him for his unstinting encouragement and guidance, as well as editorial comments on the manuscript. Joseph Seubert gave untiringly of his time and expertise, helping me to locate source materials in Japan and translating sections of one book. He and Midori Deguchi have been a tremendous aid to me in making the arrangements for the Japanese loans. Sasaki Jōhei and Kōno Motoaki have generously served as consultants, providing introductions and assistance during my research trips to Japan. I am also indebted to Roger Keyes and Tim Clark for their advice regarding women ukiyo-e artists, Louise Cort for her counsel on Rengetsu's ceramics, Hiroshi Nara for assisting the Museum by preparing documents in Japanese, and Susan Gronbeck-Tedesco for her suggestions on grant proposals.

In translating the Japanese and Chinese-style poetry written by women, I have received the assistance of a number of scholars. I wish to acknowledge the help of Fumiko and Akira Yamamoto, as well as the late Yabumoto Sōshirō, in reading and interpreting *waka*. I am especially grateful to Fumiko Yamamoto for her essay which is a significant addition to the catalogue. I would also like to thank Andrew Markus for his aid in deciphering the meaning of an inscription. For help in translating Chinese inscriptions I relied heavily upon Joseph (Tsenti) Chang, Wan Qing-li, and Kwan S. Wong. Grace Fong also kindly assisted in the interpretation and translation of a number of Chinese verses. I assume full responsibility for any errors that may remain.

Lastly I would like to express my sincere gratitude to the supportive staff at the Spencer Museum of Art. In particular, I wish to acknowledge the assistance of Karen Gerhart, curatorial intern, who has facilitated my work by helping with all aspects of the preparation of the manuscript and exhibition. I am also grateful to the Honolulu Academy of Arts for hosting the exhibition in Hawaii.

Patricia Fister
Curator of Oriental Art
Spencer Museum of Art

Introduction:
The World of Women in Japan, 1600-1900

Between 1600 and 1900, a dramatic flowering of women artists occurred in Japan. Yet these women lived in a society that theoretically limited their every move. What did talented women do when they were enmeshed in a structured social order? What outlets were open to them? One of the goals of this exhibition and catalogue is to lead toward an understanding of women artists of these three hundred years in relation to the political, social, and economic conditions in Japan.

During the Edo period (1600-1868), so named because the capital was the city of Edo (present-day Tokyo), Japan was ruled by a series of shoguns from the Tokugawa family. This shogunate provided more than 250 years of peace and security after the country had been devastated by civil wars for almost a century. The stimulation of Japan's industry and commerce led to the growth of large urban centers and a materialistic culture, a trend that had begun in the preceding Momoyama period (1568-1600). The townspeople benefited the most from the rise in economic prosperity, and the living standards of merchants and artisans rose dramatically. The early decades of the seventeenth century also saw a rapid expansion of Japanese activity abroad, due to the shogun's enthusiastic promotion of foreign trade. However, by 1640 a seclusion policy was put into effect which virtually closed the country to the outside world. This policy was adopted in part to stop the influx of Christianity, which was linked with foreign aggression and thus threatened the power of the shogunate. No foreigners were permitted into Japan except authorized Chinese and Dutch traders, and Japanese were forbidden to make voyages abroad.

Early in the seventeenth century, Tokugawa Ieyasu (1543-1616) enforced the division of the populace into four major social classes. In descending order they were: samurai, farmers, artisans, and merchants. Excluded from these four classes were members of the imperial family and the aristocracy (who retained their high status), and the clergy. Mobility within the system's framework was restricted; in theory no man could rise above the class into which he was born. Samurai were the most privileged class and received fixed annual stipends based upon the rice harvest in their domains.[1] Second in rank, theoretically, were farmers, because agriculture was the basis of the national economy. In reality, however, the life of the peasants was usually wretched as they were continually oppressed by the feudal lords controlling the land they toiled upon. Artisans and particularly merchants soon came to enjoy the greatest prosperity, even though they were relegated to the lower positions on the social ladder.

What happens to a society when it is restricted and isolated in this fashion, and at the same time is enjoying a period of peace and prosperity? In Japan, education and cultural values became very important; since the country was no longer at war, people had more time and energy for creative expression. Without external stimulation, the Japanese began to look internally, leading to new developments in art and literature. The government responded by instituting a system of education that led to a rapid spread of learning and literacy among all classes.

The new peace and prosperity with increased education and high respect for culture, combined with the lack of other opportunities, spurred Japanese artists to extraordinary achievements. Patrons of art existed at many levels of society, with different classes cultivating arts to express their own views and interests. The Edo period is now celebrated as an age of great artistic ferment and diversity. The renaissance in the arts included a significant increase in the number of women artists, a remarkable feat considering the tight restrictions placed upon their lives. Under certain conditions, women did break away from the socially approved role of wife and mother. The succeeding essays will illuminate the ways in which cultivated women rose above what was expected of them and won an honored standing in art and literature.

Economic and Social Position of Women

The position of women in Japan was a lowly one under the patriarchal system which became entrenched after 1600 when Japan was unified under a feudalistic government. Prior to the ninth century, however, the descriptions of female deities in myths, and the numerous women rulers indicate that the status of women was similar to that of men.[2] However, the feminine image suffered drastic changes as a result of the influences of Buddhism, Confucianism, and the growth of feudalism. Many Buddhist texts taught that women's nature was inherently evil, associating them with attachments to the sensual world as opposed to the spiritual realm. Some texts went as far as to declare that women had no hope for salvation until their rebirth as men.[3] Consequently, once Buddhism began to permeate the fabric of Japanese society, the status of women began to deteriorate.

The position of women declined even further in Japan after the adoption of the Chinese philosophy of Confucianism. From the seventeenth century on, the Tokugawa government fervently promoted Confucian teachings which generally regarded women as inferior to men, reinforcing the doctrines of Buddhism. The lowliness of women was a fundamental principle of Confucianism, which had originated in the strict Chinese patriarchal society. This idea was elaborated in the metaphysical theory of *yin* and *yang*, central to the Neo-Confucianism which flourished in Tokugawa Japan.[4] *Yin* and *yang* are the two principles whose interaction is responsible for the creation of the universe: *yang* is the positive, bright, male principle, and *yin* the negative, dark, female principle. A husband and wife therefore symbolized *yang* and *yin* or, in broader terms, heaven and earth. In moral instruction books for women we find the words "A woman regards her husband as heaven. She must respect and fear him."[5] Other Confucian texts stressing male superiority also include the following:

> Woman has the quality of *yin* (passiveness). *Yin* is of the nature of the night and is dark.
> Hence, because compared to man, she is foolish, she does not understand her obvious
> duties . . . She has five blemishes in her nature. She is disobedient, inclined to anger,
> slanderous, envious, stupid. Of every ten women, seven or eight will have these failings.
> In this respect she falls short of man . . . Therefore, since she is foolish, in everything she
> must submit to her husband.[6]

Such texts were widely disseminated, and consequently Confucian attitudes came to prevail in Japan. Since women were considered inferior, moralists urged them to deport themselves with humility and to accept the guidance of their wiser male relatives. Economically, a woman was dependent first on her father, then on her husband, and eventually on her son.[7] Within the feudal structure, a woman's purpose in life was to marry and produce heirs to safeguard the family succession. Depending on social class, most women were married between the ages of fifteen and twenty-five. Marriages were arranged by families; the upper levels of society frequently used daughters as tools in manipulating political or financial relationships. The Momoyama and Edo periods were eras in which *seiryaku kekkon* (political marriages) were notorious. This custom was practiced especially by feudal lords, who when arranging peace treaties with hostile parties, often contracted marriages between members of their respective families as guarantees of good faith. Under the guise of marriage, women were used as hostages, and in numerous cases, they were divorced from one husband and married off again according to their family's wishes in order to expedite another relationship. Because of the deceptions carried out in these political marriages, warnings were issued maligning women's sincerity, causing their image to sink even further.[8]

A husband's power over his wife was almost absolute. Limitations were placed upon her physical activity, and she was discriminated against with regard to property and divorce.[9] A husband could easily secure a divorce by writing a short statement of his intention,[10] and the *shichi-kyo* (seven reasons for divorcing a wife)[11] were reiterated in moral instruction books. A woman's only recourse in an intolerable marriage was escape. There were a few so-called temples of divorce (*engiriji*) which were permitted to give distressed wives sanctuary, and if they could show sufficient reason, to negotiate divorces for them.[12] Adulterous women were dealt with severely, and the *Tokugawa hyakkajō* contains the following regulations: "A wife who commits adultery shall be put to death with the man involved" and "it is no crime for a husband to kill an adulterous wife and her partner if there is no doubt of the adultery."[13] Women were encouraged to remain within the home, even to the extent of forgoing religious ceremonies at temples and shrines. Special permits, which were difficult to procure, were required for them to travel beyond the confines of their hometown. In short, women were virtually devoid of legal rights during the Edo period.

The restrictions for women outlined above were promulgated by members of the samurai class. Although the common people were expected to follow the samurai norms, there is evidence that they did not always draw such sharp distinctions between the rights of men and women in their everyday lives. Women from peasant, artisan, and merchant classes were often given greater responsibility and participated more actively in the family occupation. Because peasant women did work that was regarded as important, to some extent they shared power with their husbands.[14] Women of the merchant class also retained greater freedom than samurai women. They were often called upon to assist in running the family business, and at times went beyond merely helping their husbands and became imaginative entrepeneurs. The most famous example may be Shuhō (1590-1676), who managed her husband's pawnbroking and *sake* business with such success that she laid the foundation for the fortunes of the Mitsui family.[15]

Women of the merchant class often had enough money and leisure to become accomplished in the arts, to visit the theater, and to dress fashionably. Their boldness and indulgence in hedonistic pleasures are documented in the plays of Chikamatsu Monzaemon (1653-1724) and the novels of Ihara Saikaku (1642-1692) and Ejima Kiseki (1667-1736).[16] Although there was never a full-fledged movement (which would have been quickly stifled), there was a growing spirit of rebellion amongst some women during the Edo period. One of the earliest and most outspoken female critics of the feudal society and the restrictions placed on women was Tadano Makuzu (1763-1825). The daughter of a Sendai physician, Makuzu grew up in a scholarly environment. She became an avid student of both Japanese and Chinese literature, and associated with scholars of Dutch studies. In her writings, Makuzu promoted Western ideas, believing that women were being held back by Japanese social mores. She wrote to the famed novelist Takizawa Bakin (1767-1848), asking for his assistance in getting her work published; although he was impressed with her writing, he replied that her criticisms were taboo and thus her manuscripts unpublishable. Nevertheless, in 1817 Makuzu did get an essay printed entitled *Hitori kangae* in which she voiced some of her opinions.[17]

For the most part, such avant-garde ideas fell on deaf ears in Edo-period Japan. However, there is evidence that by the nineteenth century, patriarchal authority had begun to wither in some families. One finds increasing numbers of women beginning to marry without parental permission, or refusing matches arranged by parents, especially among women of the merchant class.[18] Popular literature and theater illuminate some of the changes that took place in the image of women and their lifestyles. In the nineteenth century, novels and kabuki plays regularly featured "bad women" who flagrantly disobeyed Confucian edicts, and also portrayed tormented female ghosts who had been maligned by their husbands. The success of such stories indicates audiences' fascination with a "new" type of woman, and their sympathy for those who were mistreated. Women were no longer viewed as simple, one-dimensional human beings. As they became educated and rose to greater prominence in society, women were conceived as multidimensional characters, capable of displaying a range of emotions and performing evil deeds as well as good.

Despite the seeming shift in public view, women did not attain equal rights in the Edo period. Feudalistic ideas had so thoroughly permeated Japanese society that it was not until the overthrow of the Tokugawa government in the succeeding Meiji period that Japanese women saw a change in status.

Influence of Moral Instruction Books

In order to teach women their proper role in life, over one thousand books on moral instruction were published during the Edo period.[19] Although literature of this nature can be found from the Muromachi period (1336-1573) on, these books began to be printed in large quantities from the beginning of the eighteenth century. All were based upon Chinese prototypes, the earliest of which, entitled the *Lieh-nü chuan* (J: *Retsujo den*, Series of Biographies of Women), was written in the Han dynasty.[20] The Japanese expanded greatly upon these moral tracts. This literature, deliberately aimed at creating the type of woman convenient for the smooth functioning of the feudal system, can basically be divided into two types: *jinbutsu setsuwa* (human stories) using famous historical women personalities as moral examples, and *tokumoku sekkyō* (advocating virtues) employing direct admonitions.[21] Both types, permeated with Confucian ideas about women's inferiority, focused on women's responsibilities in the home. The earliest publications were verbose and difficult to read, but later they were shortened and written in a simpler style of script which most women could understand.

Whereas in China most of the moral instruction books had been by women, in Japan they were primarily written by men. This was partly due to the fact that in Japan, men received better educations, and hence were the first to be able to read and interpret foreign literature. Furthermore, it was men who wanted to keep women in their place. Many of the important Confucian scholars of the Edo period wrote moral essays for women, including Nakae Tōjū (1608-1678), Kumazawa Banzan (1616-1697), Yoshida Shōin (1831-1860), and Sakuma Shōzan (1811-1864).

The Japanese scholar most influential in defining the role of women was Kaibara Ekken (1631-1714). His *Onna daigaku*[22] (Greater Learning for Women) became a part of nearly every Japanese household, and its "wisdom" became the primary educational text for women. In many cases, it was the only book that they were expected to read. Consequently, the principle it expounded of *danson-johi* (predominance of men over women) was thoroughly embedded in the psychology of Japanese society. Conditioned from childhood to regard herself as lowly and to recognize her proper realm of responsibility as the home, the Japanese woman was forced into a subordinate niche. The feminine ideal of this age can be summed up as obedience and self-effacement.[23]

Education and Women

In general, women were not encouraged to assert themselves intellectually; more important were practical skills of household management along with sewing and weaving. The majority of girls receiving any education were tutored at home, using the accepted books on moral instruction which emphasized the cultivation of virtuous qualities. The Confucian attitude toward education of women was quintessentially summed up by the statesman Matsudaira Sadanobu (1758-1829) who wrote: "A woman does not need to bother with learning; she has nothing to do but be obedient."[24]

Learning to read was not forbidden, but officials were divided in regard to the most appropriate literature for women. Some scholars such as Kumazawa Banzan felt that women should concentrate on the Japanese classics, consisting of poetry and novels of the Heian period (794-1185) such as the *Genji monogatari*. This literature was written primarily in the native phonetic syllabary which was much easier to master than Chinese characters. Other scholars, the foremost of which was Kaibara Ekken, strongly resented the wide popularity enjoyed by the *Genji monogatari*, considering the work low in moral tone and totally unfit for young women's perusal. Kaibara set forth guidelines on the education of women in his *Wazoku dōjikun*[25] which may be summarized as follows: Up to the age of seven, girls were to be instructed in the same way as, and together with boys; but beyond that age they were to be segregated. Thereafter, they were to be taught reading and writing principally through the medium of *kana* syllabary, while they were also to learn to make supplementary use of Chinese characters. They were to commit to memory ancient poems of a classical type, to become acquainted with the primary Chinese classics, and also to read treatises on women by orthodox scholars. After the age of ten they were not to be allowed to go outside their homes, where they were to be taught sewing, weaving, and arithmetic at the same time that their attention was directed to household economics.

It is clear that as long as women remained under the yoke of this sort of teaching, there was little chance for them to freely develop their talents. Those women who acquired significant literary skills were cautioned not to make any outward display of their knowledge. Matsudaira Sadanobu cited a number of Chinese examples to prove that "When women are learned and clever in speech it is a sign that civil disturbance is not far off."[26]

There was a general shift in educational trends at the end of the eighteenth century which had some effect on the type of instruction women received. In the seventeenth and early eighteenth centuries, education had been primarily the prerogative of aristocrats and high-ranking samurai. However, by the late eighteenth century some fiefs had begun to show concern for the wider education of their subjects, which led to the establishment of village schools or *gōgaku*.[27] To be sure, the feudal lords who encouraged study among the people in their fiefs usually had the motive of improving moral standards rather than the desire to raise the intellectual level of the populace. Nevertheless, popular education proceeded with official approval, and toward the end of the eighteenth century Japan witnessed a rapid expansion of schools for commoners called *terakoya*.[28]

Village schools served practical and vocational needs, providing training in the basic skills of reading, writing, and arithmetic. These schools varied considerably in size; the average *terakoya* had about thirty pupils.[29] The teachers were generally local priests, doctors, well-to-do farmers, or village officials. Although schools were established with teaching boys in mind, girls were also permitted to attend. Statistics are hard to establish, but at the time of the Meiji Restoration in 1868 it is estimated that forty percent of boys and ten percent of girls in Japan were acquiring some kind of formal education outside of their homes.[30] This percentage may seem small, but it represents a significant rise over the preceding centuries. The ten percent figure for girls is, in fact, surprisingly high considering the social structure of Edo-period Japan.

Furthermore, by 1800, children of merchants or well-to-do farmers could enter one of the numerous private schools (*shijuku*) specializing in Chinese studies and/or Japanese classics which had been established primarily for samurai.[31] As a result, in the nineteenth century, successful merchants and village headmen were often as learned as the average samurai, and literacy continued to spread at the lower levels of society. This led to a boom in the publishing business, which responded with woodblock-printed books of all types ranging from medical treatises, travel guides, novels, and poetry collections to storybooks for children.

Young women who attended schools received a much more extensive education than had been the case previously. As more women became literate, writers responded by creating special books for this new audience beyond the traditional moral tracts. In the first half of the nineteenth century, several novels were published which were aimed specifically at women.[32] Most popular were stories put out in serials about women's secret loves and sexual adventures. Since so many women had now mastered at least the native Japanese syllabary, publishers found this new market a lucrative commercial enterprise. Literacy made it possible for women to be aware of things outside their own immediate experience, and it was one of the few means they had to escape from social pressures. It allowed women to conceive of lifestyles that differed from those they were familiar with, and in some cases it must have encouraged them to explore possibilities hitherto off-limits to women.

Women in Literature and Art

There is a definite correlation between the vast expansion of the educational system and the broadening range of roles for women. This is illustrated by the dramatic increase in the number of women artists active in the nineteenth century. Although women of the elite classes (noble and high-ranking samurai families) continued to practice the arts during the Edo period, it was primarily women from lower-level samurai and townsmen families who achieved recognition as artists. Members of these latter classes tended to favor educating their daughters, either through private tutors or by sending them to school. The success of women was thus closely linked with the type of education they received and the literary skills they developed.

The great majority of Japanese women artists were also talented poets. There is a long tradition of women active in literature in Japan, beginning with Murasaki Shikibu who wrote the *Genji monogatari* around the year 1000. It was also during the Heian period that many court ladies became highly skilled in the form of poetry known as *waka*. Fujiwara no Kintō (966-1041) included several women in his compilation of poems entitled *Sanjūrokuninsen*, representing Japan's thirty-six great poets. There are many parallels which can be drawn between women active in the arts during the Heian and Edo periods, eras both characterized by closed-door policies and a flourishing of indigenous culture. Because so many women of earlier ages were renowned for their novels, diaries, and *waka*, the Edo-period literary world was prepared to accept women; in effect, literature was one of the few sanctioned intellectual outlets open to women.

Following the dictums of Japanese Confucian treatises and moral instruction books, *waka* was initially considered the literary form most appropriate for women. The first recognized women poets of the Edo period were members of the court nobility or upper samurai class, who as part of their general education received training in *waka*. However, as education began to filter down into the lower echelons of society and more and more women became literate, their literary possibilities increased. Some women became active in haiku and Chinese poetry societies, and others wrote novels and travel diaries. In fact, women writers seem to have been so much in vogue in some circles during the eighteenth and nineteenth centuries that several important male teachers began to especially encourage female pupils.[33] A testimonial to the popularity of pre-modern women authors are the hundreds of published books written by them.[34]

Once they had achieved recognition as poets and authors, it was easier for women to gain entrance into the art world, in which there was a great deal of respect for those with literary talents. Painting and poetry were not considered to be two distinct art forms in traditional Japan, but instead were frequently united. It was common for artists to write poems on their paintings, or to request a friend to add an inscription. On the other hand, those who were primarily poets often took up the brush and painted. Following in the footsteps of their male colleagues, many female poets, particularly those skilled in haiku or Chinese poetry, developed artistic talents which earned them praise. This extremely strong link with literature is thus an important feature of art by Japanese women when viewed as a whole. Very few women were simply painters, as was common in the male-dominated art world. In comparison with men, the possibilities for women interested in the arts were severely limited; the two principal schools of painting which allowed creative women into their ranks were *bunjinga* (see chapters six, seven, and ten) and ukiyo-e (see chapters three and eight) which were not bound to any established cultural tradition.

The Impact of the Meiji Restoration on the Lives of Women

New opportunities unfolded for women after the Meiji Restoration in 1868, when Japan opened up its doors and allowed Western ideas to flow in. Japanese society underwent the transformation from a semi-feudal to a modern state, heralding important changes in the status of women.[35] The abolishment of the feudal system meant the dissolution of the samurai class and the establishment of basic legal equalities for all people. Despite some resistance, the status of women slowly began to improve. Special schools for girls were created in response to the growing demand for educational reform. Following Western models, in 1872 a national system of compulsory education was initiated by the new Meiji government which required that both boys and girls of all classes must enter school at the age of six.[36] Nevertheless, because of dominant conservative forces, it took several decades before women were given primary and secondary educations equal to those of men and had access to higher education. Among the avid supporters of women's rights was Mori Arinori (1847-1889), who promoted learning for women and a single standard of morality. The famous educator Fukuzawa Yūkichi (1834-1901)[37] also supported equal opportunities for women. Laws which discriminated against women were gradually repealed, and by the mid-twentieth century women came to enjoy more social and political equality.

Several of the women represented in this exhibition lived into the Meiji era, which was characterized by greater opportunities and gradual public recognition of women's rights.

Noguchi Shōhin (1847-1917) was appointed professor of painting at a women's school in 1889, and later became an official artist for the imperial family. She and other women painters actively submitted works to domestic and international expositions, a practice that was clearly borrowed from the West. Women also became members of large art societies created by the government. All of these factors indicate the growing acceptance of women who practiced art as a profession.

Although they may have found it difficult to break away from the norm dictated by Confucian moralists, the women represented in this exhibition were far from ignored in their day. Many of them earned the plaudits of their male peers and rose to prominent positions in both literary and artistic circles. Their names are listed alongside men in such publications as the *Heian jinbutsu shi* (Who's Who in Kyoto) in sections on artists, poets, and musicians. Compared with most women of their day, these women led unconventional lives. The following essays will focus on each of the ten sections of the exhibition, discussing the social and cultural milieu of the different categories of women and introducing major artists.

Notes

1. There were many levels of samurai; the shogun and high-ranking feudal lords called daimyo formed what can be termed a samurai elite class, while under them were middle- and low-ranking samurai.
2. Empresses of Japan include Suiko (r. 593-628); Kōgyoku (r. 642-645), also reigned under the name of Saimei (r. 655-661); Jitō (r. 686-697); Genmei (r. 707-715); Genshō (r. 715-724); Kōken (r. 749-758), also reigned under the name Shōtoku (r. 764-770).
3. For more information on Buddhist attitudes toward women, see Diana Y. Paul, *Women in Buddhism*.
4. Joyce Ackroyd, "Women in Feudal Japan," 53.
5. From the *Onna daigaku*. Quoted from Ackroyd, 53.
6. Ibid., 53-54.
7. This reflects the Chinese doctrine of the *sanjū* (three obediences) which was incessantly preached: "A woman has no way of independence through life. When she is young, she obeys her father; when she is married, she obeys her husband; when she is widowed, she obeys her son." From the *Lieh Tzu*. Quoted from Ackroyd, 57.
8. Ackroyd, 50.
9. Earlier in Japanese history, during the Kamakura period (1185-1333), women were legally permitted to own property. Daughters inherited property under the same conditions as sons, and it was common for husbands to leave their estates to their widows. However, the picture changed in the succeeding Muromachi period, an age of weakening central authority and warring feudal states. Clans depended heavily upon their material strength for survival, and struggled to keep their land holdings intact. Instead of dividing property up amongst all the children, the estate was usually bequeathed in one piece to one son named as chief heir. Ackroyd, 38-45.
10. These letters of divorce were known as *mikudari-han* (three lines and a half) indicating their brevity.
11. These stated that a wife could be divorced for disobeying her husband's parents, for failing to give birth to a son, for gossiping, for stealing, for jealousy, for loose conduct, and for disease.
12. Ackroyd, 65.
13. Ibid., 58.
14. Miyashita Michiko, "Noson ni okeru kazoku to kon'in," in Josei Shi Sōgō Kenkyū Kai, *Nihon josei shi*, vol. 3, 31-32.
15. Mary R. Beard, *The Force of Women in Japanese History*, 109-111. For further information on the role of women in the Mitsui family, see Hayashi Reiko, "Chōka josei no sonzai keitai," in Josei Shi Sōgō Kenkyū Kai, *Nihon josei shi*, vol. 3, 96-105.
16. For example, see Saikaku's *Kōshoku gonin onna* (Five Women Who Loved Love), *Kōshoku ichidai onna* (The Life of an Amorous Woman), and Kiseki's *Seken musume katagi* (Characters of Worldly Young Women).
17. For more information on Makuzu, see Seki Tamiko, *Edo kōki no joseitachi*, 117-137.
18. Ibid., 18.
19. Ackroyd, 53. The *Joshirō ōrai mono bunrui mokuroku* lists 1,109.
20. This book by Liu Hsiang contains 110 episodes, including acts of virtuous women as well as examples of women who had caused dynasties to fall. A similar type of book published in the late Han period called the *Nü chieh* (J: *Jokai*, Women's Admonishments) was written by Pan Chao, the daughter of a Confucian official. She allegedly wrote it for her daughter in order to prepare her for marriage. The Japanese scholar Kitamura Kigin translated the former book and published it in 1655 under the name *Hiragana retsujo den*. See Kakei Kumiko, "Chūgoku no *jokun* to Nihon no *jokun*," in Josei Shi Sōgō Kenkyū Kai, *Nihon josei shi*, vol. 3, 292.
21. Ibid., 290.
22. This book represents a compilation of Kaibara's writings which was put together and published after his death. For English translations, see Basil Hall Chamberlain, *Japanese Things* (Rutland, Vermont and Tokyo: Charles E. Tuttle Co., Inc., 1971), 502-508, and Takaishi Shingoro, *Women and Wisdom of Japan*.
23. As Joyce Ackroyd points out, the subservient treatment of women was a concomitant of feudalism everywhere. One has only to compare Japanese books of ethics with the book of the Chevalier de la Tour Landry for the instruction of his daughters, written around 1371-1372, which includes the phrase "words of authority belong to the husband, and the wife's duty requires that she listen in peace and obedience." See Ackroyd, 67-68.
24. Ackroyd, 56. Quoted from Takamure Itsue, *Josei no rekishi*, vol. 2, 268.
25. The following summary of guidelines was adapted from Naruse Jinzō's "The Education of Japanese Women," in Ōkuma Shigenobu, *Fifty Years of New Japan*, 194.

26. Ackroyd, 268.

27. R.P. Dore, *Education in Tokugawa Japan*, 31. See also Herbert Passin, *Society and Education in Japan*.

28. Dore, 253. The word *terakoya* reflects the fact that in the sixteenth and still much of the seventeenth century, Buddhist temples (*tera*) were the main centers of formal education. *Terako* (temple children) came to mean simply pupils and *terakoya* came to refer to schools, which were usually rooms in private homes or temples.

29. Most were individual enterprises run by a single teacher, sometimes helped by his wife and one or two senior pupils. Sometimes a teacher was brought in as a cooperative endeavor by people living in the village.

30. Dore, 254.

31. For more information on these private schools, see Richard Rubinger, *Private Academies of Tokugawa Japan*.

32. Jinbo Gobi, "Kinsei bungaku to joryū," in Yoshida Seiichi, ed., *Nihon joryū bungaku shi*, 6.

33. For example, the haiku poet Matsuo Bashō (1644-1694), the *kokugaku* scholar and poet Kamo no Mabuchi (1697-1769), and the scholar of Chinese studies, Rai San'yō (1780-1832).

34. For a comprehensive listing, see Joshi Gakushūin, *Joryū chosaku kaidai*.

35. For an in-depth discussion, see Koyama Takashi, *The Changing Social Position of Women in Japan*.

36. For further information, see Naruse, 203-213. See also Passin, chapter 4.

37. Fukuzawa wrote two essays denouncing the *Onna daigaku* as behind the times: *Shin onna daigaku* (New Greater Learning for Women) and *Onna daigaku hyōron* (A Critique of the Greater Learning for Women). Naruse, 222.

7. Yukinobu, *Murasaki Shikibu* (detail)

13. Ryū-jo, *Courtesan Viewing Cherry Blossoms* (detail)

23. Ōhashi, *Waka on Decorated Paper*

34. Raikin, *Landscape with Fisherman*

清風高露浄孤芳只見東籬占晩涼珠用偏
宜黄吟手去宋都珊珊悟念此中点立原氏
如春川詩画

39. Shunsa, *Chrysanthemums and Rock*

61. Kakuju-jo, *Kanadehon Chūshingura*

75. Rengetsu, *Mizusashi*

81. Seiko, *Cranes*

Seventeenth-Century Women Artists

Chapter One: **Noblewomen Artists**

Many of the recognized women artists of the seventeenth century were members of the upper echelons of the samurai class, often allied to the imperial court. As stated in the introduction, these women led the most restricted lives of all women in the Edo period, confined to their homes and the inner quarters (ō-oku) of castles or palaces, where they devoted themselves to "womanly" pursuits set forth in treatises like the *Onna daigaku*. Their main function was to serve their husbands or fathers, to raise children, and to manage household affairs.

If women were members of the court nobility or the upper samurai class, however, they had servants who performed the routine household duties.[1] This allowed them a certain amount of leisure time which they spent enjoying various pastimes and amusements. One was dressing and adorning themselves according to fashion standards of the day. There were prescribed types of clothing for all members of an aristocratic or elite samurai household, indicative of their status. Apart from daily wear, garments for special occasions and ceremonial functions were also important. Judging from the elaborate textiles that have been preserved, as well as those shown in genre paintings and woodblock-printed books depicting the activities of noblewomen, a tremendous amount of thought was put into the selection of fabrics and the combinations in which they would be worn for a wide variety of occasions.

Another pastime considered appropriate for women was the game of incense identification (kō-awase). Incense was introduced into the realm of amusements centuries earlier during the Heian period, and it grew into an elaborate game replete with its own special accouterments. To properly enjoy the incense game, women would set out a large beautiful lacquer box, containing as many as twenty different utensils and smaller boxes. The incense was placed on tiny wafers and burned, whereupon the participants would try to distinguish the type and submit "ballots" with their choice.

Card games were also popular; the most famous consisted of cards with poems written on them representing each of the one hundred classical poets of Japan. The reader would be provided with a hundred cards, each bearing the name of one of the poets and the opening line of the corresponding poem. Another set of one hundred cards with the closing line of each poem was scattered on the floor in front of the competitors. To play this game, the reader would recite the opening line of a poem from her set of cards, and the participants would vie with one another to find the card with the correct closing line. The winner was the person who made the most correct matches, and thus this game was a true test of literary skills.

A similar game was played with shells (kai-awase). Two identical sets of 180 shells were required, each with a different miniature painting on its smooth interior. The paintings were taken from well-known poetry anthologies like the *Kokinwakashū* or popular works of classical literature like the *Genji monogatari*. One set of shells was placed face down before the players, while the shells from the other set were exposed one at a time so that each painting could be seen.[2] The players then tried to find the matching shell from the other set by turning over these shells one at a time. Since they were turned face down again if there was no match, the competitors needed good memories. The woman who discovered a shell's mate would be awarded the pair of shells, and the player with the most shells at the end of the game would be declared the winner.

The board games *go* and *shōgi* were also favorite diversions of women, and lavish lacquer sets were a customary component of a well-born bride's trousseau in the Edo period. Another form of entertainment was Nō drama, brought into the castles, where women could attend. This traditional performing art enjoyed widespread popularity among members of the samurai class, and Nō drama came to occupy an official ceremonial function during formal receptions.

1. *Noblewomen in a Daimyo's Castle*
   From the *Ehon imayō sugata*, 1802

For the wives and daughters of the upper class (shogun, court nobility, and daimyo), personal artistic interests could be indulged only when they did not interfere with family duties, but we know that some of these women did devote considerable time not only to reading but also to writing poetry. Women born into high-ranking families were likely to receive training in calligraphy and in composing the traditional Japanese form of poetry known as *waka*.[3] These skills enhanced their femininity and were considered essential to women of their stature. An illustration in the 1802 *Ehon imayō sugata* (Figure 1) depicting the inner quarters of a daimyo's castle shows a wife with her attendants busily engaged in literary activities.

A position as lady-in-waiting at the imperial palace in Kyoto or in one of the many castles in Japan was considered very prestigious for samurai-class women, and consequently families competed with one another to secure posts for their daughters. Not only did such a post make a woman more attractive as a marriage candidate, but it might also strengthen the political and economic position of her family. Several women represented in the exhibition served as attendants in the imperial palace or in a daimyo's castle. One of the beneficial aspects of such positions for them personally was that they were surrounded by other cultivated women and had a certain amount of time to devote to artistic pursuits. Two seventeenth-century women, who were widely recognized for their literary and calligraphic skills, are Ono Ozū and Ryōnen Gensō.

Ono Ozū (1559 or 1568-1631)

The confusion surrounding the biography of the woman known as Ozū or Otsū is staggering. To begin with, scholars are divided as to how her name should be pronounced. The character nowadays usually read *tsū* seems originally to have been pronounced *zū*.[4] Secondly, there are many conflicting versions of Ozū's biography,[5] as well as her birth and death dates.[6] The identity of her father is unclear, although the most knowledgeable scholars seem to believe that he was Ono Masahide, the lord of a fief in Mino (Gifu prefecture) who was an ally of Oda Nobunaga (1534-1582).[7] When Masahide was killed in battle in 1562, Nobunaga allegedly took pity on the young child and had her placed in the care of his attendants. Ozū later went to Kyoto where she took up the study of many arts, including *waka* with the high-ranking noble Kyūjō Tanemichi (1507-1594). As a result of her burgeoning talents, she was welcomed into aristocratic circles. Ozū was not only skillful at composing poetry, but she also became adept at calligraphy, painting, music (playing both wind and stringed instruments), and the tea ceremony. A portrait of her holding a *shamisen* appears in a later compendium of famous Japanese women (Figure 2).

There are diverse reports about Ozū's activities in Kyoto: some biographers relate that she became a lady-in-waiting to Yodogimi (1567?-1615), the beloved concubine of Toyotomi Hideyoshi (1536-1598); others say that she was an attendant of Hideyoshi himself. Almost all sources agree that Ozū married Shiokawa Shima no Kami, a retainer of the Toyotomi family, although the year is unknown. Because of her husband's humiliating drinking habits, Ozū later obtained a divorce from him and went off on her own, supporting herself by tutoring high-born young ladies.[8]

Ozū's talents attracted the attention of Tokugawa Ieyasu, who apparently summoned her to Suruga (Shizuoka prefecture) to give instruction to his wife and daughter. While in his service, Ozū's prowess as an artist was also recognized, and on the occasion of Ieyasu's seventy-second birthday, the second Tokugawa shogun Hidetada (1578-1632) requested her to do a portrait of his father.[9]

Ozū was held in such high regard that when arrangements were made for Hidetada's daughter Sen Hime (1597-1662, later known as Tenjuin) to marry Toyotomi Hideyori (1593-1615) at Osaka Castle, Ozū was asked to accompany her. According to some biographies, Ozū also served Shinjōtōmon'in (1545-1620), the mother of Emperor Go-Yōzei, and Hidetada's fifth daughter, Kazuko (later known as Tōfukumon'in, 1607-1678). Kazuko was married to Emperor Go-Mizunoo in 1620 at age fourteen.[10] She served as a model for high-ranking women of her era because of her connections with both the shogun and the emperor as well as her cultural accomplishments. Kazuko herself became a fine calligrapher, perhaps under the guidance of Ozū.

Although Ozū actually may not have held all of these august positions, it is clear that she was far from an ordinary lady-in-waiting. She was in demand because of her literary talents, which extended to an early form of *jōruri* (chanting),[11] and she most likely acted as a poetry and calligraphy teacher to the women she served. Examples of Ozū's writing were disseminated in several woodblock-printed books which were used as models for young women to copy.[12] There is no question that her style of calligraphy was extremely influential upon upper-class samurai women of her day,[13] and her elegant script was to remain popular for close to 150 years.

The fact that Ozū lived through the tumultuous Momoyama and early Edo epochs may account for the veil of confusion encompassing her life. It was an age of bloodshed, with provincial feudal lords battling one another for power. Families were broken up by warfare and records were lost or destroyed, resulting in a paucity of accurate documents. According to existing accounts, Ozū may have served all three of the great warlords who united Japan: Nobunaga, Hideyoshi, and Ieyasu. To gain their recognition was no easy feat for a woman, indicating the extraordinary status that Ozū attained.

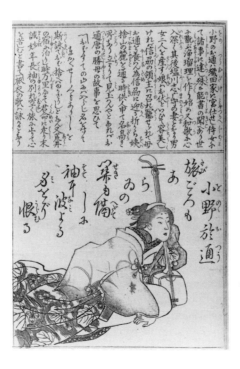

2. *Ono Ozū*
From the *Teisō setsugi kokin meifu hyakushu*, 1881

Ryōnen Gensō (1646-1711)

Like Ono Ozū, Ryōnen was born into a prominent family, but in her case the information is more reliable.[14] The period in which she lived was definitely a more stable one, for by the middle of the seventeenth century the Tokugawa family had quelled any signs of rebellion and established a firm base of power. Ryōnen's father was Katsurayama Tamehisa (1600-1673), a descendant of the famous warrior Takeda Shingen (1521-1573); her mother was a member of the noble Konoe family. As a child in Kyoto, Ryōnen followed her mother's example and served at the imperial court. Since her mother was an attendant of the imperial consort Tōfukumon'in, Ryōnen became a companion of Tōfukumon'in's grandchildren. She learned various arts and accomplishments at this time, including calligraphy and *waka* poetry.

As was customary, Ryōnen entered into an arranged marriage at the age of seventeen or eighteen; her husband was the Confucian scholar and doctor Matsuda Bansui (1630-1703). Although accounts differ, they apparently had several children. In 1672, after ten years of marriage, Ryōnen made the momentous decision to leave her family and become a Zen nun.[15] Her husband was apparently agreeable, and after arranging for a concubine to take care of her family, Ryōnen entered the Kyoto temple Hōkyōji which was headed by Emperor Go-Mizunoo's daughter. Dissatisfied with a "women's temple," after six years at Hōkyōji Ryōnen went to Edo for more intensive Zen study.

In Edo Ryōnen first visited Kōfukuji to have an audience with the Ōbaku Zen monk Tetsugyū (1628-1700), who rejected her by saying she was too beautiful to enter his temple where she would be a distraction to the other monks. She received the same response from the Ōbaku monk Hakuō (died 1682) at Daikyūan. Since her physical beauty was holding her back from the Zen training she desired, Ryōnen responded by burning her face with a hot iron that left her with a permanent scar. This drastic action made her famous, and it was memorialized by a woodblock illustration (Figure 3) in the *Kinsei meika shogadan* (Famous Calligraphers and Painters of Recent Ages, second series, Edo, 1844).[16] Hakuō was so impressed at Ryōnen's dedication that he allowed her to enter his temple; she became his leading pupil, earning her certificate of enlightenment in 1682.

Hakuō died in that same year, and Ryōnen determined to build a temple in his honor. It took time to obtain permission, but in 1693 she was granted some land in Ochiai, just outside of Edo, and there she renovated an old temple called Renjōin. Hakuō was posthumously named founder of the new Renjōin, and Ryōnen became the second abbot.

Ryōnen's temple, later called the Taiunji,[17] became a center of learning, and children from the nearby villages came to receive their educations. Ryōnen herself became celebrated for her achievements in poetry, calligraphy, and painting, and she stands along with Ono Ozū as one of the outstanding women artists of the seventeenth century. Although their styles of brushwork were quite different from each other, they both represented the aristocratic tradition of their time.

3. *Ryōnen Burning Her Face*
   From the *Kinsei meika shogadan*, 1844

1. Ono Ozū (1559 or 1568-1631)

Hotei and Child, 1624
Hanging scroll, ink on paper, 86.3 x 45.5 cm.
Signature: Ono-shi Zū-jo shoga
Yanagi Takashi Collection
Published: Kuroda Tōtōan, ed., *Cha kake kanshō* (Tokyo: Kōgei Shuppan, 1972), 129.

Ono Ozū has been most celebrated as a calligrapher, but her paintings are also highly admired. They are somewhat rare and usually depict figures accompanied by calligraphic inscriptions; in addition to Hotei, portraits exist by Ozū of Daruma, Hitomaro, and Kitano Tenjin.[18] These were all subjects often painted by Zen monks, while Hitomaro and Kitano Tenjin have literary connections as well.[19] Ozū's own literary interests make her choice of the latter two figures easy to understand, but it is mysterious that she should choose to render primarily Zen subjects in a simplified ink style. There is no indication that she ever studied Zen Buddhism. One might have guessed that she would be drawn to the more colorful, decorative style of painting practiced by professional court artists. Instead she seems to have been influenced by the works of Konoe Nobutada (1565-1614), a prominent Kyoto court noble active in the same period.

Nobutada was known as a great calligrapher who revived the rugged strength of early styles. After becoming a pupil of the Zen monk Takuan Sōhō (1573-1645) at Daitokuji, he began to create ink paintings in the rough, bold style traditionally associated with Zen.[20] Ozū's style of brushwork recalls that of Nobutada, with thick gray lines dominating. Since Nobutada's favored subjects were Daruma and Kitano Tenjin, she was apparently influenced by him in subject matter as well.[21]

In this painting, Ozū has depicted Hotei leaning sleepily on his large bag, gazing fondly at the small child standing at the left.[22] The child reaches out to touch the bag with both hands, his curiosity brimming over. Because of Hotei's good luck connotations and his love of children, this type of painting would be especially appropriate to display on Boys' Day, the fifth day of the fifth month. The poem also alludes to children:

Yoshiashi no	Not knowing of
Koto no wa shiranu	"Goodness" or "evil,"
Mitori ko o	The young child
Tomo to suru mi zo	Is taken as a companion
Sukashi karikeri	By this pure spirit.

Ozū has written the poem from left to right, the opposite of standard practice in China and Japan. In doing so, she was influenced by a tradition associated with Zen painting in which the inscriptions were written in the direction opposite to that which the figure faces. Since Hotei is facing left, Ozū began her poem at the left and moved toward the right.

Ozū's brushlines in both writing and painting are primarily curvilinear, rarely displaying sharp angles or ragged edges. Particularly in her calligraphy, the lines range from thick and full to wiry and threadlike, exhibiting extreme changes in width for dramatic effect. Characteristic of her writing are the attenuated flourishes of the brush, especially in strokes forming the long vertical of the syllable *shi*. Ozū may have been trained in the aristocratic tradition of the Shōren'in school of calligraphy (also known as the O'ie tradition) which was founded by Prince Son'en (1298-1356) in Kyoto.[23] However, the fluency and elegance of her script established a new precedent in calligraphy styles, which came to be known as "Ozū *ryū*."

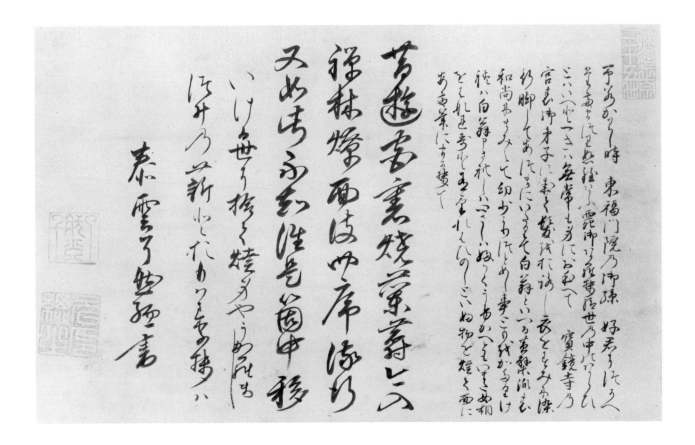

2. Ryōnen Gensō (1646-1711)

Autobiographical Poems
Hanging scroll, ink on paper, 27.9 x 44.6 cm.
Signature: Taiun Ryōnen kinsho
Seals: Rinzai shōshū sanjūgodai; Ryōnen; Gensō no in
Shōka Collection
Published: Addiss, "The Zen Nun Ryonen Gensho," *Spring Wind–Buddhist Cultural Forum*, vol. 6, nos. 1-3 (1986), 182.

Ryōnen is primarily recognized for her skills in both *waka*[24] and the Chinese-style poetry which she occasionally wrote out in her bold, distinctive script. She also painted portraits of important Ōbaku Zen abbots,[25] probably for use in temple ceremonies. Examples of her brushwork are rare; this calligraphy begins with a short autobiographical prose passage, followed by her two most famous poems composed upon burning her face, the first a Chinese quatrain and the second a *waka*.

> When I was young I served Yoshinokimi, the grand-daughter of Tōfukumon'in, a disciple of the imperial temple Hōkyōji. Recently she passed away; although I know that this is the law of nature, the transience of the world struck me deeply and I became a nun. I cut my hair and dyed my robes black, and went on a pilgrimage to Edo. There I had an audience with the monk Hakuō of the Ōbaku Zen sect. I recounted to him such things

as my deep devotion to Buddhism since childhood, but Hakuō replied that although he could see my sincere intentions, I could not escape my womanly appearance. Therefore I heated up an iron and held it against my face, and then wrote as my brush led me:

Formerly to amuse myself at court I would burn orchid
  incense;
Now to enter the Zen life I burn my own face.
The four seasons pass by naturally like this,
But I don't know who this is amidst the change.

Ikeru yo ni	In this living world
Sutete taku mi ya	The body I give up and burn
Ukaramashi	Would be wretched
Tsui no takigi to	If I thought of myself as
Omowazariseba	Anything but firewood.[26]

Ryōnen's Japanese-style writing, seen in both the prose section and *waka*, bears some resemblance to the style of Shōkadō Shōjō (circa 1584-1639), who was one of the most gifted calligraphers of the seventeenth century.[27] In particular, their calligraphy shares a suppleness combined with nervous energy. Hair-fine characters contrast with more thickly brushed ones, all written in rich black ink.

Ryōnen wrote out the Chinese quatrain in a somewhat larger and thicker script, causing it to be the center of focus. The brushwork forming the characters is rounded and flowing, showing stylistic traits of calligraphy by Ōbaku Zen monks. In particular, the manner in which her horizontal strokes curve downward to the left recalls the writing of Ōbaku Ingen (1592-1673). Yet Ryōnen's writing exhibits a personal intensity and vigor which is purely her own. The full range of her calligraphic skills are exhibited in this unique combination of Japanese prose, *waka*, and Chinese-style poetry.

3. Ryōnen Gensō

A Single Lump of Iron
Hanging scroll, ink on paper, 77.5 x 15.2 cm.
Signature: Taiun nidai Daikyū Ryōnen kinsho
Seals: Rinzai shōshū; Mumei betsu azana Hakumei
Private collection

Bold and forceful single lines of calligraphy are an important genre of Zen brushwork; many examples were written to be hung in a Japanese *tokonoma* alcove during the tea ceremony. Because of the striking simplicity and the meditative nature of the messages, such large-character calligraphy was highly praised and sought after by tea enthusiasts.

Examples of single lines by Zen nuns are extremely rare, making this work by Ryōnen exceptional. The reason for their scarcity may be accounted for by the fact that traditionally, large-character calligraphy was brushed only by Zen abbots, and Ryōnen was one of the few women who achieved this position. Single lines commonly consist of a phrase of five or seven Chinese characters, often steeped in complex Zen meanings. The five characters here can be translated "Everything is contained in a single lump of iron." This phrase was not invented by Ryōnen, but was a well-known Zen expression. Interpretation of such Zen maxims is difficult, but the meaning underlying these five characters relates to one of the goals of Zen Buddhism–to reach a state of mind in which one is completely self-contained with no imperfections. It refers to a primordial state of being, where elements are undifferentiated. This phrase may have had special significance for Ryōnen because of her rejection at first because she was a woman; the reference to iron may also allude to the incident of burning her face.

The large-scale rendering of the characters creates a bold visual statement which does indeed cause one to stop and contemplate the meaning. Ryōnen's characters show traces of Ōbaku influence, although not as prominently as in her smaller script. Here she has exploited the technique known as "flying white," letting the brush run dry while moving it quickly in order to let areas of white paper show through the ink. The resulting rough, dry texture of the "flying white" areas contrasts nicely with more heavily inked ones, creating a work which is visually as rich as its Zen meaning.

Notes

1. The wives, daughters, and concubines of the shogun, high-ranking feudal lords, and members of the imperial court were surrounded by women attendants of various rankings. There were 250 women attendants living in the *honmaru* of Edo Castle, and another 125 serving in the *nishi no maru*. For an explanation of the hierarchical order of women attendants, see Tsubota Itsuo, ed., *Nihon josei no rekishi*, no. 2 (*Shogun to daimyō no fujin*), 140.
2. This is very similar to a modern card game called "Concentration."
3. Composed of thirty-one syllables arranged in five lines of 5-7-5-7-7.
4. In the collection of Sanboin at Daigoji there is a *tanzaku* poem sheet signed "Zū," with voiced consonant marks added over the *hiragana*. In addition, vol. 2 of the 1685 *Kōeki shoseki mokuroku* contains a list of calligraphy manuals which includes the *Ono no Zū tehon*, once again exhibiting a voiced consonant mark. See Komatsu Shigemi, ed., *Nihon shoseki taikan*, vol. 13, 238.
5. Iwahashi's article "Ono Otsū shū den" in *Rekishi chiri* gives an extensive outline of the different versions of her life, noting the sources and quoting the information which they give. Unfortunately, scholars are not able to confirm many of the facts. I have relied primarily on Sudō Motome's *Ono Otsū* since he has written the most extensively on Ozū.
6. Her birthdate is given as 1559 or 1568, and deathdate as 1616 or 1631. The 1631 death date is more feasible, since there are two paintings extant bearing the date 1624. See Cat. 1.
7. Other biographies state that she was the daughter of Ono Izumi from Mito, or the daughter of Naganuma Kichibei who was later adopted by Ono Noto. However, both Komatsu and Sudō believe that she was the daughter of Masahide.
8. She may have remarried or become a concubine, but accounts differ widely. According to some biographies she also had a child.
9. This portrait is in the collection of Zōjōji in Shiba. Ozū had previously painted a portrait of Hideyoshi which is kept at Kōdaiji in Kyoto.
10. This was a political move by her father, the second Tokugawa shogun, who wished to strengthen ties with the imperial family. When Emperor Go-Mizunoo abdicated, Kazuko became a Buddhist nun and adopted the name Tōfukumon'in.
11. One of the other controversial accomplishments of Ozū is her authorship of the *Jōruri junidan sōshi*. Prior to Ozū's time, this story had been chanted to the accompaniment of a *biwa*. It was Ozū's idea to use a *shamisen*, and she was assisted by Sawazumi Kengyō who helped set the tale to new music. Some consider this to be the origin of *jōruri*, but modern scholars question Ozū's role.
12. These books include *Johitsu tehon nisatsu Ono Tsū-jo*; *Ono no Zū tehon*; *Ono Otsū tehon*; *Ono Otsū ryū den so*; *Johitsu haru no nishiki: Ono Otsū*. See Maeda Toshiko, "Ono Otsū," *Nihon bijutsu kōgei*, no. 389, 44.
13. Komatsu has noted that Yodogimi's handwriting shows the strong influence of Ozū. See *Nihon shoseki taikan*, vol. 13, 238.
14. The most comprehensive sources of information on Ryōnen's life are Mori Senzō, "Ryōnen-ni" and Nagata Tairyō, ed., *Shijitsu Ryōnen-ni*. For an English language article, see Stephen Addiss, "The Zen Nun Ryonen Gensho."
15. In her decision to enter the Zen life, Ryōnen may have been inspired by her two younger brothers who had become Zen monks.
16. The illustration is by Kō Ryūko (dates unknown) after a design by Hishikawa Moronobu (circa 1618-1694).
17. In 1701 the Renjōin was expanded and became a full monastery called the Taiunji.
18. For reproductions, see Komatsu, *Nihon shoryū zenshi*, vol. 2, 161-162.
19. Kakinomoto Hitomaro (active circa 685-705) was a famous court poet, and Kitano Tenjin is the deified name of Sugawara Michizane (845-903). Michizane was a scholar, poet, and distinguished government minister who died in exile as a result of false charges brought against him by a rival. After his death he came to be considered as a god of poetry and art, and Shinto shrines dedicated to him can be found all over Japan.
20. Nobutada and the Daitokuji monks he associated with were all actively reviving Muromachi-period Zen styles. For more information on this revival, see Stephen Addiss, "The Revival of Zen Painting in Edo Period Japan," *Oriental Art*, vol. 31, no. 1 (Spring 1985), 50-61.
21. Nobutada's daughter, Tarokimi, also did ink paintings of Zen subjects which were heavily influenced by her father. This indicates that the Zen ink painting tradition became popular among amateur painters of the court, a phenomenon undoubtedly incited by Nobutada and the prestige attached to his work.

22. An almost identical painting which is dated to a different month of 1624 is in the Burke Collection; however, the poetic inscription is different. This painting is reproduced in the exhibition catalogue published by the Tokyo National Museum, *A Selection of Japanese Art from the Mary and Jackson Burke Collection* (Tokyo, 1985), no. 75.
23. According to Torie Shōji's *Isetsu machimachi*, she was a pupil of Matsuura Iwami, a practitioner of the Son'en style. The *Hisseki ryūgi keizu*, published in the mid-nineteenth century, lists her as a follower of Emperor Go-Yōzei, who although trained in the Shōren'in tradition, sought greater diversity as he matured. See Maeda, "Ono Otsū," 44.
24. Ryōnen wrote a collection of *waka* entitled *Wakamurasaki* in 1691 which no longer exists.
25. Ryōnen's portraits of Ingen and Mokuan are in the collection of Hōdenji. For reproductions, see Nagata, *Shijitsu Ryōnen-ni*, 62.
26. Both poems and the prose passage were translated by Stephen Addiss.
27. Shōkadō had turned away from the prevailing Shōren'in tradition and revived the styles of such Heian-period calligraphers as Ono no Michikaze, Fujiwara no Yukinari, and Fujiwara no Teika. His own calligraphy represents an integration of a wide range of stylistic influences.

Chapter Two: Atelier Professionals

Professional artists during the Edo period were by and large males, for this occupation was not considered fitting for women who were expected to fulfill certain household duties. Two exceptions were Kiyohara Yukinobu (1643-1682) and Sasaki Shōgen (active late seventeenth-early eighteenth century) who became famous for their painting and calligraphy, respectively. Both were the daughters of artists, which played a critical part in their breaking away from the traditional role of women. The fathers of Yukinobu and Shōgen encouraged their daughters' artistic talents and permitted them to adopt this male-dominated vocation.

What was it like to work for a professional workshop in Japan? The Kano school, with which Yukinobu was affiliated, was by far the largest and most influential painting atelier in Edo-period Japan. Its origins extend back to the fifteenth century when Kano Masanobu (1434-1530) secured a position as an official painter to the Ashikaga shogunate. His son Motonobu (1476-1559) expanded on Masanobu's teachings to create the orthodox Kano style, and instituted an atelier system organized around a familial structure which insured the perpetuation of the school.[1] Throughout the four centuries of its history, the Kano school was favored by the patronage of leading feudal lords and government officials. The heads of the Kano school cultivated increasingly close ties with the controlling figures of the day; this led to the creation of an organization of artists who worked within a complex hierarchical system.

Stimulated by the appointment of three leading Kano artists (Tan'yū, Naonobu, and Yasunobu)[2] as *oku-eshi* or "painters of the inner quarters of Edo Castle" in the mid-seventeenth century, the Kano atelier evolved into a vast network which spread throughout Japan. The title of *oku-eshi* was a prestigious one, for the Tokugawa shogunate presented designated artists with generous stipends and property which could be passed on to heirs along with their titles. Furthermore, *oku-eshi* were also permitted in the presence of the shogun and allowed to wear double swords, privileges ordinarily extended only to members of the samurai class.

One step lower than the *oku-eshi* and their schools were many ateliers run by the branch houses of relatives and students who were allowed to establish independent workshops. They constituted the middle level of artists within the hierarchy of the Kano school, and were called *omote-eshi* or "official painters." *Omote-eshi* also received commissions from the shogunate as well as from daimyo, but they were not allowed to wear double swords, and their stipend was not hereditary although the succession of property was permitted.

In response to the needs of well-to-do townsmen, a third group of Kano artists came into existence called *machi-eshi* or "town painters." Most *machi-eshi* were students from one of the various Kano ateliers. In general they used their own family names, but there were a few exceptions who were allowed to use the Kano surname. As time went by, countless numbers of *machi-eshi* appeared, comprising the bottom layer of the Kano school organization.

The proliferation of the different levels of Kano workshops succeeded in safeguarding the family's dominant position in the artistic world of Edo-period Japan. Official status, gained through connections with the Tokugawa family and other daimyo, was central to the survival and success of the Kano school. For the most part, Kano artists were remarkably consistent in maintaining and transmitting the family tradition, and the style associated with the Kano name changed very little throughout the two-and-a-half centuries of the Edo period. This remarkable feat was accomplished through guidelines such as those set forth by Kano Yasunobu (1613-1685) in his *Gadō yōketsu* (1680). This text stressed the importance of preserving the stylistic norms of the Kano tradition and passing them on accurately to future generations.[3] Creativity was considered of secondary import, and cultivation of personal styles was discouraged. Yasunobu described in detail the correct styles and methods of painting, the manner of handling and moving the brush, and even the quality of paper and inkstones. Through these kinds of guidelines, the Kano style was codified. Artists who were not able or willing to follow these precepts were forced to abandon their affiliations with the school.

The structure of a Kano atelier was classified into master (family head), senior, and junior assistants. Assistants were most commonly the sons or relatives of the master. If gifted family members were lacking, new talent was adopted into the family. Commissions were contracted through the master and then parceled out to his assistants. Wages were proportionate to an artist's status within the atelier.[4]

Not all Japanese ateliers were as formally structured as those which functioned within the orbit of the Kano school. Many artists ran small operations, with only one or two apprentices. As a matter of course, sons (and more rarely daughters) learned the family trade and took over when their father retired. The two women included in this chapter represent the divergent poles of professional artists. Whereas Yukinobu worked successfully as a member of the vast Kano school network, Shōgen followed her father's example and established herself as an independent calligrapher.

Kiyohara Yukinobu (1643-1682)

Kiyohara Yukinobu was one of the rare women painters affiliated with the Kano school who achieved recognition in her day.[5] Her father was Kusumi Morikage (circa 1620-1690), and her mother Kuniko was a niece of the *oku-eshi* Kano Tan'yū.[6] Morikage was one of Tan'yū's most outstanding pupils, who for reasons unclear left the Kyoto Kano atelier between 1675 and 1680 and went to work for the Kaga clan in Kanazawa. Yukinobu lived in Kyoto for most of her life, and married another pupil of Tan'yū named Kiyohara Hirano Morikiyo. Tan'yū undoubtedly played a role in arranging Yukinobu's marriage, as he had done previously with her parents. The fact that Yukinobu, her mother, and grandmother were all married to Tan'yū's pupils is evidence of the strong familial bonds characteristic of the Kano school and of Japanese culture in general.[7]

Yukinobu probably first studied painting with her father Morikage, but there is reason to believe that she also took lessons from her great-uncle Tan'yū,[8] perhaps studying together with her husband. Since Yukinobu's style is extremely close to that of Tan'yū, it seems that he had the greatest influence upon her development as a painter. Tan'yū's popularity reached its peak in the second half of the seventeenth century, and therefore it is understandable that Yukinobu would want to emulate him.

As a professional Kano painter, Yukinobu produced works of great variety on formats ranging from large screens to hanging scrolls and small albums. She was trained in the academic Chinese styles used for painting landscapes, birds and flowers, and figures. Depending on the subject and format, she would employ a formal descriptive mode or informal cursive mode of brushwork, the former being most common. In addition, Yukinobu was adept in the decorative Japanese style known as *yamato-e* which was traditionally used for rendering narrative tales or portraits. Certain works by Yukinobu represent a synthesis of Chinese and Japanese styles, a feature also apparent in some of Tan'yū's paintings.

Like most Kano painters, Yukinobu's thematic range was diverse. What distinguishes her from her colleagues is the high percentage of paintings depicting women: most prominent are colorful portrayals of famous Chinese beauties. Yukinobu also painted Buddhist deities, Chinese figures, portraits of Japanese classical poets (often female), scenes from Japanese narrative tales, birds and flowers, and, more rarely, landscapes. Her style can be described as jewel-like, exhibiting meticulous linework and delicate application of opaque colors as well as light washes. Occasionally she would paint in a bolder manner primarily with ink, exemplified by the pair of screens in the exhibition (Cat. 4).

Most of Yukinobu's works are painted on silk and mounted as hanging scrolls, suggesting that she was most comfortable with this format. There is no record that she participated in any large-scale wall decoration in which labor was divided among atelier members. Although Yukinobu was certainly as skillful as other Kano artists of the day, smaller paintings were probably considered more suitable and ladylike. Social norms would also have prevented her from traveling to the site of a castle or temple in order to assist in painting sliding door panels and other architectural decoration. Within a Kano workshop, smaller commissions such as scrolls were executed by one artist who, depending upon his or her rank, would stamp on it either the master's or a personal seal. The fact that there are so many extant paintings signed and sealed with Yukinobu's own name implies she had achieved enough fame that patrons specifically commissioned works to be done by her. In his novel *Kōshoku ichidai otoko* (The Life of an Amorous Man), Ihara Saikaku relates a story in which the Kyoto courtesan Kaoru commissioned a painting from Yukinobu.[9] Yukinobu's unusual position as a female Kano artist surely contributed to her success, for owning a painting by a woman would have been a novelty in the seventeenth century, especially when it showed the high level of skill and refinement that Yukinobu possessed.

Sasaki Shōgen (active late seventeenth-early eighteenth century)

Sasaki Shōgen was as celebrated for calligraphy as Yukinobu was for painting. Shōgen's father was the eminent Kyoto calligrapher Sasaki Shizuma (1619-1695) who developed a personal style of writing called "Shizuma *ryū*." Shōgen married a retainer of the Takakura family named Awazu Shinanonosuke.[10] The year is unknown, but after her husband's death Shōgen became a nun.[11] To occupy her time she began to teach calligraphy like her father, and before long she had become famous enough to have scores of pupils, among them noblemen and women such as the princess Hōkyōji no Amamiya (1725-1764).[12] Unlike Ono Ozū (see chapter one), Shōgen did not serve the shogun or the court in any official capacity. She was purely a professional calligrapher who gave lessons to people of all classes. She probably taught most students in her own home or studio,[13] but proper etiquette would have required her to go to the homes of her upper-class pupils. It is doubtful that Shōgen operated any sort of atelier, but as a calligraphy master she would have received many requests from patrons for examples of her writing. Any moderately well-to-do family in Edo-period Japan would have enjoyed having scrolls of famous Chinese or Japanese texts or poems to display in their homes. Would-be patrons sought out artists whose style they admired, and paid them for their efforts in either cash or the equivalent in food or some other commodity. Shōgen achieved such notoriety that she was included in the *Zoku kinsei kijin den* (1798), a compilation of biographies and anecdotes relating to eccentric personalities of the Edo period.[14]

At first glance, Shōgen's calligraphy looks anything but feminine, characterized by bold sweeps of the brush and dramatic flourishes. According to the *Kinsei ijin den* (1879) she modeled her style upon the Chinese master Yen Chen-ch'ing (709-785).[15] But there is no question that she was trained by her father, and hence was strongly influenced by his personal manner of calligraphy which combined Japanese and Chinese traditions.[16] Shōgen became proficient at both Chinese and Japanese scripts, exemplified by the long handscroll in the exhibition containing passages in many different styles (Cat. 11). Several books were published containing woodblock-printed examples of Shōgen's calligraphy which were intended as models to be copied by students learning to write.[17] These books served to spread Shōgen's name throughout Japan, and consequently her personal style was widely admired and imitated.

4. Kiyohara Yukinobu (1643-1682)

Taoist Immortals
Pair of six-fold screens, ink, colors, and gold on paper, each
150.5 x 306 cm.
Signature: Kiyohara-shi onna Yukinobu hitsu
Seals: Yukinobu; Kiyohara-jo
Mr. and Mrs. Leighton R. Longhi Collection

The aura of magic and supernatural powers possessed by legendary Taoist immortals has long fascinated the Japanese, who learned about them through imported Chinese art and literature.[18] Artists in both China and Japan were fond of representing gatherings of immortals, frequently in groups of eight. Specific immortals can often be identified by their iconographic attributes. Yukinobu has included eight, along with one child, in this pair of screens.[19] The two immortals most popular in Japan have been Gama and Tekkai (Ch: Hsia-mo and T'ieh-kuai), appearing here in the right screen. Tekkai sits at the far right, blowing his spirit out of his body in order to travel the world at will. To his left sits Gama, who is admiring the dance of his three-legged white toad. Identification of the other figures is more difficult. The man standing to the left of Gama and Tekkai, dressed in leafy garments and carrying a basket resembles Shin Nō (Ch: Shen Nung), the legendary Chinese emperor who taught the arts of agriculture and the properties of medicinal herbs. He is also believed to have written a book on medicine containing the secrets of immortality. In the left screen, the man flying away on the back of a crane could be any number of immortals. A long-standing symbol of

longevity, the crane was considered to be a messenger of Taoist divinities; it served as the aerial courser of various *sennin* including Wang Tzu-ch'iao, Kung Ho, Su Shê, and Huang Pei.[20] The other figures are not given attributes specific enough to identify them as particular immortals.

This pair represents the only known screen paintings by Yukinobu. The composition extends across both screens, beginning and ending with massive tree trunks so that the figures are neatly contained within the central panels. The immortals are of primary interest; typical of Kano paintings of this genre is the inclusion of only enough landscape elements to suggest a setting. To establish the prominence of the figures, Yukinobu outlined their robes in bold black and gray strokes, setting them apart from the background of light ink wash and gold. Yukinobu's ink paintings are almost always brushed in the free, spontaneous style associated with Zen art, as modified by the Kano school.[21] Due to the large-scale format, Yukinobu used a thicker brush than usual when painting in a cursory manner. Her brushwork is very fluid, emphasizing smooth and rounded contours rather than rough, angular strokes.

In these screens, Yukinobu followed Kano prototypes which were based ultimately upon Chinese images. For example, the pose of Tekkai is almost identical to one of a pair of paintings attributed to the Chinese artist Yen Hui (active fourteenth century) in the collection of the Kyoto temple Chion'in.[22] However, Yukinobu's brushwork is quite different from the original. Typical of the Japanization process are her simplified forms and sinuous brushstrokes which give these screens their dramatic visual impact.

5. Kiyohara Yukinobu

Apsara
Hanging scroll, ink and colors on silk, 116.8 x 44.8 cm.
Signature: Kiyohara-shi onna Yukinobu hitsu
Seal: Kiyohara-jo
The Mary and Jackson Burke Collection

Yukinobu occasionally painted Buddhist figures,[23] most frequently the white-robed Kannon who is closely associated with Zen Buddhism. In most cases the figures are elegant and feminine, beautiful to behold but lacking the spiritual power of Buddhist art of prior centuries. This secularization of Buddhist imagery was not unique to Yukinobu, but a phenomenon which occurred in Edo-period Japan in response to the dwindling spiritual power of religion in this era. While families were required to be affiliated with Buddhist temples, interest gradually shifted away from religious ideals to everyday, earthly concerns.

This painting may originally have been part of a triptych, since single scrolls of this subject are rare. In Asian art, flying deities called *apsara* (J: *tennin*), sometimes equated with angels, are usually shown hovering around a Buddha. Arms outstretched in preparation to strike a musical note, Yukinobu's *apsara* descends amidst swirling clouds. The celestial deity is garbed in robes decorated with intricate gold patterns which Yukinobu painted with an extremely fine brush. Scarves, ribbons, and filaments of jewels flutter elegantly in the breeze. Although the coloring is minimal, the background of light ink wash causes the figure to appear radiant.

In spite of its heavenly environment, Yukinobu has thoroughly humanized the *apsara* by depicting a face no different from that of her court ladies, with flawless skin painted opaque white. Yukinobu was doubtlessly responding to a patron's taste for paintings of Buddhist deities which reflected the worldly affluence and refinement of the upper echelons of Japanese society.

6. Kiyohara Yukinobu

Hanrei and Seishi
Hanging scroll, ink and colors on silk, 71.8 x 32.3 cm.
Signature: Kiyohara-shi onna Yukinobu hitsu
Seal: Kiyohara-jo
Museum of Fine Arts, Boston (The Weld-Fenollosa
Collection, bequest of Charles Goddard Weld)

This seemingly idyllic scene, rendered in soft pastel colors, represents a famous Chinese "Pygmalion" tale involving intrigue and seduction. The hero was the minister of the state of Yüeh, Hanrei (Ch: Fan Li), who assisted his ruler in ending twenty years of war with the kingdom of Wu by conceiving the stratagem of sending the beautiful girl Seishi (Ch: Hsi Shih) to divert the king of Wu from his official duties. Seishi was originally of low birth, but Hanrei trained and dressed her to carry out his ploy. Some accounts say that Hanrei later drowned Seishi because of her boastful threat to captivate the Yüeh ruler as she had the king of Wu. In paintings, Hanrei and Seishi are usually represented together in a boat on lake T'ai, alluding to Seishi's imminent tragic death.

Yukinobu has enclosed the figures in a soft, misty landscape, rendered primarily in broad strokes of wash. Dark, jagged texture strokes were brushed over the rock in the lower left foreground, bringing the viewer's attention to the two figures just beyond. Both Hanrei and Seishi have somber expressions, as though they have resigned themselves to fate. The melancholy mood is intensified by Yukinobu's use of cool blue and green colors and the overcast sky. Her forte was this kind of figural subject, rendered with the sensitivity and precision that won her public acclaim.

7. Kiyohara Yukinobu

Murasaki Shikibu
Hanging scroll, ink and colors on silk, 92.5 x 37 cm.
Signature: Kiyohara-shi onna Yukinobu hitsu
Seal: Kiyohara-jo
Mr. and Mrs. Peter Brest Collection

The Heian court lady in this exquisite painting can be identified as Murasaki Shikibu, author of the celebrated *Genji monogatari*. This novel was widely read and admired in Yukinobu's day, with many scholars promoting it as a literary masterpiece especially suitable for women. Yukinobu may well have identified herself with the multitalented Murasaki who was also skillful in calligraphy and painting.

In her depiction of Murasaki and other female poets, Yukinobu followed the tradition of the Tosa school, a hereditary line of painters specializing in *yamato-e* subjects who were patronized by the imperial court from the fifteenth century on. By the seventeenth century, many Kano artists were also expert in the *yamato-e* style, the foremost being Tan'yū. Yukinobu may well have learned this style from her mentor, but there is also evidence that she may have associated with Tosa Mitsuoki (1617-1691).[24]

Here Murasaki is shown in the act of writing, either her diary[25] or perhaps the *Genji monogatari*; a finished portion of her text lies partially unrolled on the writing desk in front of her. Seated amidst a splendid array of brightly colored robes, she contemplates her composition with brush in hand. The overlapping layers of brocade and silk, rendered with unusually fine brushwork, represent the formal dress of court ladies of the Heian period. Also typical of Heian court women is the cascading long black hair; here it is almost hidden in the folds of the robes except for the few strands which flow over Murasaki's right shoulder.

Above the figure is a *waka* by Murasaki, believed to have been inscribed by the court calligrapher Konoe Motohiro (died 1722).[26] The poem reads:

Meguri aite	A chance encounter–
Mishi ya sore tomo	But who was it that I saw?
Wakanu ma ni	I could not be sure;
Kumo kakure ni shi	Obscured by the passing clouds,
Yowa no tsuki kana	The midnight moon.

8. Kiyohara Yukinobu

A Palace Scene in a Snowy Landscape
Hanging scroll, ink and colors on silk, 43 x 57.5 cm.
Signature: Kiyohara-shi onna Yukinobu hitsu
Seal: Kiyohara-jo
Los Angeles County Museum of Art,
The Shin'enkan Collection
Published: *The Shin'enkan Collection of Japanese Painting*
(Kyoto: Kyoto Shoin, 1984), no. 124.

Yukinobu's fascination with Heian-period female personalities and their literary works can be observed again in this painting which represents a scene from Sei Shōnagon's *Makura no sōshi* (Pillow Book). Like Murasaki Shikibu, Sei Shōnagon was a lady of great beauty famed for literary accomplishments at the imperial court. One of the most famous incidents in her life is depicted here; Sei Shōnagon is rolling up a bamboo blind (*sudare*) in order to reveal the snow-covered garden. The story is as follows: One day the snow lay thick on the ground and it was so cold that the lattices had all been closed. Surrounded by her ladies-in-waiting, the empress asked Shōnagon "How is the snow on Hsiang-lu peak?," alluding to a verse by the Chinese poet Po Chü-i.[27] Shōnagon immediately recognized the allusion; in response she had the lattice raised and proceeded to roll up the blind as had Po Chü-i. Her quick comprehension of the classical reference earned her great praise.

Yukinobu's painting represents a slight variation on this episode, for the figure partially visible behind the closed blinds is not the empress, but a male, perhaps the emperor. Nevertheless, the woman unrolling the blinds in order to expose the snow-covered landscape must be Sei Shōnagon. Both figures are dressed in layers of sumptuous textiles conforming to Heian courtly fashion. Shiny black tresses and stiff folded robes trailing behind her, Shōnagon's profile is arrestingly beautiful. Yukinobu was expert at the meticulous, refined brushwork requisite for traditional *yamato-e* subject matter. She has imbued the composition with a quiescent mood through the smooth horizontality of roof lines, veranda, garden stream, and layered distant mountains. The soft, muted brushwork forming the surrounding landscape is closer in spirit to the Tosa style than to Kano, once again exhibiting Yukinobu's versatility as an artist.

9. Kiyohara Yukinobu

Peonies and Chrysanthemums
Pair of hanging scrolls, ink and colors on silk,
each 98 x 38.6 cm.
Signatures: Kiyohara-shi onna Yukinobu hitsu
Seals: Kiyohara-jo
Harvard University Art Museums (Arthur M. Sackler
Museum), Hofer Collection of the Arts of Asia

Yukinobu's ethereal touch is nowhere better
demonstrated than in her bird-and-flower paintings.
Peonies were among her specialties, here paired with
another scroll depicting chrysanthemums. Both species of
flowers have symbolic meanings in Japan where they are
associated with royalty. The two compositions are
complementary; whereas the chrysanthemums and a stalk
of bamboo grow rigidly upward, slicing the picture plane
in half vertically, the peonies bend gracefully inward.
Furthermore, Yukinobu has skillfully balanced the lush
fullness of the peonies against the sparse chrysanthemums.
In typical Kano fashion, she has outlined each individual
leaf and flower petal; however, the lines were done with an
extremely fine brush so as not to be overbearing. Within
the outlines she has applied colored washes of graded
intensity so that the plants have a slight sense of three-
dimensionality. Yukinobu seems to have preferred
understated coloring: she applied her pigments in such
light layers that the texture of the silk shines through,
producing a warm glow.

10. Sasaki Shōgen (active late 17th-early 18th century)

Poem by Tu Fu
Hanging scroll, ink on paper, 132.6 x 57.1 cm.
Signature: Shōgen sho
Seals: Sasaki-shi jo; Seishidō
Shōka Collection

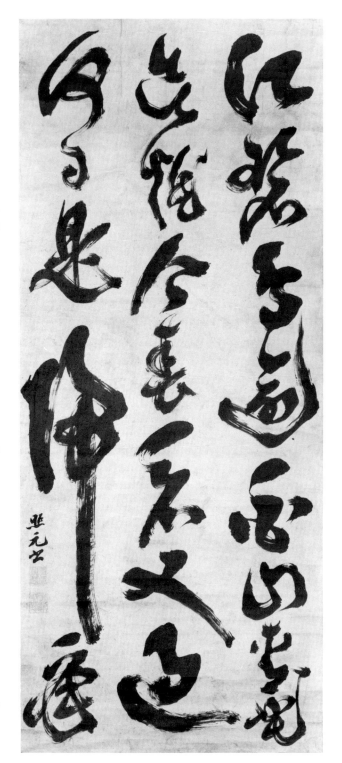

Sasaki Shōgen's brushwork is described as being strong and forceful, for a woman,[28] a trait well exemplified in this quatrain by the Chinese poet Tu Fu (712-770) which she wrote with a bravura and velocity suitable to the large-sized Chinese characters. The poem reads:

Over the blue river, the birds seem especially white.
In the green mountains, the flowers are about to become
    ablaze.
This spring will soon pass by–
But when will the time come for me to return?[29]

Shōgen was adept in many scripts and styles in both Chinese and Japanese calligraphy; here she has chosen to use a semicursive running script, in which strokes are simplified and written in a continuous movement without lifting up the brush. In Chinese script Shōgen is said to have followed the T'ang-dynasty calligrapher Yen Chen-ch'ing, and her writing here does indeed share a robustness and vitality characteristic of the Chinese master. In his more informal works, Yen Chen-ch'ing cultivated an eccentric flavor by playfully juxtaposing large characters with small ones and exploiting dramatic variations in line width.[30] When writing out Tu Fu's poem, Shōgen also deliberately varied the size of the characters in order to achieve an irregular and consequently more vigorous rhythm. Whereas her first column contains eight characters, the third has only five. The second-to-the-last character meaning "to return," written in enormous size compared to the others, is a bold and dramatic feature also employed by Yen Chen-ch'ing.

Although Shōgen's Chinese-style calligraphy shares some qualities with Yen Chen-ch'ing, her brushwork is tempered with features of the Daishi tradition learned from her father Shizuma.[31] For example, she has rendered some of her strokes with a quivering motion causing them to fluctuate in width. An electric tension is created through abrupt stops and shifts in movement of the brush. Also characteristic of the Daishi style are the brushstrokes continuing out from underneath forms which resemble long tails, most evident in the fourth character. Drawing upon divergent models, Shōgen has masterfully blended both Chinese and Japanese script styles in this poem, achieving a grandeur and vitality that are unmistakably her own.

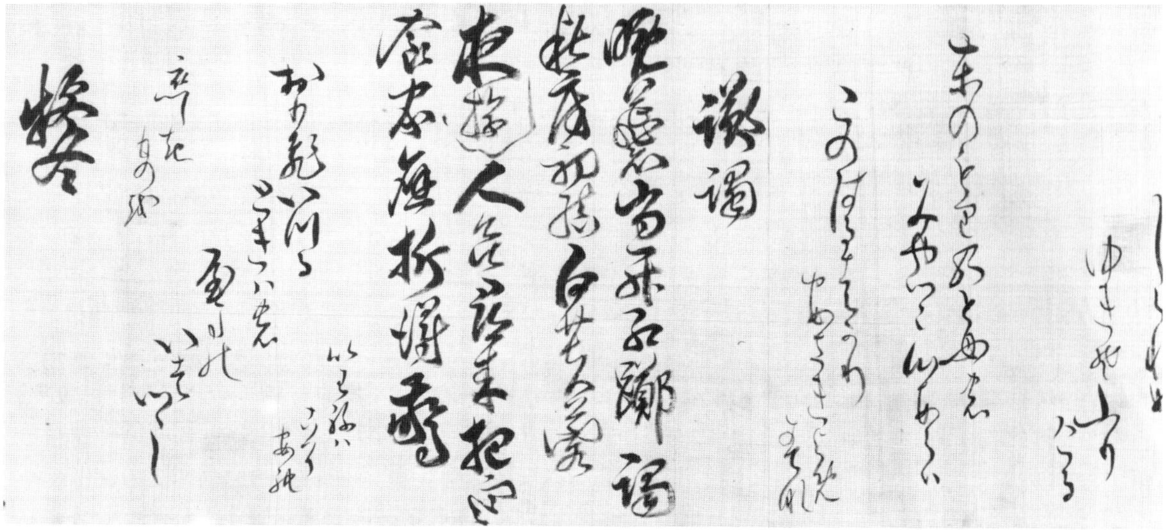

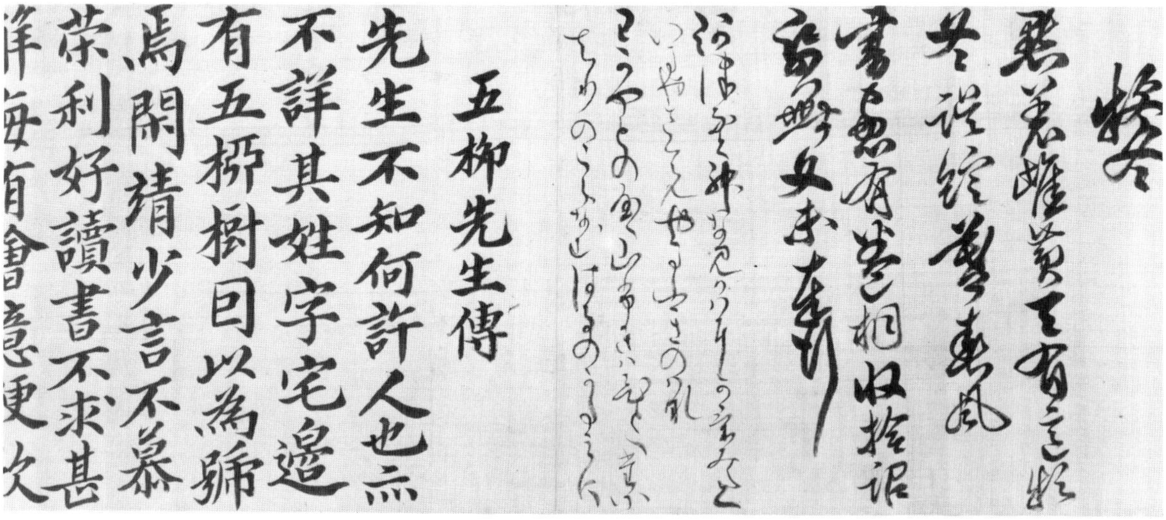

談調

五柳先生傳

先生不知何許人也亦
不詳其姓字宅邊
有五柳樹因以為號
焉閑靖少言不慕
榮利好讀書不求甚
解每有會意便欣 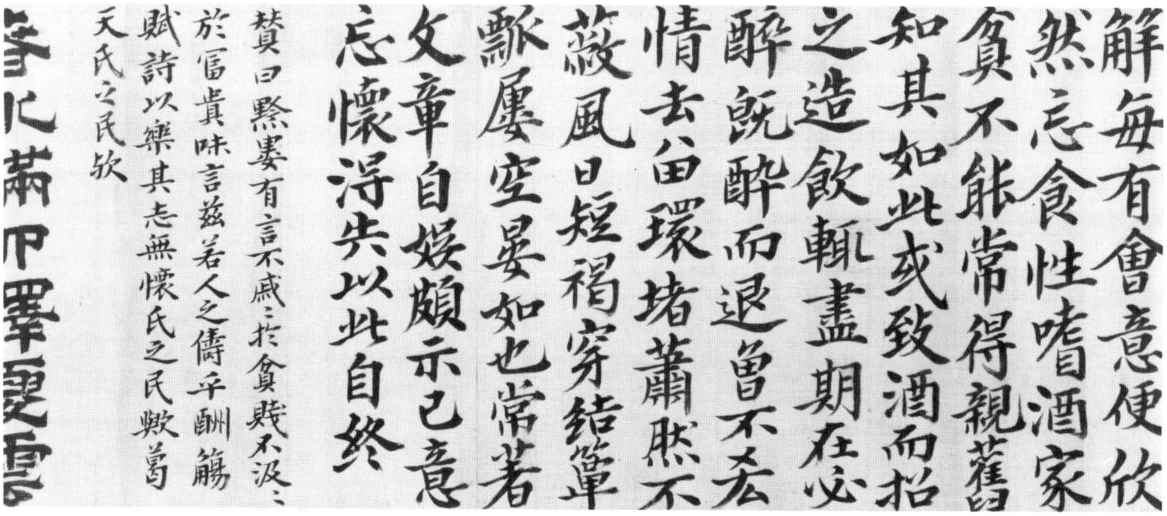
然忘食性嗜酒家
貧不能常得親舊
知其如此或致酒而招
之造飲輒盡期在必
醉既醉而退曾不吝
情去留環堵蕭然不
蔽風日短褐穿結簞
瓢屢空晏如也常著
文章自娛頗示己意
忘懷得失以此自終
贊曰黔婁有言不戚
戚於貧賤不汲
汲於富貴味言茲若人之儔乎酬觴
賦詩以樂其志無懷氏之民歟葛
天氏之民歟

44

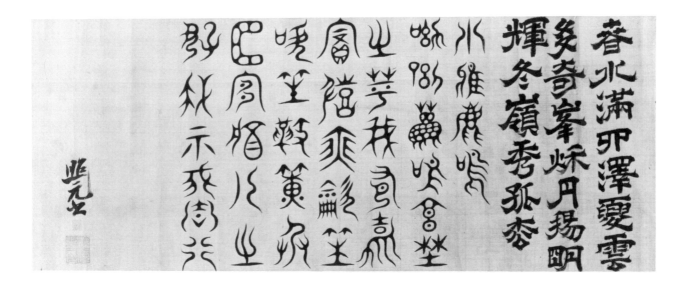

11. Sasaki Shōgen

Calligraphy in Various Scripts
Handscroll, ink on silk, 31 x 643 cm.
Signature: Shōgen sho
Seals: Geisokaku; Seishidō; Shōgen no in
Hakutakuan Collection

A common practice of professional calligraphers during the Edo period was to demonstrate the range of their skills by writing out texts or poems in different scripts sequentially in a single handscroll. Prior to the seventeenth century this custom was almost unknown; its popularity seems to have been related to the tastes of Edo-period calligraphers who were fascinated with various scripts. Although many styles of Chinese calligraphy had been introduced to Japan previously, scholars now began to investigate them with new fervor, publishing manifold compendiums of different forms of script.[32] This handscroll by Shōgen falls into that genre; a virtuoso performance, it exhibits a full spectrum of both Chinese and Japanese styles of calligraphy.[33] Included are Chinese poems and prose passages written in bold running script (*gyōsho*), regular script (*kaisho*), clerical script (*reisho*), and seal script (*tensho*); these were alternated with *waka* inscribed in the Japanese syllabary known as *kana*. After several sections of poems, Shōgen added a biography of T'ao Yüan-ming (372-427), a sign of her great respect for the Chinese poet.

Shōgen leaves one script and goes into another with ease, flaunting her competence and ingenuity. Her calligraphy is so imbued with personal flavor that it is difficult to distinguish its sources. Nevertheless, Shōgen's Chinese regular and running scripts owe a debt to Yen Chen-ch'ing, and her *kana* writing bears a striking resemblance to her father Shizuma's style. Shōgen's interest in diversity extended even to her *kana* syllabary, for in this scroll she employed three different compositional arrangements including one known as *chirashi gaki* with the columns of poetry scattered diagonally across the paper.

The end of the scroll contains some of the most extraordinary passages. The climax is two Chinese poems; the first written in clerical script, and the second in an ornamental form of seal script called "bird" script, in which the characters are wonderfully pictorial.[34] These final two verses read:

Spring waters fill the four valleys,
Summer clouds envelop the strange pinnacles,
The autumn moon raises its bright radiance,
Winter peaks dominate the lone pines.

Deer Cries

Yu, yu, cry the deer
Grazing in the fields.
I have an honored guest;
We strum the zither, blow the panpipes,
Blow the panpipes, trill the reeds.
Take up the basket of offerings–
Here is a man who cares for me
And will teach me the ways of Chou.

Notes

1. For further information on Motonobu's influence, see Carolyn Wheelwright, "Kano Painters of the Sixteenth Century A.D.: The Development of Motonobu's Daisen-in Style," *Archives of Asian Art*, vol. 34 (1981), 6-31.

2. Each of these artists established an atelier in Edo which came to be referred to by its location: Tan'yū's in Kajibashi, Naonobu's in Kobikichō, and Yasunobu's in Nakabashi.

3. See Sasaki Jōhei, *Edo kaiga I, Nihon no bijutsu* series, no. 209 (Tokyo: Shibundō, 1983), 47.

4. For more detailed information on the inner workings of Kano ateliers, see Yoshiaki Shimizu, "Workshop Management of the Early Kano Painters, circa A.D. 1530-1600," *Archives of Asian Art*, vol. 34 (1981), 32-47.

5. Yukinobu's name is recorded in a list of painters in the 1672 *Bengyoku shū*, and *Koga bikō* notes a painting dated 1666 signed "Kiyohara-shi Yukinobu hitsu," indicating that she had established herself as an artist by the age of 25-30. See "Kiyohara Yukinobu hitsu O Shō-kimi zu," *Kokka*, no. 597, 239. Ilustrations in later woodblock-printed books such as the *Hanasugata joshoku jinkan* by Utagawa Kuninao (1793-1854) show women labeled as *onna-eshi* (women professional painters) painting fans. However, they remain nameless as they did not sign their works, indicating that they were members of lower-class *machi-eshi* ateliers. See Hanasaki Kazuo, *Zue Edo onna hyaku sugata*.

6. Kuniko's mother was a sister of Tan'yū named Nabeko who married Kōtari Kōun (died 1702), one of Tan'yū's four major pupils.

7. Yukinobu may also have had a daughter named Harunobu who painted, but no works by her are extant. This information is recorded in Shirai Kayō, *Gajō yōryaku*, vol. 2, 140.

8. According to the *Gajō yōryaku*, Yukinobu studied with Tan'yū, as did her brother Hikosaburō. See Soeda, "Onna Yukinobu no hanashi," 9.

9. Kaoru commissioned Yukinobu to paint a picture of an autumn scene on plain white satin, and then asked eight court nobles to inscribe verses. The result was a design of breathtaking beauty which Kaoru had made into a robe for herself rather than a hanging scroll. For an English translation of this passage, see Hamada Kengi, *The Life of an Amorous Man* (Rutland, Vermont and Tokyo: Charles E. Tuttle Company, 1964), 185.

10. The *Kinsei sōgo* (1816) records that she married someone in the Yoshimi household, but according to a grave inscription, it was Shōgen's daughter who married Yoshimi. See Yoneda Yatarō, "Shizuma ryū to karayō ni tsuite," 144.

11. It was at this time that she adopted the name Shōgen. This information is included in the *Shoga benran* and the *Zoku kinsei kijin den*. See Yoneda, 144-145.

12. The daughter of Emperor Chūgomon, Hōkyōji no Amamiya took the tonsure in 1733, becoming a nun at the Kyoto temple Hōkyōji. This temple was specifically for women; Ryōnen had served as a nun there before going to seek instruction in Edo (see chapter one).

13. One of her seals bears the name "Seishidō" (Hall of Quiet Thoughts) which may have been the name of her studio.

14. Mikuma Katen and Ban Kōkei, *Zoku kinsei kijin den*, 415-417.

15. Komatsu, *Nihon shoryū zenshi*, vol. 1, 682.

16. Shizuma was initially a pupil of Fujiki Atsunao (1582-1649), founder of the Daishi calligraphy tradition. However, after visiting with the Chinese immigrant painter/calligrapher Chen Yüan-yün (1587-1671), Shizuma was stimulated to learn Chinese script forms. He seems to have studied Chinese calligraphy independently, perhaps learning from woodblock books, and developed a unique style.

17. The following four books by Shōgen were listed at the back of Shizuma's book entitled *Senjibun* (1726): *Senjibun* (two volumes, various scripts); *Toshi zekku* (three volumes, grass script); *Chōkon waka* (one volume, running script); *Ekashiko shinshō* (two volumes, grass script). See Komatsu, *Nihon shoryū zenshi*, vol. 1, 682. Other woodblock books with Shōgen's calligraphy include: *Sekiheki fu* and *Ken Shin-shō (Ch: Hsien Ch'en-sung) ishizuri*. See Yoneda, 148-149.

18. For a discussion of the Chinese origins of these immortals, (called *sennin* in Japanese) and their appearance in Japanese art, see Janet Carpenter, "*Sennin*: The Immortals of Taoism," in *Japanese Ghosts and Demons: Art of the Supernatural* (New York: George Braziller, Inc. in association with the Spencer Museum of Art, 1985), 57-65.

19. The immortals depicted here are not the standard group of eight represented in Chinese art.

20. Will H. Edmunds, *Pointers and Clues to the Subjects of Chinese and Japanese Art* (London: Sampson Low, Marston & Co., Ltd., 1934), 317.

21. Like her great-uncle Tan'yū, Yukinobu associated with Ōbaku Zen monks, who sometimes added poetic inscriptions to her paintings.

22. Many Japanese artists made copies of this pair, including Kano Motonobu.

23. Two other known examples by Yukinobu featuring Buddhist deities depict Bukan with his tiger, and Benzaiten.

24. There is an album of paintings by Yukinobu depicting thirty-six women poets, the inside cover of which was painted by Mitsuoki. See Narazaki Muneshige, "Kiyohara Yukinobu hitsu nyōbo sanjūrokkasen zu," 255.

25. Entitled the *Murasaki Shikibu nikki*.

26. The poem is not signed, but the painting's box lid bears an inscription attributing it to Motohiro.

27. Po Chü-i's poem was:
The sun has risen in the sky, but I idly lie in bed;
In my small tower-room the layers of quilts protect me from the cold;
Leaning on my pillow, I wait to hear I-ai's temple bell;
Pushing aside the blind, I gaze upon the snow of Hsiang-lu peak.
(Translation by Ivan Morris)

For a complete translation of this passage, see Ivan Morris, *The Pillow Book of Sei Shōnagon* (New York: Columbia University Press, 1967), 241-242.

28. Komatsu, ed., *Nihon shoseki taikan*, vol. 19, 246.

29. Translated by Stephen Addiss.

30. For reproductions, see Nakata Yūjirō, ed., *Shodō geijutsu* (Tokyo: Chūōkōronsha, 1970), vol. 4, pls. 108-112.

31. Shizuma's teacher Fujiki Atsunao was the founder of the Daishi *ryū* or lineage. Atsunao initiated a revival of the ornamental calligraphy style of the great monk Kōbō Daishi (774-835) which featured tremulous brushlines full of sweeping curves. For examples of Daishi-style calligraphy, see Komatsu, *Nihon shoryū zenshi*, vol. 2, 9-16.

32. This activity was stimulated by imported woodblock books from China containing examples of unusual scripts. Ming-dynasty calligraphers are well-known for their revival and reinterpretation of old forms of writing. Chinese immigrants to Japan, such as the Ōbaku Zen monks and Tōkō Shin'etsu (Ch: Hsin Yüeh, 1639-1696), also brought books with them, arousing interest in clerical and seal scripts which were rare in Japan until the seventeenth century.

33. A woodblock book was published which featured various scripts by Shōgen entitled the *Senjibun* (One Thousand Character Classic). Her father was also fond of executing calligraphy in different manners, exemplified by a modelbook in the Shōka Collection which consists of the *One Thousand Character Classic* written in regular script but utilizing a variety of brushwork styles.

34. The last poem (written in seal script) is from the *Shih Ching* (Book of Songs, circa 600 B.C.). I have based my translation on Arthur Waley, *The Book of Songs* (Boston and New York: Houghton Mifflin Company, 1937), 192.

Eighteenth-Century Women Artists

Chapter Three: **Ukiyo-e Painters**

Women artists working in professional ateliers were still a novelty in the eighteenth century; they were most visible among the urban ukiyo-e artists. The pleasure districts of the great cities of Edo, Kyoto, and Osaka were the spawning grounds of urban culture in Edo-period Japan. Overflowing with brothels, theaters, teahouses, public baths, and other places of entertainment and assignation, these quarters were termed *ukiyo* or "floating worlds" because the hedonistic pleasures they offered were so fleeting.

Ukiyo-e is the term for paintings and prints depicting activities and personages of the "floating world." Stimulated by the growth of popular culture, writers and artists responded to the tastes of the lower- and middle-class townsmen patrons and created an art form that all could enjoy. Among the most popular subjects were plebian scenes from daily life, especially people at leisure and enjoying diversions of various kinds. Mirroring the interests of their clientele, ukiyo-e artists focused their attention on life in the amusement quarters. In particular, they took as their subjects the idols of the day, kabuki actors and courtesans. These two subjects make up the majority of the ukiyo-e produced in the eighteenth century.

In view of the tremendous pressure that Japanese society placed on individuals to conform to the rigid rules of Confucian behavior, the entertainment districts which offered escape from the heavy responsibilities of family and occupation were essential safety valves against social unrest. Although the shogunate always maintained some surveillance over them, these quarters were to a large extent self-governing. Unlike the conservative Kano school, ukiyo-e ateliers were not bound by a fixed set of restrictive rules and regulations, nor were they dominated by familial ties. It was also possible for artists who were not part of an established atelier to make a successful living producing ukiyo-e. Furthermore, because of the relative freedom of behavior in the pleasure quarters, the ukiyo-e world was more receptive to women painters than were traditional art workshops. The more liberal

4. Masanobu, *Mu-me Painting Bijinga*
From the *Ehon fūga nana komachi kinki shoga*
Prof. Dr. Med. Gerhard Pulverer Collection

view toward women was reflected in the popular fiction of the day which often depicted women as daring and brazen, not the meek creatures praised in Confucian texts.

In the metropolitan centers of Edo, Kyoto, and Osaka, several women ukiyo-e artists were able to achieve success in the late seventeenth and eighteenth centuries. At least three women were followers of the leading master Hishikawa Moronobu (circa 1616-1694): San (active 1688-1703),[1] Ran-jo (active 1711-1715), and Yamazaki Ryū-jo (active 1716-1735). In Kyoto, Mu-me (active 1716-1735), the daughter of Nishikawa Terunobu (active 1716-1735), produced ukiyo-e, as did Tsuna-jo (active 1688-1710), a pupil of the illustrator Yoshida Hanbei (active 1660-1692). In the later eighteenth century, several women studied with notable ukiyo-e artists in Edo, including Chiyo-jo[2] with Kitagawa Utamaro (1753-1806) and Kiyu-jo (active 1781-1788) with Kitao Shigemasa (1739-1820). Tsukioka Settei (1710-1786) in Osaka had two female followers, Shunko-me (active in the eighteenth century) and Inagaki Tsuru-jo (active in the late eighteenth century). Another Osaka woman ukiyo-e artist was Katsura Miki (active 1781-1788), a pupil of Katsura Sōshin. Unfortunately, works by most of these women are extremely rare, and in some cases no paintings or prints are known to be extant. Mu-me's painting activity, for example, is documented by an illustration (Figure 4) of her at work from a book designed by Okumura Masanobu (1686-1764). The two best known women ukiyo-e painters of the eighteenth century were Yamazaki Ryū-jo and Inagaki Tsuru-jo, whose works are plentiful and well represented in Western as well as Japanese collections.

Yamazaki Ryū-jo (active 1716-1735)

Ryū-jo (also known as Joryū and Oryū) was the daughter of Yamazaki Bunzaemon, a shogunal vassal in Edo. As a child she loved to paint, and from the age of six or seven Ryū-jo was allegedly producing fine ukiyo-e. She also avidly studied *waka*, and frequently inscribed poems on her paintings. Ryū-jo's childhood talents are documented by the fact that she often included her age when signing her works, especially those of her youthful years.[3]

According to many biographies, Ryū-jo studied painting with Hishikawa Moronobu;[4] however, modern scholars perceive this information as doubtful, suggesting instead that she was probably self-taught.[5] If Ryū-jo had formally been Moronobu's pupil, she probably would have adopted one character from his name and called herself Mororyū or Noburyū. Furthermore, her earliest works are not fully within the Moronobu tradition, but share stylistic characteristics with paintings by the Torii and Kaigetsudō ateliers, as well as with those by Nishikawa Sukenobu (1671-1751). Ushiyama Mitsuru believes that Ryū-jo was born around 1708, fourteen years after Moronobu's death.[6] He arrived at this date by comparing Ryū-jo's works inscribed with her age to dated contemporary works which he speculates may have served as her models. For example, there is a painting by Ryū-jo at age fourteen depicting women dressing their hair which closely resembles Sukenobu's illustrations in the woodblock book *Hyakunin jorō shina sadame* published in 1723. Using this as the foundation for a chronology, Ushiyama believes that Ryū-jo probably began learning how to paint around 1714-1716, perhaps from woodblock-printed books by Moronobu and Sukenobu. Moronobu's style was overwhelmingly popular, so it is not surprising to find similar features appearing in works of artists outside of his immediate pupils.

Most of Ryū-jo's known paintings depict fashionable courtesans either alone, with female attendants, or, occasionally, accompanied by a male guest. Ryū-jo favored bright colors, especially red, blue, and green. Her extant works dated to the age of thirteen show a rather childish handling of the brush, but she quickly mastered the art of painting and by age fourteen was producing very skillful ukiyo-e. One of Ryū-jo's more unusual works, highly praised by the novelist and critic Santō Kyōden (1761-1816), is a parody on scenes of the Buddha's death. Instead of the Buddha, it depicts the death of the ninth-century poet and hero of the *Ise monogatari*, Narihira.[7] This work was painted with her distinctive delicate brushwork, yet it is imbued with a humor typical of the playful atmosphere of the "floating world." However, Ryū-jo is most well-known for her depictions of sinuously posed beauties.

Inagaki Tsuru-jo (active late eighteenth century)

There is little biographical information about Tsuru-jo.[8] She lived in Osaka, and was active during the second half of the eighteenth century, specializing in paintings of *bijin* (beautiful women) that closely resemble those by the Osaka painter and illustrator Tsukioka Settei. It is not known whether or not he was actually her teacher, or if she was connected with an ukiyo-e atelier.

Like Ryū-jo, Tsuru-jo focused her attention on courtesans and other beauties of the day rather than famous kabuki actors. These two artists were obviously fascinated with the women who reigned over the pleasure quarters in Edo and Osaka. What led them to paint in the ukiyo-e manner? Were they affiliated with an atelier, or self-taught as has been suggested in the case of Ryū-jo? What attracted them to the world of the courtesan? Unfortunately, these questions cannot be answered without more detailed biographical information. One can only speculate that their interest in painting was stimulated by family or friends who were somehow involved in the ukiyo-e world. The question as to why they chose to paint primarily courtesans is quite provocative. It is clear that men found courtesans alluring, but how were they viewed by other women? Given the restrictive nature of Edo-period society, one might surmise that women looked upon the courtesans with envy. Famous courtesans were glamorized in popular novels, and to outsiders, they appeared to lead exciting, pampered lives. They were the fashion models of the day, flaunting the latest styles in dress and hairdos. Courtesans were the trend-setters for women, and the idols of every man. Compared with most women who were expected to stay home and take care of their families, high-ranking courtesans enjoyed more freedom. Their work was perceived as play, and despite the moral issues involved, many women would have gladly exchanged places with them. By painting the beauties of the demimonde, might Ryū-jo and Tsuru-jo have been acting out a dream?

12. Yamazaki Ryū-jo (active 1716-1735)

Courtesan
Hanging scroll, ink and colors on paper, 70.3 x 27.9 cm.
Signature: . . . Joryū jūsansai hitsu
Seals: ?; Yamazaki-shi hitsu
Private collection, The Hague

This scroll is important as one of the earliest known paintings by Ryū-jo, inscribed as having been brushed at age thirteen.[9] Damage to the paper seems to have obliterated the first part of her signature, which originally would have been prefaced by her surname to read "Yamazaki-shi Joryū jūsansai hitsu." In her early works, she usually called herself Joryū, but later used Joryū interchangeably with Ryū-jo. Japanese art publications usually refer to her by the name Ryū-jo.

Courtesans were social figures of great importance in Edo-period Japan, and became the subject and stimulus for a vast body of literature and art. In some respects they were prostitutes, for their favors could be exchanged for money. Yet at the same time these women enjoyed a considerable degree of freedom and influence within their restricted worlds. Many of them began, between the ages of five and seven, as apprentices serving as attendants to high-ranking courtesans called *tayū*. They received extensive training in many arts, and were ranked according to their class origin, beauty, charm, and skill.

The arresting pose struck by this courtesan, who pauses to look coyly over her shoulder, is an imitation of a design popularized by Kaigetsudō school artists (active in the eighteenth century), who specialized in paintings and prints of seductive courtesans. Ryū-jo's painting is rather naive in comparison with her ultra-sophisticated Kaigetsudō models, indicative of her immature artistic skills at the age of thirteen. Nevertheless, this work documents the typical Japanese learning process, that of developing and refining one's skills through the copying of a recognized master's work. Ordinarily, an artist would learn by imitating his or her teacher's work, but as the daughter of an Edo warden, Ryū-jo probably had to be content with copying designs from woodblock-printed books or illustrations. The charm of this painting lies in the bold, vivacious manner in which Ryū-jo has brushed her worldly subject.

13. Yamazaki Ryū-jo

Courtesan Viewing Cherry Blossoms
Hanging scroll, ink and colors on silk, 78.8 x 27.8 cm.
Signature: Joryū hitsu
Seal: undecipherable
Mr. and Mrs. Leighton R. Longhi Collection

This painting of a courtesan out with her attendant
viewing cherry blossoms represents the heights that Ryū-jo
achieved as an artist; it is one of her most sophisticated
works. In typical Japanese fashion the scene is permeated
with a mood of melancholy, with the courtesan staring
wistfully at the blossoms that have fallen to the ground.
The period of blossoming of the Oriental cherry is
extremely brief, but the element of impermanence makes
this flower all the more beautiful in the eyes of the
Japanese. The courtesan is reminded that life is transitory,
especially within the "floating world" that is her milieu.
The romantic image of courtesans found in ukiyo-e
obscured their often unhappy lives. Many had been sold to
brothels by their families while they were still children.
They were bound by contracts to work for a fixed number
of years, usually retiring by the age of twenty-five. If a
courtesan could find a patron willing and able to buy out
her contract, she was free to leave. However, as long as
she remained licensed, she was in bondage. There was a
high death toll among women in this profession, from both
illness and abortions. Beauty and fame quickly faded in
the "floating world," as courtesans were replaced each year
by fresh "blossoms." Ryū-jo's *waka*, written out in thin,
spidery calligraphy to the right of the tree branch, adds a
literary dimension to the work.

Fumeba ashi	To tread on them is bad;
Fumaneba ikan	Yet if she doesn't step, she cannot
Kata mo nashi	move,
Kokoro zukushi no	And there is nowhere else to go.
Yamazakura	Scattered here for her pleasure–
	The mountain cherry blossoms.

Landscape settings were somewhat rare for Ryū-jo,
who usually represented her figures in interior scenes or
against a blank background. The theme of a beauty
standing beneath a tree, however, had been popular for
centuries in Asia, and continued to be depicted by ukiyo-e
artists. Ryū-jo has painted the foreground bank, the tree,
and the winding river almost entirely with ink, causing the
brightly colored robes of the courtesan to stand out vividly.
The lineament defining the contours of her garment is
strong and fluid, displaying the confidence that comes
through mastery of the medium.

Like many ukiyo-e artists, Ryū-jo did not invent new
themes but fashioned her paintings after those popularized
by the leading designers of the day. The pose, as well as
the shape of the courtesan's face and coiffure, are more
refined than Cat. 12, recalling the graceful type of beauty
popularized by Nishikawa Sukenobu. Despite the fact that

he was active in Kyoto, Sukenobu established such a great reputation that even though Ryū-jo lived in Edo, she would have been aware of his work. Although Sukenobu produced a number of fine paintings, it is likely that Ryū-jo learned his style through illustrated books which were more readily available. Ryū-jo shared with Sukenobu a vision that women were graceful, docile creatures. In her designs she presented an idealized version of the feminine image which met with a receptive audience among the thriving townspeople of Edo.

14. Yamazaki Ryū-jo

Young Actor Holding Narcissus
Hanging scroll, ink and colors on paper, 82 x 24.8 cm.
Signature: Yamazaki-shi Joryū ga
Seal: Sanshikyo
Idemitsu Art Museum
Published: Idemitsu Bijutsukan, ed., *Shoki fūzokuga to nikuhitsu ukiyo-e ten zuroku* (Tokyo: 1972).

Extant works reveal that Ryū-jo painted primarily courtesans, but she occasionally depicted the other favored subject of eighteenth-century ukiyo-e, kabuki actors. This willowy actor is shown portraying a young woman, since by this time females were no longer allowed to perform on stage. He adopts a feminine stance with practiced grace, demurely looking downward. In his left hand he holds a stalk of narcissus, probably alluding to a scene within a particular kabuki play.

The garments worn by the actor are quite striking, with a rust-colored *haori* overlaying a black *kosode* decorated with white plum blossoms. Ryū-jo's brushwork defining the figure and robes is smooth and flowing. She added slender lines of glittering gold paint as accents on the actor's cap and the upper portion of his black *kosode*. Although the type and pose of the figure once again recall Sukenobu, the painting exudes Ryū-jo's intrinsic charm and refinement, with the additional fascination of a woman portraying a man portraying a woman.

15. Inagaki Tsuru-jo (active late 18th century)

Courtesan with Attendant
Hanging scroll, ink and colors on silk, 85.9 x 30.9 cm.
Signature: Inagaki-shi Tsuru-jo hitsu
Seal: Azana Senrei etsu
Estate of Louis Vernon Ledoux

All that is known about Inagaki Tsuru-jo is that she
was active in Osaka during the second half of the
eighteenth century, and that she painted in the style of
Tsukioka Settei. This enigmatic woman artist is all the
more interesting because numerous works by her have
come to light, all of them exquisitely painted.

Judging from her extant works, Tsuru-jo specialized in
paintings of courtesans. We cannot be sure that she
studied with Settei, but the fact that he had at least one
other woman pupil, Shunko-me, makes this premise
feasible. Settei was a prolific artist who achieved great
fame in Osaka during the late eighteenth century, and
Tsuru-jo was only one of many painters who followed his
style.

Tsuru-jo's debt to Settei is apparent in this work
depicting a courtesan talking with her attendant who
carries a *shamisen* over her shoulder. The two women
might well be on their way to a special party. Both women
are elegantly garbed in flowing silk brocades. Settei's
influence is evident in the stance of the figures, the shape
of their faces, and the way in which the robes pool around
their feet like water. The garments are brilliantly
decorated, reflecting the bold designs so popular among
women of the pleasure districts. Tsuru-jo reproduced the
woven patterns with great delicacy and detail, her
threadlike strokes of gold paint effectively imitating the
lustrous quality of brocade. Tsuru-jo's fastidious
brushwork is also evident in the faces of the two women,
rendered with the precision and sensitivity that were the
hallmarks of her style.

16. Inagaki Tsuru-jo

Courtesan
Hanging scroll, ink and colors on silk, 77.2 x 27.5 cm.
Signature: Inagaki-shi Tsuru-jo hitsu
Seals: Ina-shi no in; Azana Senrei etsu
William Sturgis Bigelow Collection
Courtesy, Museum of Fine Arts, Boston
(not in exhibition)

This seemingly modest courtesan deliberately assumes an elegant pose as she pauses to glance back over her shoulder, voluminous sleeves swinging at her sides. One hand is entirely hidden within her sleeves, but the other holding a sprig of fern makes a subtly enticing gesture. Although perhaps only mildly sensuous to us, such paintings were quite appealing to Edo-period Japanese. Some courtesans were revered like Buddhist deities, for they offered love and compassion, be it worldly rather than spiritual.

The willowy, sinuous figure of this courtesan closely resembles the type of woman painted by Tsukioka Settei, and it is easy to understand why Tsuru-jo is believed to have been his pupil. Similarities include the pose of the courtesan and the manner of brushwork, but in particular the type of face and hairstyle.[10] As always, Tsuru-jo's linework and application of color show an incredible degree of refinement. Especially notable is the exacting fashion in which she rendered the facial features and hair of the courtesan with thin, almost microscopic lines. The brushwork defining the robes is bold in comparison, especially in the right lower sleeve where the inner lines exhibit dramatic flourishes. The skill of this painting indicates the high level of professional work done by women ukiyo-e artists in the eighteenth century.

Notes

1. San was the daughter of Moronobu's son, Morofusa (active 1685-1703). She is recorded as having done a painting at age twelve depicting two women.
2. Chiyo-jo may have been Utamaro's wife.
3. Her earliest recorded work painted at age twelve was a picture of Kitano Tenjin, according to Akai Tatsurō, ed., *Nikuhitsu ukiyo-e*, vol. 2, 54.
4. Sources which record that Ryū-jo studied with Moronobu are Kikuoka Tenryō, *Kindai seijidan*, vol. 4 (1734), and Okada Heiji, ed., *Kinsei itsujin gashi*.
5. See Ushiyama Mitsuru, "Yamazaki Ryū-jo kō," 1-18; Akai, ed., *Nikuhitsu ukiyo-e*, vol. 2, 54.
6. Ibid., 6.
7. This painting is in the Nogata Collection in Yokohama, and has a box inscription dated 1801 by Santō Kyōden. For an illustration, see Akai, ed., *Nikuhitsu ukiyo-e*, vol. 2, no. 26.
8. In comparison with other schools of Japanese painting, it is frequently the case that we have only scant information about the lives of ukiyo-e artists.
9. Other known early paintings include a *bijin* leaning out from underneath a mosquito net reading a letter (age thirteen), in a private Japanese collection; a *bijin* carrying an umbrella (age fourteen), in the MOA Museum of Art; two *bijin* standing by a horse (age fourteen), in a private Japanese collection; and a courtesan entertaining a male customer (age fourteen), in the Otani Collection. For reproductions, see Ushiyama Mitsuru,"Yamazaki Ryū-jo kō" and Akai, ed., *Nikuhitsu ukiyo-e*, vol. 2, 55.
10. The hairstyle worn by this courtesan is post-1772 in date, indicating that the painting, too, was done after that time.

Chapter Four: Haiku Poet-Painters
Chiyo and Kikusha: Two Haiku Poets

By Fumiko Y. Yamamoto

The poetry of brevity and evocation, haiku,[1] gloriously blossomed during the late seventeenth century in the works of Matsuo Bashō (1644-1694). This master poet expressed his profound empathy with the human and natural worlds in concise three-line poems of only seventeen syllables (the first and third lines contain five syllables, and the second line has seven). His haiku reflect a sensitivity to many diverse aspects of nature: he delights in the fragile beauty of tiny, frail creatures and humble weeds, as well as in the more monumental grandeur of landscapes enveloped by the incessant flow of the four seasons. Using the direct and unadorned vocabulary of everyday life, Bashō sketches the fleeting and piquant encounter between heightened human sensibility and the ephemeral natural environment. Because of its simplicity of expression and earnest sentiments, haiku became widely admired by commoners. Bashō's succinct, redolent poetic style inspired a number of poets throughout Japan to compose in the haiku idiom, including many women.[2]

The women who succeeded in distinguishing themselves in haiku were frequently directly connected with Bashō or his pupils. The male poet Kagami Shikō (1665-1731), who came from the Mino area (Gifu prefecture), was among Bashō's so-called ten disciples.[3] After Bashō's death, Shikō energetically spread the art of haiku throughout Mino and in the surrounding areas.[4] Two women haiku poets emerged from Shikō's Mino school: Kaga no Chiyo (Chiyo of Kaga) and Kikusha. Eventually their haiku became more popular than that of Shikō. Chiyo and Kikusha are special among women haiku poets because they also brushed paintings to accompany their verses. This chapter will focus on their lives and the development of their literary and visual arts.

Chiyo (1703-1775)

Chiyo was born in 1703 in the town of Matsutō in Kaga (Ishikawa prefecture), the daughter of the scroll mounter Fukumasuya.[5] Information about this gifted child's early poetry is incomplete although she was supposed to have composed her first haiku at age seven. Chiyo's name became well-known in poetic circles after she became Shikō's pupil. The haiku master had journeyed to Kaga where one of his local pupils, Kitagataya Taisui, recommended that Shikō meet Chiyo. Shikō was so impressed with Chiyo's poetry that he eagerly accepted her into his school. He enthusiastically praised the sixteen-year-old Chiyo in a letter to one of his followers, calling her "a marvelous expert [poet]." Shikō might have had an ulterior motive in inviting this young girl to join his school, for her talent would have enhanced its reputation, especially since women poets were still rather rare at that time.[6]

It is uncertain whether or not Chiyo ever married. If she did, it was at an early age for a brief period of less than two years while she lived in the neighboring town of Kanazawa. By the time she was twenty, she had returned to her parents' home in Matsutō. When she was twenty-three, Chiyo traveled to Ise (Mie prefecture) to visit another of Bashō's students, Bakurinsha Otsuyū (1675-1739). Although Shikō was her official teacher, Chiyo became affiliated with Otsuyū and was accepted into his poetic coterie in order to expand her study of the art of haiku. This association lasted for more than ten years, until Otsuyū's death. Both Shikō and Otsuyū included Chiyo's poems in several of their edited collections of haiku, an indication of their great respect for her poetry.

When Chiyo was between the ages of thirty and forty, a succession of deaths occurred in the Fukumasuya family: her parents, her older brother, and his wife all died. Chiyo was left alone to carry on the family business. During this ten-year period she wrote very few haiku, apparently because of pressing business needs. Not until she was almost fifty years old did she find time to compose poetry once again, after she became free of her familial responsibilities by adopting a married couple as the successors to her household.[7] After arranging that the Fukumasuya family business would be carried on by her adopted children, Chiyo became ordained as a Buddhist nun in 1754.[8] At this time she added the suffix *ni* (nun) to her name and became known as Chiyo-ni (Nun Chiyo).[9] On the day of her tonsure, Chiyo wrote that she was not seeking to denounce this wretched world, but instead she was searching for a new way "to enhance my heart to take after pure water which flows day and night."[10] Chiyo commemorated the occasion with a haiku:

Kami o yuu	Not coiffuring my hair
Te no hima akete	Will leave my hands free
Kotatsu kana	To spend my time at the *kotatsu*.[11]

A *kotatsu* is a type of footwarmer; the haiku suggests that Chiyo felt she would now have time to relax and to compose haiku. She did not live in a temple as did conventional nuns, but instead stayed at Fukumasuya. Becoming a nun gave her a certain amount of freedom—with a heart as free as flowing water she would not be hindered or disturbed by worldly cares.

Her status as a nun gave her another advantage—the privilege to travel and to fraternize with other poets. During the Edo period, women of the samurai and merchant classes were subject to a strict Confucian code of conduct promulgated by the military government. Women's main sphere of activity was restricted to their homes, where they were required to obey the male members of their families. To freely associate with outsiders, especially males, was socially taboo. Buddhist nuns, however, were not bound to these restrictive social codes, and because of their religious status they were granted a measure of respect.[12]

Many haiku poets now came to visit Chiyo, and she took several trips to seek kindred souls. Her acquaintance with two female poets is noteworthy. One of them was Shisen, who lived in Kanazawa. During one visit Chiyo and Shisen composed two sets of thirty-six linked verses. Shisen wrote in the foreword that the verses were made "when Chiyo, a friend who plies her pole in the same stream [of haiku writing as mine] came to visit."[13] The poems were dedicated to the temple Gyōzenji in Matsutō.

Chiyo also enjoyed a close association with another female poet who lived in her hometown of Matsutō, Suye of the Aikawaya household. Suye, who was sixteen years younger than Chiyo, respected Chiyo as her haiku teacher. They frequently exchanged haiku as well as letters, and Suye was also Chiyo's traveling companion on several journeys. Their friendship continued until Chiyo's death, after which the Aikawaya family built a memorial in Matsutō in her honor.

When Chiyo was fifty-eight, she went to Kyoto to attend a Buddhist ceremony held at Higashi Honganji and then traveled to Nagoya to see the poet Yokoi Yayū (1702-1783) and the painter Naitō Tōho (?-1788). During this visit, Chiyo wrote out two of her most famous poems, one about morning glories and the other about one hundred gourds; Tōho then added paintings to her calligraphy. The morning glory haiku is perhaps the best-known of Chiyo's verses.

Asagao ni	By morning glories
Tsurube torarete	The well-dipper has been ensnared—
Moraimizu	I will borrow water.

Many modern critics argue that the poem is too logical to be truly poetic, but despite these criticisms the poem is widely admired and the name of Chiyo has come to be associated with the morning glory.[14] The delicate morning glory, with its tenacious vine and flowers blossoming anew everyday, is a suitable emblem for Chiyo who dedicated most of her life to crystalizing in words the fleeting beauties of nature.

The gourd poem had been composed while Chiyo visited the Zen temple Eiheiji in Echizen (Fukui prefecture) when she was twenty-four. The abbot of the temple asked her to write a haiku on the Buddhist theme "three worlds in one heart."[15] Chiyo responded with the following verse:

Hyakunari ya	One hundred gourds—
Tsuru hitosuji no	All from
Kokoro yori	The heart of a single vine.

This haiku refers to the Buddhist understanding that there is no reality outside human consciousness, and that the three worlds of unenlightened men spring from the human mind, just as a single vine produces a multiplicity of gourds of various shapes.[16] It is evident that this haiku was one of Chiyo's favorites, since she wrote out this poem when she visited Nagoya. Chiyo was also skilled at *haiga*, the combination of simplified painting and haiku verse.[17] An example of her *haiga* taking as its theme the gourd poem follows.

17. Chiyo

Hut and Gourds
Hanging scroll, ink with light color on paper,
95.7 x 28.5 cm.
Signature: Chiyo-ni
Seal: Chiyo
Private collection

In this scroll, Chiyo has written her haiku out in three lines, creating a fluent diagonal movement from left to right. The thickly brushed top and bottom columns counterbalance the delicate middle column, creating a subtle rhythm. The calligraphy is offset by the painting of a hut at the lower left. The tip of the vine on the roof extends as if to capture the last word of the flowing calligraphy. Chiyo's written signature and her seal impressed in red at the end of the eaves repeat the dotted pattern of the gourds. The painting is serene yet not static: the graceful movement of the vine and the gentle bobbing rhythm of the gourds swaying in the wind infuse the space with vibrant nature.

In 1763, the monk-poet Mugaian Kihaku collected and published a number of Chiyo's poems in the *Chiyo-ni kushū* (Collection of Nun Chiyo's Verses). This edition contained 546 haiku. At the time, Chiyo was sixty years old; it was rather rare to have a collection of poems published during a poet's own lifetime, and therefore this publication attests to the contemporary recognition of Chiyo as a poet.[18] In the same year, another incident which confirms her fame took place. She was commissioned by the Maeda daimyo of Kaga to inscribe twenty-one of her poems on six scrolls and fifteen fans which were then included as gifts from the ruling Tokugawa government to Korean envoys. Among these poems, she included the haiku of one hundred gourds.

As she aged, Chiyo suffered from asthma and was often bedridden, but despite her physical decline she continued composing haiku. The following haiku alludes to her days confined in a room as if in a hermitage.

Shigururu ya	Late autumn drizzle–
Hitoma ni kinō	In one room, my yesterday
Kyō mo kure	And today, too, have passed away.

Chiyo died in the ninth month of the year 1775, at the age of seventy-two.[19] In her last poem, her recollection that she had savored many of nature's gifts, including the pleasure of moon-viewing, led her to accept with serenity her approaching death.

Tsuki mo mite	I've also viewed the moon
Ware wa kono yo o	From this world
Kashiku kana	Now I too shall wane.

Several other haiku written in 1775 also seem to reveal her awareness of impending death:

Chō wa yume no	A butterfly wanders into
Nagori wakeiru	The remnant of dreams–
Hanano kana	A field of flowers.

Shimizu suzushi	Spring water is cool
Hotaru no kiete	A firefly faded
Nani mo nashi	And nothing remains.

Chiyo was a butterfly chasing the fictional world of haiku. She also resembled a firefly, flickering within the light of creation for an instant, before becoming engulfed by the constant welling of time and vanishing without any regrets. At the end of her days these two delicate insects became vehicles for Chiyo's reflection on her creative life. Chiyo seems to have been particularly fond of the butterfly, an image which accompanied her to her last days.

Chōchō ya	A butterfly–
Nani o yume mite	What dream
Hanezukai	Is making your wings flutter?

Mono hitotsu	It did not utter a word
Iwade kochō no	And a little butterfly's spring
Haru kurenu	Has passed away.

The subject of a butterfly's dream commonly refers to the fourth-century B.C. Chinese philosopher Chuang Tzu who dreamed he was a butterfly. When he awoke, he could not decide whether he was a man dreaming he was a butterfly, or a butterfly dreaming he was a man. However, in Chiyo's poem the reference to the Chinese episode is not essential to understanding the poet's imaginary assimilation into the butterfly's tiny cosmos. Chiyo also created *haiga* inspired by the theme of butterflies.

18. Chiyo

Butterflies
Hanging scroll, ink on paper, 100.5 x 26.7 cm.
Signature: Chiyo-ni
Seal: Soen
Private collection
Published: Rosenfield, *The Japanese Courtier: Painting, Calligraphy, and Poetry from the Fogg Art Museum, the Philip Hofer Collection* (Santa Barbara Museum of Art: 1980), 40 (no. 25); Rosenfield and Cranston, *The Courtly Tradition in Japanese Art and Literature* (Tokyo: Kōdansha, 1973), 124.

Chōchō ya	A butterfly
Onago no michi no	On a maiden's path–
Ato ya saki	Now behind, now in front.

Chiyo's graceful calligraphy moves effortlessly from the center to the right, and then to the left, as if to trace a butterfly's curving course of flight. In reality Chiyo may have seen one butterfly escorting a girl. In the scroll, however, she painted two butterflies to achieve spatial harmony. The two insects seem to pay close attention to the fluid lines of the calligraphy. In the first line, the writing and the larger butterfly are so well integrated that it is difficult to discern which was put on the paper first. In the lower right, Chiyo's signature and seal alight on a clump of fine grass as though they, too, were insects.

Chiyo's attraction to butterflies indicates her preference for delicate objects; her status as a nun did not alter her refined feminine sensitivity. She composed several haiku which convey many of the manners and feelings entertained by women living at the time.

Nani kitemo	Whatever robe she wears
Utsukushū naru	She transforms to beauty
Tsukimi kana	The moon-viewing time.

Kaketaranu	Perhaps these are not enough?
Onna-gokoro ya	Her woman's heart ponders
Doyōboshi	On the summer airing day for clothes.

Tsukimi ni mo	Even at moon-viewing
Kage hoshigaru ya	Do they want to have shades?
Onago-tachi	These modest women.

Mononui ya	In sewing new clothes
Yume tatamikomu	All her dreams are enfolded–
Shiwasu no yo	The last night of the year.

Beni saita	My lips I took care to rouge–
Kuchi mo wasururu	I forget them
Shimizu kana	At the bubbling water.

Because of the haiku's economy of language, the subjects of the poems are often open to interpretation; in the haiku just quoted Chiyo could well be the heroine. The germinal idea for this last haiku was conceived when Chiyo was about twenty-five. She revised this poem several times and wrote it in its present form sometime after she was sixty. All of her poems about women reflect the sentiments of women of her era, and Chiyo shared these emotions.

Women were sensitive to the charm of natural phenomena and to their own beauty. They sought to find a tenuous balance between their vanity which urged them to show off their wealth, and their desire not to appear ostentatious. They were demure and often shied away from the curious eyes of others, yet their dreams unfolded quietly and richly through the elements they employed in their daily tasks.

Just as Chiyo was responsive to the feminine awareness of self and to the women's sphere, she was also keenly perceptive of the subtle inflections of each season. In early spring, Chiyo discerned an extraordinarily minute change on the branches of a tree:

Asa yū ni	Each morn and eve
Shizuku no futoru	The dew swells
Ki no me kana	On buds of trees.

In summer she discovered flowers capturing light:

U no hana wa	White deutzia flowers
Hi o mochinagara	Are absorbing the light
Kumorikeri	Even on a cloudy day.

She tried to find respite from the summer heat:

Suzukaze ya	Cool breeze–
Tamoto ni shimete	I will enclose it in my sleeves
Neiru made	Till I fall asleep.

The approach of autumn is implied through a change in touch:

Kaya no nami	The waves of the mosquito net
Kao ni nururu ya	Wet my face
Kesa no aki	Autumn of this morn.

As autumn matures, drenching rain fills the air:

Oto soute	Accompanying the rain
Ame ni shizumaru	The sounds are quieting–
Kinuta kana	The fulling block.

Winter is a bleak season, but Chiyo found many objects which harbor life in spite of the algid air:

Fuyu-gare ya	Winter withering,
Hitori botan no	The peonies alone
Atatamari	Embrace warmth.

Cha no hana ya	The blossoms of tea bushes
Kono yūgure o	Are glowing, to halt
Sakinobashi	This deepening dusk.

Fuku kaze no	In the blowing wind
Hanare-banare ya	All separated, separated
Fuyu-kodachi	A clump of winter trees.

Except for the winter peonies and small white tea blossoms, not many flowers bloom in the winter. Yet Chiyo reveals an unexpected flower in the following work.

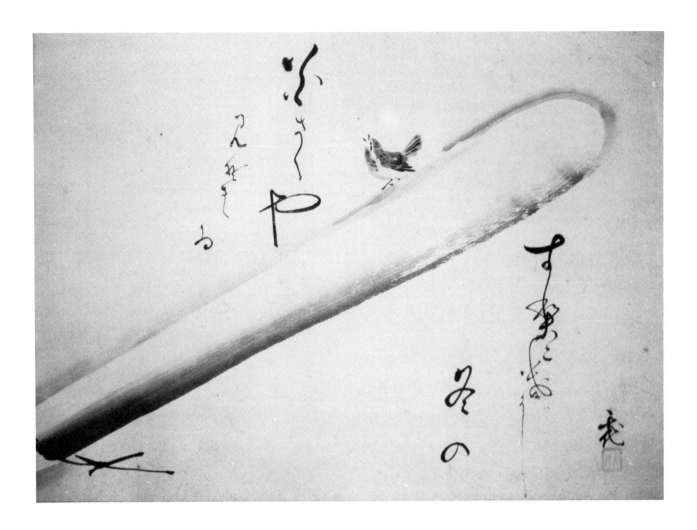

19. Chiyo

Wren and Pestle
Hanging scroll, ink on paper, 38.1 x 49.5 cm.
Signature: Chiyo
Seal: Chiyo
Mr. and Mrs. William Rushton Collection

The bold line of the pestle which diagonally cuts across the surface of the painting is balanced by the calligraphy which is divided into two parts, below and above the pestle. Chiyo's poem reads:

Surikogi ni	On the pestle
Fuyu no hana saku ya	A winter flower is blooming
Misosazai	But only a wren[20]

As in all of Chiyo's works, her use of space is masterly.[21] The word *hana* (flower) appears above the wren which seems to be singing homage to the word. The wren is aware that it is the point of brightness in Chiyo's vision. The last word, *misosazai* (wren), is written in small characters suggestive of the bird's tiny frame. The signature "Chiyo" implies that the work dates from the time before she became a nun, and therefore the poem was written in Chiyo's early or mid-career.

Chiyo was a creative poet who spent her life finding grace and charm in unassuming objects and illuminating them with simple words. Because of her uncomplicated expression and quiet praise of the immanent life force shared by humans and other inhabitants in nature, Chiyo's haiku touch the hearts of many readers. After her death, her poetry remained popular. She was frequently included in paintings depicting groups of famous haiku poets, and toward the end of the Edo period, she appeared in woodblock prints. Kitagawa Utamaro (1753-1806), Utagawa Toyokuni (1769-1825), and Utagawa Kuniyoshi (1797-1861) included Chiyo in their series of prints depicting famous women.[22] In Kuniyoshi's design of Chiyo from his series *Ken'yū fujo kagami* (Figure 5), the poetess is shown surrounded by morning glories recalling her famous haiku.

賢勇婦女鏡

千代女

5. Kuniyoshi, *Chiyo*
From the *Ken'yū fujo kagami*
Museum of Fine Arts,
Springfield, Massachusetts:
The Raymond A. Bidwell
Collection, 60.D05.281

Kikusha (1753-1826)

Kikusha was a woman poet whose name literally means "hut of chrysanthemums."[23] Unlike the summer's morning glory, the chrysanthemum endures the winter frost, and this poet differed from Chiyo both in temperament and in poetic expression.

Kikusha, in her youth called Tagami Michi, was born in 1753 in a samurai household at Chōfu in Nagato (Yamaguchi prefecture). She was the daughter of Tagami Yoshinaga and his wife Tane. Yoshinaga was a poet of Chinese-style verse, and since Kikusha was an only child until her brother was born when she was sixteen, she is believed to have received a good education which included composition of poetry. She married into the Murata family when she was sixteen, but her husband died eight years later. They did not have children, and Kikusha soon went back to her parents' home. It is not certain when Kikusha started creating haiku, but in 1780 at the age of twenty-seven, she decided to travel to the Ōu and Tōkai areas[24] to search for poetic inspiration, following the tradition of many poets in the past, including Bashō. At the beginning of her journey, she visited a temple in Hagi where she became a nun of the Shin sect of Pure Land Buddhism, the same sect to which Chiyo had belonged. Kikusha's reasons for becoming a nun were similar to those of Chiyo: she sought complete self-immersion in an artistic life, and readily abandoned worldly, mundane interests. Kikusha revealed her attitude towards a journey she was planning in the following haiku:

Tsuki o kasa ni	Wearing the moon for a hat
Kite asobaya	I will disport myself
Tabi no sora	Under the sky on my journey.

Just as she declared in her poem, Kikusha spent the rest of her life traveling and pursuing artistic activities.

After taking the tonsure, Kikusha went to Osaka and Kyoto, then visited the haiku poet Chōboin Sankyō (1726-1792) in Mino to ask for permission to become his pupil. Sankyō accepted her with delight, and gave Kikusha the name Ichijian. After leaving Mino, she continued on to Kaga to visit Chiyo's home. Chiyo had passed away seven years earlier, but Kikusha became acquainted with Chiyo's adopted son, Hakuu. At his house Kikusha wrote a poem with Chiyo's graceful figure in mind:

Hana miseru	To reveal the flower
Kokoro ni soyoge	Of your heart
Natsu-kodachi	Sway, you summer grove.

To this poem, Hakuu added the next two lines to commemorate Kikusha's moonlike visit to his humble house.[25]

Yabureshi kaya ni	To the tattered mosquito net
Utsuru tsukikage	Shifts the light of the moon.

Kikusha's journey then took her to the coast of northwest Japan. Although she enjoyed the beautiful scenery, the venture was often arduous. One of her poems was composed while she was lost in the mountains:

Yamanaka ya	Amidst the deep mountains
Kasa ni ochiba no	On my hat
Oto bakari	Only the sounds of falling leaves.

The poem portrays the treading of a lonely wayfarer, but Kikusha's enjoyment of carefree roving apparently outweighed the hardships of the journey.

When Kikusha reached Niigata during this trip, she studied calligraphy with a local master named Goshō (Five Pines) who is believed to have influenced the development of her strong and free brushwork. From the northern tip of the main island, she went across to the Pacific Ocean side and finally reached Edo, where she stayed for three years. Her name must have been known to the poets in the new capital, because she was invited to many poetry meetings and tea gatherings. In 1784 she left Edo, taking the Tōkaidō (Eastern Coastal Way) to return home. Before she reached Chōfu, she stopped at Mino again. There she formally learned the art of tea ceremony under Itō Munenaga, and was thereafter frequently invited to attend many elegant tea parties.

When she at last joined her parents after an absence of five years, Kikusha expressed her joy at the reunion which occurred at the start of a new year:

Tokete yuku	Thawing and melting
Mono mina aoshi	All are green
Haru no yuki	In spring snow.[26]

Her stay at home, however, did not last very long, and after a year she left for the southern part of Japan and visited the Kyūshū and Kinki areas. After this journey, Kikusha set off for Kyoto again in 1790 to participate in the centennial ceremony on the anniversary of Bashō's death. After attending the ceremony, she visited the Ōbaku temple Manpukuji in Uji, an area famous for its superb tea. Manpukuji was strongly influenced by Chinese culture, and Kikusha commented "I felt as if I had been on Chinese land." When she left the temple, the contrast of the foreign elements with her native country must have touched her deeply and she composed one of her best-known haiku:[27]

Sanmon o	Leaving the mountain gate,
Izureba Nihon zo	I found Japan, indeed–
Chatsumi-uta	The song of the tea leaf pickers.

During this trip to Kyoto, Kikusha started composing *waka* poetry in addition to haiku. One of her first *waka* was created when she visited Mount Yoshino, renowned for its masses of cherry blossoms which had been extolled in poetry for centuries. It was summer when Kikusha went to the mountain, and there were no traces left of the cherry blossoms. Remembering that in Bashō's book, *Oi no kobumi* (Notes in a Straw Satchel, circa 1690), the haiku master had expressed a poetic vision in which "anywhere a poet looks, there are flowers," Kikusha composed the following *waka*:

Natsu kitemo	Even though I've come in summer,
Hana ka to miete	They appear like flowers
Yoshinoyama	On Mount Yoshino;
Mine no aoba ni	Over the green-leafed peak–
Kakaru shirakumo	Draping white clouds.

She succeeded the *waka* with a haiku:

Natsuyama ni	Above the summer mountain–
Kumo mite sumasu	Satisfied by clouds
Yoshino kana	Here at Yoshino.

The *waka* solemnly explains the logic behind the artistic composition, while the terse haiku reveals the poet's stance in a brief flash: the anticipated occasion of flower viewing is supplanted by a complete absorption in the beauty of the clouds. The haiku presents a casual connoisseur's approach to the heavy traditional canon of beauty. Because of its fresh and light quality, the haiku is more appealing than the *waka*.

In 1793 Kikusha revisited Edo, and at this time Kikuchi Tōgan taught her to play the seven-stringed *ch'in*, an instrument traditionally beloved by Chinese poets and sages. She left Edo the following year, and traveled along the Tōkaidō again. Along the road, she composed haiku and sometimes accompanied them with paintings. The following *haiga* by Kikusha made on a different trip recalls the poem and painting combinations she made during this journey on the Tōkaidō.

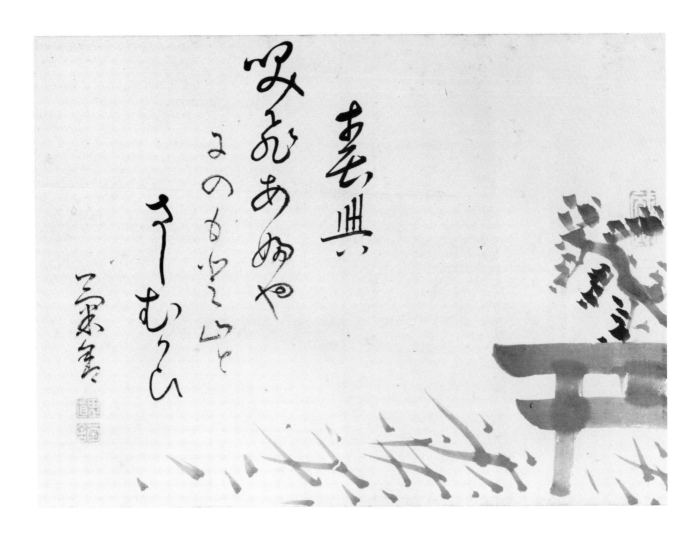

20. Kikusha

Spring Inspiration
Hanging scroll, ink on paper, 20 x 28.6 cm.
Signature: Kikusha
Seals: Tagami Michi, Kikusha; Gishu
Kato Shōshun Collection

Entitled *Shunkō* or ''Spring Inspiration,'' the poem reads:

Waraiau ya	Smiling at each other
Ni no Motoyama to	Motoyama with a red gate
Sashimukai	And I stand face to face.[28]

This haiku seems to commemorate Kikusha's visit to Motoyama, the site of a Shinto shrine, and it may have been written during her journey to northern Japan when she visited Akita. The auspicious beginning of a new year is reflected in her haiku. The Japanese new year begins with spring, and during this holiday season people pay homage at Shinto shrines. A red gate called *torii* marks the entrance to these shrines. Kikusha used a soft thick brush to paint the *torii* gate and pine tree, both propitious symbols. The pointed blades of grass direct the viewer's eyes to the left, where the calligraphy is executed in a spontaneous and graceful hand. The title and eloquent first line include weighty Chinese characters and are followed by a lightly inked and somewhat angular second line that contrasts with the smooth and clear third line. The structure of this work attests to Kikusha's skillful blending of poem and painting: the image and calligraphy form two counter balanced diagonal masses that suggest composure and harmony.

One of the most famous barriers for regulating traffic to and from Edo was established at Hakone on the Tōkaidō. When passing through this barrier, Kikusha chanted one of her most charming haiku which she composed along the road.

Te ni nosete	Placing it on my palm
Seki no to koemu	I will cross the barrier gate–
Sumiregusa	A wild violet.

The gate, which was rigidly guarded by officials, was linked with the small purple flower by her poetic imagination, thus mitigating human restrictions and marking her passage with a humble and natural adornment.

Kikusha sought almost avariciously to develop her talents, and when she was in Kyoto she furthered her *ch'in*-playing skills by studying with a courtier, Lord Hiramatsu. Through the art of *ch'in* playing, Kikusha must have come to be well-known in Kyoto's high society. A former minister invited her to his musical gatherings and gave her personal *ch'in* the name *Ryūsui* (Flowing Water).

Kikusha acquired more artistic associates on her second trip to Kyūshū in 1796. At this time she befriended Confucian scholars and poets who wrote in the Chinese style, and consequently she began to compose poems in this manner as well. In contrast to *waka*, which utilizes only Japanese words, haiku include words of Chinese origin. Kikusha's talents seemed appropriate for haiku, and therefore the Chinese poetic style may have been easy for her to master. In her late years she became increasingly occupied with writing poems in the Chinese manner.

In 1803 Kikusha was invited by Mōri Baimon, the daimyo of Nagato who was also a poet, to create a joint work of poetry and painting with Watarai Bunryūsai,[29] a prominent painter. Lord Baimon was eager to associate with Kikusha; on several occasions he sought her verses, and he also deigned to give her several of his own poems. Just as Chiyo's poetic achievements were recognized by the authorities who selected her poetry as a gift to the Korean envoys, so, too, were Kikusha's artistic endeavors acknowledged by high society in her region when Baimon became interested in her poetry.

Kikusha spent many years traveling until she died in Chōfu in 1826 at the age of seventy-three.[30] It is believed that she visited the Kyoto area seven times and Kyūshū four times, in addition to numerous trips to neighboring areas. On each journey, she met poets and attended poetry gatherings, musical performances, and tea ceremonies. One of her most memorable experiences occurred when she visited the temple Hōryūji in Nara in 1812. She was allowed to play an ancient Chinese *ch'in* which was one of the temple's treasures. Kikusha played before the statue of Prince Shōtoku, who had founded the temple in 607, and she honored this happy occasion with a haiku:

Kaoru kaze ya	A fragrant breeze
Morokoshi kakete	Is blowing from China
Nana no o ni	Over these seven strings.

It must have been indeed an unusual opportunity for a commoner to touch this precious instrument.[31] This event was obviously an unforgettable highlight in her life and Kikusha concluded her published collection of poems, *Taorigiku* (Handpicked Chrysanthemums), with this experience. Printed in 1813 by the Kyoto publisher Tachibana Jihei, the *Taorigiku* consists of four sections: the first part contains a travelogue with haiku that Kikusha composed during her first trip to the Ōu and Tōkai areas; the second part includes haiku and paintings of some of the Tōkaidō's fifty-three stations made during her 1793 journey; the third and fourth parts consist of Chinese poems with related haiku.[32]

In the third part of the *Taorigiku*, Kikusha described her philosophy of life at age fifty-seven:

> It is said that a man less than one hundred years old has the worries of one thousand years. In contrast to this saying, I have the enjoyments of one thousand years. In my life, entertainment is my trade and I entertain myself alike with those I know and with those whom I do not know. I enjoy years spent in traveling and I also enjoy returning home. I enjoy both criticism and praise. I have devoted myself to enjoyment and I hardly have time to fold my fingers to count my age.[33]

The previously discussed haiku in which she wears the moon as her hat appears at the beginning of part one in the *Taorigiku*. Kikusha's youthful decision to journey under the open sky expressed in this haiku, and the description of her enjoyment of life quoted in the passage above, testify to her aim of living a life in which she could savor artistic diversions. Most of her poems reflect joy upon viewing a beautiful scene, meeting another individual of the same taste, or attending a memorable event. The only time when sorrow visited this strong-willed poet seems to have been at the time of inevitable separation from people by death. Since she was an only daughter, she enjoyed her parents' love and attention; her father's death left Kikusha with a profound sense of loss. Many of her haiku are devoid of sentimentality and partially because of this, a sense of pathos is infrequent in her poetry. The poems composed at her father's death in the summer of 1807, however, are full of personal feelings. Her Chinese-style poem mourns:

> Human life is like the morning dew;
> It yields to the wind and falls before my eyes.
> Frail are the dewdrops on the morning glory
> As drop by drop, they return to the spring of eternity.

Her haiku which follows this Chinese poem sighs at evanescence:

Chirishi hito wa	The life now perished–
Kesa o kagiri no	Limited as of this morn
Asagao ka	To morning glory time.

The autumn of that year left her with a painful realization which pierced her total being:

Mi hitotsu no	My body all alone
Aki ka to zo omou	In this autumn, I feel–
Ame no kure	The dusk in rain.

These pensive moments are, however, rather rare for Kikusha, and most of her poems reveal a positive acceptance of this world. In contrast to Chiyo, who seems to have preferred to pose herself quietly before an object and to then observe it until she became assimilated into it, Kikusha was an individual of action who rigorously sought out the source of her interest. The following two works are representative of her life-view, symbolized in the images of flowers.

21. Kikusha

Orchid
Hanging scroll, ink on paper, 29.3 x 46.7 cm.
Signature: Kikusha
Seals: Kinshin; Tagami Michi, Kikusha; Gishu
Private collection

The orchid, a symbol of modesty and purity to Chinese scholars, is one of the celebrated "four gentlemen" plants along with bamboo, plum, and chrysanthemum. It became a common subject for scholar-amateur painters in both China and Japan. Kikusha was fond of Chinese poetry and must have felt a strong affinity with the orchid. Her boundless inner energy is echoed in the vigorous rhythm in the descending lines of writing as well as in the orchid flowers and leaves. Expanding outward and upward, the leaves actively extend out of the picture plane. The blossoms have a thriving existence of their own, imbued with such sprightly movement that they resemble winged insects about to take flight. A comparison with orchids by other artists (Cat. 45 and 78) reveals the vibrant personal nature of Kikusha's brushwork. Within the total composition, the balanced spacing between the characters

and flowers adds dignity to the work. Kikusha accompanied her orchid with a haiku instead of a Chinese poem, creating a blend of Chinese and Japanese traditions that shows the broad range of this multifaceted artist. The haiku reads:

Amari sakite	While blooming too much
Kaori wasurezo	Do not forget your fragrance
Ran no hana	Orchid flowers.

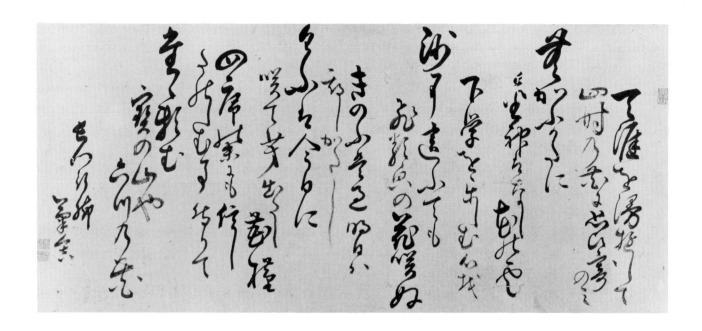

22. Kikusha

Four Haiku
Hanging scroll, ink on paper, 24.8 x 56.7 cm.
Signature: Kikusha
Seals: Kinshin; Tagami Michi, Kikusha
Shōka Collection

The four haiku included in this scroll appear at the end of part one in the *Taorigiku*. Each one refers to a season, starting with spring cherry blossoms, and each is prefaced with a comment.

Spending my life wandering on the road while keeping only the flowers of the four seasons in my thoughts:

Mukau kata ni	On my way
Konjin wa nashi	No spirit of ill fortune–
Hana no kumo	The clouds of flowers.

Enjoying learning from common things:

Suna ni hautemo	Even creeping on the sand
Hirugao no hana	A bindweed
Sakinu	Gives forth its flowers.

Yesterday has passed and tomorrow is yet uncertain:

Kyō wa kyō ni	Today, again, today
Saite medetashi	Its new blossoms are felicitous
Hanamukuge	A rose of Sharon.

Having something which I believe in and enjoy even at the end of the seasons:

Tada tanomu	My only creed–
Takara no yama ya	The mountain of treasure
Mutsu no hana	The six-petaled flowers of snow.

Kikusha's brushwork occupies the entire space with force and vitality. At the beginning of each poem the brush was dipped anew, and the strong ink tones create accents which strengthen the total composition. Some of her lines fluctuate dramatically in width, adding vigor to the calligraphy. Her signature prefaced with the words "While traveling in Nagato" is also boldly written, attesting to the confidence of the creator. From both the poems and the calligraphy emerges the figure of the poetess who willfully directed her life beyond the narrow frame of activities imposed on many women during an era of constrictive feudalism.

Both Chiyo and Kikusha pursued the beauty of flowers in each season, yet their poetic stance and consequently their artistic products are quite different. Chiyo envisioned a wren as a winter flower, and Kikusha took snow for winter blossoms. Chiyo's view is modest and intuitive, while Kikusha's vision is grand and cerebral. In spite of the differences, however, both poets are similar in one respect: they both achieved fame during their lifetimes through their intense devotion to art in a period when freedom of expression was restricted for women.[34]

Notes

1. The procedure of linking the first three lines of a *waka* (with a 5-7-5 syllable pattern) by one poet, with two final lines by a different poet (with a syllable pattern of 7 and 7) developed into a new poetic form called *renga* (linked verse). *Renga* was often created conjointly by a group of poets. *Hokku* (the starting verse of 5-7-5 syllables) was usually composed by the most prominent poet and this convention laid the groundwork for establishing the independent poetic form of haiku. Haiku is a modern term for *haikai*, an abbreviation for a type of *renga* called *haikai no renga* (comical linked verse). Bashō's haiku evolved out of this *haikai no renga* form. For a detailed description of the development of linked verse, see Howard S. Hibbett, "The Japanese Comic Linked Verse Tradition," *Harvard Journal of Asiatic Studies*, vol. 23 (1960-1961), 76-92; Earl Miner, *Japanese Linked Poetry* (Princeton, New Jersey: Princeton University Press, 1979). For *haikai* (haiku) and Bashō, see: Harold G. Henderson, *An Introduction to Haiku* (New York: Doubleday Anchor Books, 1958).

2. The proliferation of women in haiku circles is documented by such books as the *Kokin haikai jokasen* (Women *Haikai* Poets of Modern and Ancient Times) written and illustrated by Ihara Saikaku in 1682, and the *Mikawa komachi* published by one of Bashō's disciples in 1702 which included one hundred haiku by women.

3. Bashō's "ten disciples" are usually considered to include Enomoto Kikaku, Hattori Ransetsu, Morikawa Kyoroku, Mukai Kyorai, Kagami Shikō, Naitō Jōsō, Sugiyama Sanpū, Tachibana Hokushi, Shida Yaba, and Ochi Etsujin.

4. Shikō seems to have been very egotistical and his boisterous acts of self-advertisement were criticized by many of his contemporaries. He was, nevertheless, successful in popularizing haiku in many local areas.

5. Fukumasuya was the business name for the family scroll mounting shop. Commoners did not have surnames and this is one of the reasons that Chiyo was known simply as Chiyo of Kaga.

6. Among the haiku poets who came after Bashō, there were over three hundred women active during the Edo period. See Yamamoto Zentarō, "Tokugawa jidai no joryū haijin," in Miwata Gendō, ed., *Nihon josei bunka shi*, vol. 2, 614. This number, however, is still much smaller than that of male poets writing haiku during the Edo period.

7. It has been a common practice in Japan to adopt a child or a married couple into a family when there is danger that the family might become extinct. The adopted person then becomes an heir. The couple adopted by Chiyo were named Rokubei and Nao. Rokubei was a haiku poet who wrote under the name of Hakuu.

8. Chiyo entered the Shin sect of Pure Land Buddhism. Founded by the monk Shinran (1173-1262), this sect taught that faith in Amida Buddha's doctrine of compassion was the vehicle for salvation.

9. Chiyo also adopted another Buddhist name, Soen, in 1755.

10. Yamanaka Rokuhiko, *Chiyo-jo to Kikusha-ni*, 14.

11. All of the translations in the text are by the author, except where noted.

12. To trace the evolution of women in Japanese history, see Joy Paulson's "Evolution of the Feminine Ideal," in Lebra, Paulson, and Powers, eds., *Women in Changing Japan*, 1-23.

13. Murakami Genzō, "Kaga no Chiyo," in Sōga Tetsufu, ed., *Zusetsu jinbutsu Nihon no josei shi*, vol. 7, 57.

14. There is another version of the haiku which has *asagao ya* (oh, morning glory) instead of *asagao ni* (by a morning glory). This version makes the captor of the well-dipper obscure, and thus lessens the logicality of the poem.

15. The three worlds represent: 1. the world of desire, whose inhabitants have appetite and sexual desire; 2. the world of form, whose inhabitants have neither appetite nor sexual desire; 3. the formless world, whose inhabitants have no physical forms. All of these worlds are creations of the human mind. See *Japanese-English Buddhist Dictionary* (Tokyo: Daitō Shuppansha, 1965), 252.

16. It is possible to speculate that Chiyo attached another meaning to the haiku. She might have been comparing herself to the vine in the poem—a single source generating a multiplicity of forms. According to this interpretation, the gourds were not mere illusions but represented haiku, the fruits of her artistic efforts.

17. It is said that Chiyo learned the Jimyōin school style of calligraphy and that she also studied painting under Go Shunmei. Yamanaka, *Chiyo-jo to Kikusha-ni*, 11. It is not clear how much the Jimyōin school style influenced her work, but her calligraphy appears to be much freer than that of the traditional school. The extent of her formal study of painting is also uncertain.

18. Chiyo also had another collection entitled *Haikai matsu no koe* (*Haikai*: Voice of a Pine) published during her lifetime.

19. Chiyo's original grave has disappeared; however, a stone memorial, museum, and Chiyo-ni-dō (Hall of Nun Chiyo) exist to commemorate her at Shōkōji, and there is another memorial tablet at Senkōji. Both temples are in Kanazawa.

20. Translated by Stephen Addiss.

21. Nakamoto Jodō comments that Chiyo's masterful use of space must be the result of her innate talent. See his *Kaga no Chiyo kenkyū*, 247.

22. See Utamaro's *Kindai shichi saijo shika* (Seven Talented Women Poets of Modern Times), Toyokuni's *Kokon meifuden* (Famous Women of Ancient and Modern Times), and Kuniyoshi's *Kenjo reppuden* (Stories of Wise and Strong Women), *Ken'yū fujo kagami* (Mirrors of Intelligent and Strong Women), and *Kenjo hakkei* (Eight Views of Intelligent Women).

23. At first Kikusha chose a name with the same pronunciation but which means "wheel of chrysanthemums"; she changed the character combination so that it meant "hut of chrysanthemums."

24. These areas include northeast and central Japan.

25. *Utsuru* (to shift) could also refer to Chiyo's figure which had passed away. The word *utsuru* is sometimes written with the Chinese character meaning "to reflect."

26. Translated by Akira Yamamoto.

27. In 1922 a stone memorial engraved with this poem was set up in front of Manpukuji.

28. I am indebted to Professor Kōno Motoaki for his interpretation of this haiku.

29. Kikusha is believed to have studied painting under this master whose fame at that time was said to be comparable to Tani Bunchō (1763-1840).

30. Kikusha's grave is marked at two sites: one is at Tokuōji and the other at Honkakuji, both temples in Chōfu.

31. A modern critic, Kawashima Tsuyu, attributes this incident to Kikusha's ability to skillfully maneuver people for her own advantage. See Kawashima Tsuyu, *Joryū haijin*, 205-206. She describes Kikusha as a person seeking to become famous, who was successful at capturing the hearts of courtiers and celebrities.

32. Besides the *Taorigiku*, Kikusha had twenty-four other poetry collections published.

33. Kikusha, *Taorigiku* in *Kasei Tenpo haikai shū*, vol. 16 of *Koten haibungaku taikei*, annotated by Miyata Masanobu and Suzuki Katsutada (Tokyo: Shūeisha, 1971), 189.

34. I would like to express my deep appreciation to Theresa Mahoney for the critical reading of this article.

Chapter Five: *Waka* Poets in Kyoto

As previously noted, *waka* is a traditional form of Japanese poetry composed of thirty-one syllables arranged in five lines of 5-7-5-7-7. Since it was the poetic form deemed most suitable for women in the Edo period, far more women mastered the basic skills of writing *waka* than any other form of verse. In the seventeenth century, recognized women *waka* poets such as Ono Ozū and Ryōnen Gensō had been members of the elite samurai class with aristocratic connections, for whom learning to compose *waka* was part of the basic training for women (see chapter one). In the eighteenth century, however, literacy became more widespread among other classes of society, and consequently more and more women distinguished themselves in *waka*.[1] Women were especially encouraged to study *waka* by some of the leading scholars involved in the *kokugaku* or "national learning" movement.

Kokugaku was the study of classical Japanese literature and ancient writings with the aim of identifying quintessential Japanese cultural elements. It was promulgated by scholars who felt that the classical literature of the past represented the true expression of national sentiments. *Kokugaku* evolved as a reaction against the prevailing Confucian and Buddhist education, with *kokugaku* scholars attempting to revive an ancient spirit that predated the introduction of foreign influences. In many respects, *kokugaku* was synonymous with Shinto studies, and the scholars associated with it promoted a national revival of the indigenous Shinto religion.

Unlike Buddhist and Confucian texts which tended to view females as lowly creatures, *kokugaku* scholars came to recognize women as being on equal terms with men. The *kokugaku* scholar and poet Kamo no Mabuchi (1697-1769) was the leader in promoting *waka* studies among women, for he is recorded as having forty female pupils.[2] Mabuchi and other scholars cited the importance of women in the founding of Japan; the imperial line traced its ancestry back to the Sun Goddess Amaterasu, and in the Asuka and Nara periods, half of the Japanese rulers were women. Mabuchi also praised the role of Japanese women in the development of classical poetry and literature. Poems by women are included in the eighth-century *Man'yōshū*, and many aristocratic women of the Heian period were celebrated for their poetry, diaries, and prose, the most famous being Murasaki Shikibu.

It was as part of a revival of past epochs of national glory that *kokugaku* scholars reemphasized the role of women in the arts. In particular, there were a number of female *waka* poets who flourished during the Hōreki era (1751-1763).[3] Biographical material is scarce, but there is enough information to sketch out the lives of some of these women. Those who won the most popular acclaim did so because their talents were visible to the public. One of the few professions in which intelligent women of the lower classes were encouraged to display artistic skills was that of the courtesan. There were many levels of courtesans; at the bottom were low-class prostitutes, but at the top were exceptionally talented women often skilled in traditional poetry and painting.

Many courtesans were celebrated for the *waka* which they composed and shared with favored customers. Collectors and connoisseurs sought out verses written by eminent women of the "floating world," and commonly had them mounted together in long handscrolls. The artistry of courtesans was also represented in woodblock prints, which frequently depict them writing out poems and occasionally painting. Torii Kiyonobu (died 1729) designed a famous print illustrating a courtesan painting a scene of willows along a river bank while her patron watches with admiration (Figure 6). Among the most well-known of the eighteenth-century Kyoto courtesans was Ōhashi, who became famous both for her *waka* and her paintings of plum blossoms. It was not only courtesans, however, who became recognized for the artistic beauty of their *waka*. Kaji, Yuri, and Gyokuran, three women who ran a teahouse in Kyoto, also became renowned for their skills in *waka*. Women of nonaristocratic birth are credited with adding a new flavor to *waka*, which had become somewhat stale in the hands of traditional court poets.

6. Kiyonobu, *Courtesan Painter*

Ōhashi (active mid-eighteenth century)

Ōhashi was one of the many Japanese women who were sold to brothels by families having financial difficulties. Although she was the daughter of a well-to-do samurai serving the Tokugawa shogunate in Edo, her life took a tragic turn when her father withdrew from official service and became a *rōnin*.[4] Relieved of his hereditary post as well as his stipend of 1,000 *koku*, he moved to Kyoto with his wife and Ōhashi (then called Ritsu). Because the family was poor, they were forced to sell their daughter to a brothel in the Shimabara entertainment district. At this time she was given the name Ōhashi.

Ōhashi surpassed the other courtesans in intelligence as well as beauty. As the daughter of a samurai, she had received training in poetry, music, and other feminine arts such as tea ceremony and incense identification. She continued her study of *waka* in Kyoto with a member of the Reizei school, and also became adept at painting. It is ironic that the artistic talents Ōhashi had begun to develop as a proper daughter of a samurai became the foundation for her success as a courtesan. However, Ōhashi was deeply humiliated at being forced into such a lowly occupation. Her physical condition weakened and she became very sick. Doctors were unable to determine the cause of her illness, and the medications they prescribed were in vain. One day a visitor asked what was troubling her. She responded by telling him of the unfortunate circumstances which had led to her becoming a courtesan. He replied that her sickness was undoubtedly provoked by her unhappiness with her present life, and that if she adopted the Buddhist path of severing attachments to this world, she would be enlightened and thus cured. Ōhashi determined to try to put into practice what she had learned from her visitor, and diligently worked toward achieving an enlightened state of mind. Her breakthrough occurred in the Enkyō era (1744-1747) during a thunderstorm. Ōhashi abhorred thunder and ordinarily would hide herself amidst bedding and mosquito netting. This time she reflected upon her visitor's words, and after calming herself, she came out of hiding and sat quietly. Just then a huge clap of thunder shook the house, and she reached a state of enlightenment. It was at this point that Ōhashi decided to give up her life in the "floating world" of pleasure and left the Shimabara. She sought out a spiritual master, and in the spring of 1751 met the Zen monk Hakuin Ekaku (1685-1768) at the home of the Yotsugi family in Kyoto. A major figure in revitalizing Zen Buddhism during the Edo period, Hakuin had already attracted scores of followers from all walks of life. His compassion for the less fortunate is well-documented, and he encouraged Ōhashi in her spiritual quest.

Ōhashi did not fully immerse herself in Zen study at this point in her life; instead she married the man-about-town Kurihara Isso. In some ways they were opposites, but they were both interested in the arts and consequently led a simple, happy life together. Her husband chanted music from Nō drama, while Ōhashi read the *Genji monogatari* and cooked simultaneously. He was proficient in Chinese poetry, whereas she loved to compose *waka*. Both continued to maintain an interest in Zen, and would go together to visit Hakuin. Ōhashi's desire to study Zen intensified over time, and in her later years she secured her husband's permission to dissolve their marriage ties in order to become a nun. It is unclear where Ōhashi went to live, but presumably she went to study with Hakuin. After becoming a nun, Ōhashi adopted the name Erin, using the character *E* from her teacher's name Ekaku.

Ōhashi's story was so unusual that she was included in Ban Kōkei's (1733-1806) *Kinsei kijin den* (Legends of Eccentrics of Recent Times, 1790). In addition to relating much of the biographical information given above, the *Kinsei kijin den* records a later meeting between Ōhashi and Hakuin in Kyoto at the home of the priest Reizei Jakujō. Hakuin recalled his earlier encounters with Ōhashi and her husband, recounting Kurihara's profligate activities. He then reminisced about how Ōhashi used to describe many of the beautiful sights in Kyoto. In particular there was a place not far from Shōgoin famous for its view of the moon; the *Kinsei kijin den* includes an illustration of Ōhashi after she had shaved her head and become a nun, pausing amidst some rice paddies in order to catch a glimpse of the full moon (Figure 7).

The extant poems and paintings by Ōhashi seem to be products of her courtesan years because they are all signed "Ōhashi." This was obviously the period in which she achieved her greatest fame as an artist. It is likely that she continued to compose poems and to paint once she had become a nun, but she was no longer in a profession where customers begged for examples of her work. Poems by courtesans have long been admired and enthusiastically collected in Japan, partly for their inherent beauty, but perhaps more because of the "star" status of the artists themselves. Would that we had an example by Ōhashi created after her long years of Zen practice to compare with the elegant, refined artworks of her courtesan days, but unfortunately there seem to be none.

Kaji (active early eighteenth century)

Like Ōhashi, Kaji led such an interesting and unusual life that she, too, was included in the *Kinsei kijin den*. Although Kaji spent her life operating a teahouse, her position was not that of a courtesan. Her teahouse, called the Matsuya, was located near the southern

7. Mikuma Katen, *Ōhashi*
From the *Kinsei kijin den*,
1790

gate of Maruyama Park, not far from a popular Shinto shrine in Kyoto's Gion district.[5] From the illustration in the *Kinsei kijin den* we know that it was an open-air establishment, serving tea to customers who sat on benches (Figure 8). Such teahouses were popular at the time, and in fact can still be found in areas of Kyoto today. The factor which distinguished the Matsuya from other teahouses was Kaji's fame as a poetess.

Kaji's birthplace is unknown, but some scholars speculate that she was the daughter of a Kyoto poet.[6] She was given an extensive literary education, and in her youth loved to read old stories. By age fourteen her skills in *waka* were recognized, and from that time on, people flocked to the Matsuya in order to hear her recite poetry. Among her steady customers over the years were famous poets and intellectuals, including Nakanoin Michishige (1631-1710) and Reizei Tamemura (1712-1774) who reputedly were great admirers of her *waka*.[7] She did not restrict herself to conventional themes like other poets of her age; instead she drew upon her own experiences. In addition to *waka*, Kaji also composed haiku. In 1703, a samurai from Owari named Asahi Bunzaemon recorded his visit to the Matsuya in his diary *Omurōchūki*, stating how impressed he was with Kaji's poetry and that her fame had spread to the Kantō (Edo) area of Japan.[8]

In 1707, 120 of Kaji's *waka* were collected by the Edo poet Ameishi (dates unknown) and published in a three-volume book entitled the *Kaji no ha* (Paper Mulberry [Kaji] Leaves, Cat. 26). This book, along with her later appearance in the *Kinsei kijin den*, served to increase her popularity and to transmit the legacy of her work. A century after her death, Kaji continued to be one of the most beloved of Kyoto women poets. The ukiyo-e artist Utagawa Kuniyoshi included portraits of her in at least three series of prints he did featuring famous women of the past.[9] His depiction of Kaji from the *Kenjo reppuden* series shows her gorgeously attired, seated on an outside bench beneath a branch of blossoming plum (Figure 9). Brush in hand and writing materials beside her, she contemplates the verses it would be appropriate to inscribe on the folding fans to her left. Her fame continues to the present day; Kaji is remembered each year in Kyoto's festival "Jidai Matsuri" held on October 22, where men and women dress up as famous personalities from various eras of Japanese history and parade through the streets.[10]

Because her poems were casually brushed for friends and favored customers, Kaji's works were treated as ephemera and extant examples are rare. The calligraphy in her few remaining works displays vigor and flair, reflecting a self-assurance and boldness of spirit that enabled Kaji both to manage a teahouse and to become respected in the Kyoto literary

8. Mikuma Katen, *Matsuya Teahouse* From the *Kinsei kijin den*, 1790

9. Kuniyoshi, *Kaji*
From the *Kenjo reppuden*
Museum of Fine Arts,
Springfield, Massachusetts:
The Raymond A. Bidwell
Collection, 60.D05.330

world dominated by men. Despite the fact that many of her poems are about love, she remained single throughout her life. She adopted a daughter named Yuri who became her successor at the Matsuya.

Yuri (1694-1764)[11]

Yuri's background is as enigmatic as her adoptive mother Kaji's. She is believed to have come from Edo, and her original family name may have been Kimura.[12] Like Kaji, Yuri was exceptionally gifted in *waka*. In 1727, 159 of her poems were published in a volume entitled the *Sayuri ba* (Leaves from a Small Lily).[13] Critics usually claim that Kaji was the better poet of the two, yet Yuri certainly inherited her mother's aptitude for *waka*.

Upon hearing of the story of Yuri's life from the Kyoto monk Yamaoka Geppō (1760-1839), the scholar-poet Rai San'yō (1780-1832) wrote a biography of her, heralding Yuri as a model for other women to follow.[14] According to San'yō, Yuri was exceptionally intelligent, and after she was adopted by Kaji she followed her mother's example and began to compose poems. Yuri spent her days serving tea to the customers who visited the Matsuya, but whenever she had a moment of leisure, she would take out her brush, paper, and inkstone and write verses inspired by the world around her. The courtier-poet Reizei Tamemura took a special interest in Yuri and became an important mentor to her. She would take her poems to him for criticism, whereupon he encouraged her and offered instruction.

Examples of Yuri's calligraphy are almost as rare as those by Kaji. She, too, wrote out verses to give to poet-friends, and undoubtedly complied with requests from Matsuya customers. In spite of the close connection between these two women, their calligraphic as well as literary styles are distinctly different. Yuri's writing is smooth and flowing, in contrast to Kaji's which is full of dramatic flourishes. Whereas Kaji's poetry seems to brim over with her own feelings, Yuri most often took nature as her subject.

Yuri was apparently a striking beauty like Kaji, and young men from wealthy and distinguished families in Kyoto were invariably attracted to her. However, Yuri fell in love with a young samurai named Tokuyama, the son of a shogunal vassal from Edo. They lived together happily for ten years and had a daughter whom they named Machi. When Tokuyama was suddenly called back to Edo to assume the position of family leader, the couple was devastated. He wanted to take Yuri and their daughter with him, but Yuri declined, knowing that her humble social position would only cause friction with his family and unhappiness for all involved. She remained in Kyoto, dedicating herself to running the Matsuya, composing poetry, and bringing up her daughter Machi (who later came to be called Gyokuran).

Machi (Ike Gyokuran) (1727 or 1728-1784)

Yuri reared her daughter with pride, frequently telling her, "Your father was a samurai. You must respect yourself as a woman–never look down on yourself!"[15] Machi received instruction in *waka* from her mother,[16] and may have begun to study painting around the age of ten under Yanagisawa Kien (1706-1758).[17] Kien was one of the first Japanese artists to experiment with the Chinese literati painting tradition, which is called *nanga* or *bunjinga*

10. Mikuma Katen, *Taiga and Gyokuran*
From the *Kinsei kijin den*, 1790

in Japan (see chapter six). Kien may have patronized the Matsuya, whereupon Yuri arranged for him to teach Machi. One of Kien's artistic names was Gyokkei (Jade Cassia), and he purportedly gave Machi the name Gyokuran,[18] by which she is most commonly known.

Since Yuri wanted to insure that Gyokuran's literary talents and artistic interests would continue to be encouraged, she was judicious in selecting a proper mate. Exactly how Taiga and Gyokuran got together is not clear, but most scholars believe that it was Yuri who cultivated Taiga and persuaded him to marry her daughter around the year 1751.[19] Rai San'yō referred to this as one of Yuri's triumphs. At that time Taiga was living in the Gion neighborhood, not far from the Matsuya. He purportedly could be found daily sitting on a mat outside the gate of Sōrinji temple, producing paintings and calligraphy as well as carving seals for passers-by.[20] All sources relate that Taiga and Gyokuran were the perfect match. Both artistically gifted, they passed their time painting, practicing calligraphy, composing poems, and making music together. Their eccentric behavior assured them a chapter in the *Kinsei kijin den*, which includes a charming woodblock-printed illustration of the couple (Figure 10) by Mikuma Katen (1730-1794). Taiga and Gyokuran are depicted sitting in a room littered with paintings, calligraphy, brushes, and other writing equipment. Oblivious to the clutter around them, they are smiling and playing music–Gyokuran the *koto* and Taiga a miniature lute. Many delightful anecdotes about this unorthodox couple have been passed down to us, including the accounts that they frequently wore each other's clothes, and that they enjoyed playing music in the nude. An overnight guest once reported that unknowingly he was given the only *futon* (bedding); when he woke up the next morning he was shocked to find Taiga rolled up in a rug and Gyokuran sleeping beneath painting paper and silk.

Neither Taiga nor Gyokuran cared about money or material possessions. Gyokuran paid little attention to clothing or makeup, and she did not shave her eyebrows as was customary for married women. They lived near Gion in a ramshackle hut believed to have been first owned by Yuri, and eked out a modest living by selling their paintings and calligraphy.[21] At first they painted lanterns for teahouses and tobacco pouches for geisha, as well as fans for all occasions. Later, however, they both achieved recognition and began receiving commissions for larger scale paintings. Although Gyokuran had learned to paint before meeting Taiga, he quickly became the major influence upon the development of her painting style.

Gyokuran, in return, gave Taiga advice in composing *waka*. They further sharpened their skills in poetry by taking lessons from Reizei Tamemura. Although Gyokuran was highly regarded as a poet, her *waka* skills were never refined to the point of rivaling her mother or grandmother. Nevertheless, eighteen of her verses were included in the compendium *Ruidai wakana shū* published in 1827,[22] and nineteen in the small volume *Shirofuyō* (White Mallow, 1910).[23] Compared to the scarcity of extant works by Kaji or Yuri, more original examples of Gyokuran's *waka* remain, due to her fame as Taiga's wife. In comparison to the relatively freely brushed calligraphy by her grandmother and mother, Gyokuran seems to have cultivated more control; consequently her writing has a polished elegance. Gyokuran also differed from her mother and grandmother by pouring most of her artistic energy into painting, which will be discussed more fully in the next chapter. Her unique background led her to create a new variation upon the literati painting tradition, combining Chinese-style subject matter with *waka* inscriptions.[24]

Gyokuran inherited the Matsuya upon Yuri's death in 1764. However, the teahouse had passed its golden age, and when the writer Takizawa (Kyokutei) Bakin (1767-1848) visited Kyoto in 1802, he noted that it had disappeared.[25] Gyokuran may have suspected that the Matsuya's heritage would soon slip away when, in 1778, she commissioned a stone monument to be erected in front of Sōrinji dedicated to her mother and grandmother. Carved into the stone were two *waka*, memorializing the artistic achievements of Kaji and Yuri. Gyokuran outlived Taiga by eight years; although he provided for her by putting aside paintings to be sold when she needed income, she also taught calligraphy to girls at a *terakoya*. She and Taiga did not have any children, nor did Gyokuran have any outstanding pupils, resulting in the termination of the legacy which Kaji had begun.

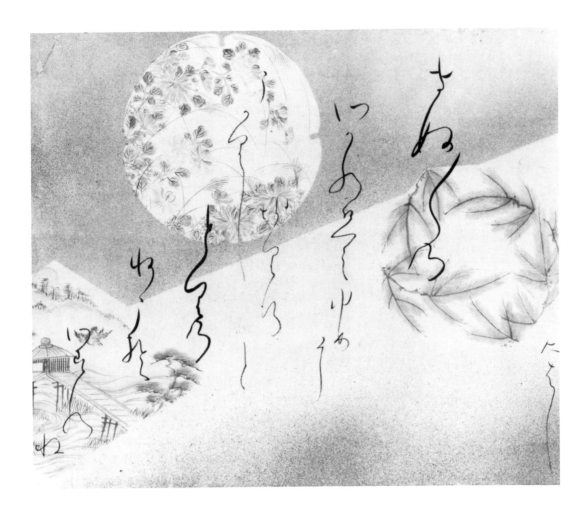

23. Ōhashi (active mid-18th century)

Waka on Decorated Paper
Hanging scroll, ink on paper, 29.6 x 36.1 cm.
Signature: Ōhashi
Tokuriki Collection

Poems written out by famous courtesans have long been treasured by the Japanese, and are still sought by collectors today. It is common to find long handscrolls containing poems by several generations of courtesans which have been gathered by connoisseurs and then mounted together.[26] This *waka* by Ōhashi is especially notable because of the highly decorated paper which she wrote upon. The designs on the paper were partially hand-painted (probably by someone other than Ōhashi); some motifs seem to have been created by the technique known as *fukizomi*, where liquid pigment is blown through a small tube. Although recognizable plant and landscape images make up the bulk of the decoration, the overall design is somewhat abstract because the motifs are confined within geometrical shapes simulating the patterns found on some textiles. A further boldness is achieved by the asymmetrical, diagonal division and subsequent contrast between the plain paper background and the area painted a sky blue.

Ōhashi positioned her poem beautifully; the lines of writing serve to bridge the division existing between the upper blue field and the plain paper below. Heavily inked strings of characters are deftly balanced against lighter ones created when her brush began to run dry. By beginning and ending her lines at irregular levels, Ōhashi was continuing a classical style used for writing *waka* known as *chirashi gaki* which literally means "scattered writing." Her calligraphy dances beautifully along the dividing line from right to left, echoing the diagonal thrust of the design. Ōhashi's poem refers to the inevitable parting between lovers at dawn, and the sadness which follows if the affair does not mature. She has created a charming variation on classic poems describing the anguish of a couple upon hearing the first cry of an early morning bird.

Kinuginu no	On the morning after,
Wakare wa yume ni	Let your parting
Nariyuke to	Be like a dream.
Ukarishi tori no	I cannot forget
Ne koso wasurene	The wretched cry of the bird.

24. Ōhashi

Plum Blossoms
Hanging scroll, ink on paper, 93 x 28.3 cm.
Signature: Ōhashi
Private collection

Ōhashi was renowned in her day for her depictions of plum blossoms. This scroll is one of the rare remaining examples of her painting, accompanied by a *waka* in the upper left.

Ume no hana	The plum blossoms—
Tagasode fureshi	On whose sleeves
Nioi zo to	Have they left their fragrance?
Haru ya mukashi no	I would like to ask the moon
Tsuki ni tohabaya	Of a springtime long ago.

The inspiration for this poem was undoubtedly an evening stroll, probably in February or early March. Ōhashi wonders who in the past may have viewed the blossoming plum trees she is now enjoying. Her painting is complementary, composed of a plum tree and a full moon, both only partially shown. The brushwork recalls the casual, simplified style of contemporary Kano artists in their informal scrolls. The trunk was brushed with light gray ink, showing "flying white" where the brush began to run dry. For contrast, the smaller branch springing from the trunk was crisply delineated with dark, black ink. One slender twig extends upward to the left as though it were pointing out the poem to the viewer. The moon, outlined by thick bands of restrained ink wash, nestles between the protruding branch and the trunk of the plum tree. Ōhashi's calligraphy here is slightly different than in Cat. 23, showing a little more angularity and tension, indicating that it may have been done during another period of her life.

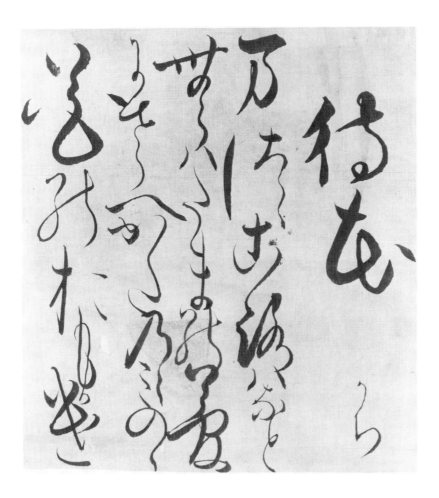

25. Kaji (active early 18th century)

Waiting for Spring Blossoms
Shikishi mounted as a hanging scroll,
ink on decorated paper, 17.1 x 15.9 cm.
Signature: Kaji
Shōka Collection

Intellectuals and poets frequented the Matsuya teahouse operated by Kaji, and in response to requests from friends and patrons, she would write out her verses for them to take away as souvenirs. Very few actual works by Kaji are preserved,[27] although many of her poems were published in the *Kaji no ha* (Cat. 26). Kaji wrote this *waka* on a small square sheet known as a *shikishi*, which was dyed a golden brown and decorated with flowering plants delicately painted in gold. The motifs form an appropriate background for Kaji's verse which she titled "Waiting for Spring Blossoms."

Matsukoro wa	As I wait,
Nado mubatama no	Even in the darkness
Yume ni sae	Of my dreams
Katano no mino no	There are visions of the
Hana no omokage	Cherry blossoms at Katano no mino.

A literal interpretation of this poem is that Kaji was longing for spring and the chance to view cherry blossoms. Yet, knowing her penchant for love poems, one could also read between the lines and infer that Kaji was recalling a past affair and yearning to fall in love again.

Kaji's calligraphy displays a frenetic energy, with lines full of tremulous movement and characters colliding with one another in wild abandon. She has exploited dramatic variations in line thickness which give this piece a theatrical brilliance. The vigor and personal flavor of her calligraphy is certainly indicative of the strong spirit which led Kaji to become one of the most widely recognized woman poets of the eighteenth century.

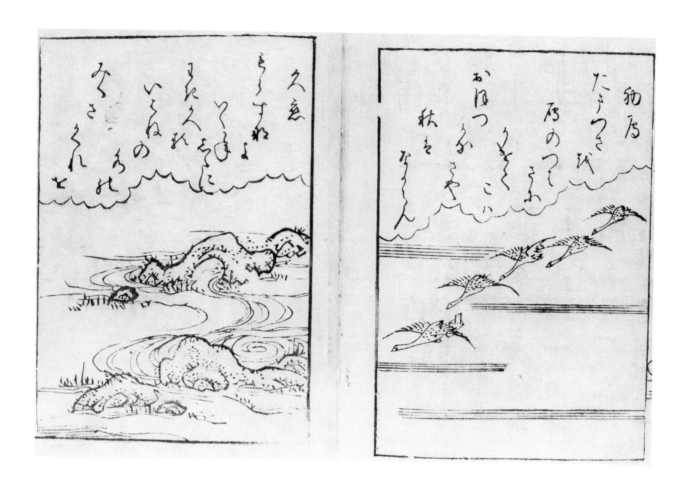

26. *Kaji no ha* (Paper Mulberry [Kaji] Leaves), 1707
Woodblock-printed book, 22.2 x 14.1 cm.
Shōka Collection

Kaji's talents were distinguished and made known to a wider public by the publication of 120 of her *waka* in three small volumes titled the *Kaji no ha*.[28] The poems were collected by the Edo poet Ameishi, who wrote the introduction for the woodblock edition which was published by Heian Shosha in Kyoto in 1707.[29] The volumes are interspersed with illustrations by Miyazaki Yūzen (died 1758), the originator of the resist dyeing technique for cloth which came to be known as Yūzen dyeing. Miyazaki's designs for the *Kaji no ha* are primarily nature scenes, although a few figures are also included. The two pages illustrated here are typical ones, with Kaji's poems contained within the cloud motifs over Miyazaki's pictures below. His designs are simple and linear, recalling in some respects the genre of poem-paintings created by haiku masters (see chapter four).

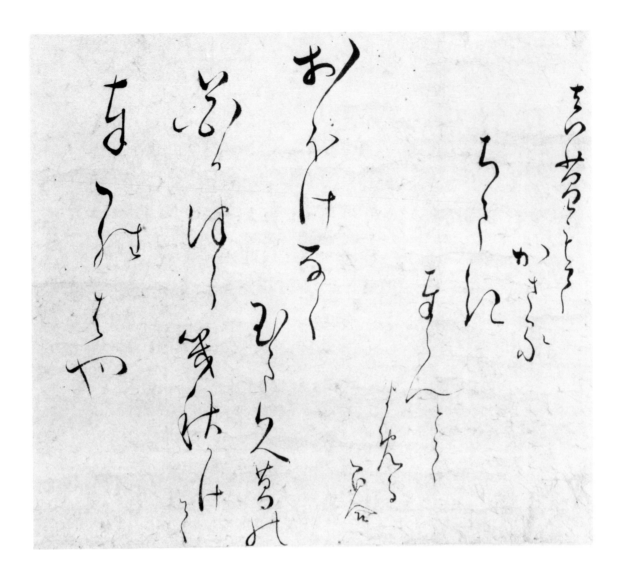

27. Yuri (1694-1764)

Waka Dedicated to Reizei Tamemura
Hanging scroll, ink on paper, 30.2 x 33.6 cm.
Signature: Yuri
Shōka Collection

Yuri's initial training in the arts of *waka* and calligraphy undoubtedly came from Kaji. Inspired by her mentor-mother, Yuri, too, developed a strong personality which is apparent in both her writing and poetry. Yuri's calligraphy is nevertheless quite different from her mother's style. Whereas Kaji's brushstrokes were assertive and agitated, Yuri's handling of the brush was more relaxed and her writing more fluid. Furthermore, Yuri allowed more space to flow in and around her characters, and she liked the irregular effect achieved by *chirashi gaki*. Yuri also chose to render the characters in simpler forms with fewer strokes.

Yuri composed this *waka* for the court noble Reizei Tamemura, who was both her friend and poetry teacher. She would visit him at the appropriate times of the year, offering small gifts and asking him to critique her poems. Yuri prefaced this poem with a short dedication to Tamemura.

For Reizei Tamemura: a poem offered with *chimaki* (rice dumpling) wrapped in an arrowroot leaf

Ohokenaku	Too humble a gift
Tamamakuzu no	Is this jadelike arrowroot's
Hanakazura	Flower coronet–
Iku aki kakete	Yet for how many autumns
Tatematsurabaya	Have I made this offering?[30]

Her brushwork appears nonchalant, the lines thickening and thinning as though they were ribbons fluttering in the breeze. Although lacking the fiery drama of her mother, Yuri's writing displays a strength of character and natural purity especially admired by traditional connoisseurs of calligraphy.

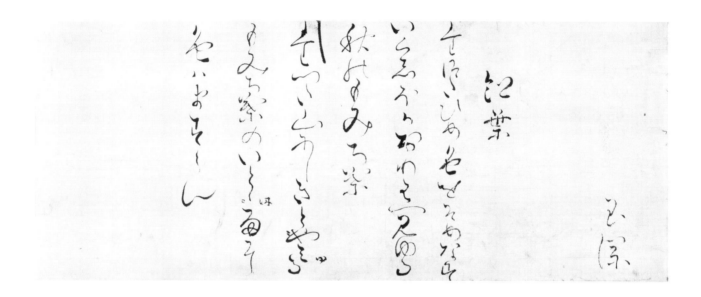

28. Ike Gyokuran (1727 or 1728-1784)

Two Waka
Hanging scroll, ink on paper, 15.9 x 39.7 cm.
Signature: Gyokuran
Shōka Collection

Gyokuran never achieved the literary fame accorded to her mother and grandmother, yet she was certainly a prolific composer of *waka*. She was first tutored by Yuri, and then later by the aristocratic poet Reizei Tamemura who had befriended her mother. Here she has written out two *waka* inspired by the autumn foliage on Mount Tatsuta in Nara.

Tatsuta hime	The Princess of Mount Tatsuta
Iro o somenasu	Dyes the colors
Ikushio ka	Time after time
Orihae miyuru	Deepening their richness–
Aki no momiji ba	The autumn foliage.

Tatsutayama	The autumn leaves
Nishiki to miyuru	On Mount Tatsuta
Momiji ba no	Looking like brocade
Itodo shigure ni	Intensify their colors
Iro wa masuran	In the autumn shower.

Just as Yuri's writing differed considerably from Kaji's style, Gyokuran's calligraphy is easily distinguished from that of her mother. Gyokuran's writing here and in many examples suggests Reizei Tamemura as a source of influence.[31] In particular, her characters have hints of Tamemura's manner of embellishing strokes with decorative flourishes and heavy accents. In comparison with Yuri, Gyokuran's characters seem to be more self-contained and show fewer vertical extensions. However, although Gyokuran's brushwork may lack some of the freedom present in Kaji and Yuri's work, her writing has a formal beauty deriving from the predominantly curvilinear brushstrokes and an overall stately rhythm.

29. Ike Gyokuran

Landscape Fan with Waka
Folding fan mounted as a hanging scroll,
ink on mica paper, 17.6 x 44.8 cm.
Signature: Gyokuran
Seals: Shōfū; Gyokuran
Shōka Collection
Published: Kurt A. Gitter and Pat Fister, *Japanese Fan Paintings from Western Collections* (New Orleans Museum of Art: 1985), no. 26; *Poem Paintings* (London: 1977), no. 11.

Whereas Kaji and Yuri were solely poets, Gyokuran was a talented artist who frequently created simple paintings on which she inscribed a verse.[32] Gyokuran rarely added poems to her larger paintings (see chapter six), but found smaller formats more intimately suited to this purpose. She was especially fond of fans, exemplified by this lovely evocation of Akashi Bay. Gyokuran limited her picture to three horizontal spits of land dense with pine trees, above which float three tiny boats. She painted the forms with great brevity, complementing her simple, flowing script which reads:

Akashigata	On Akashi Bay
Koyoi no tsuki no	This evening's moon is now
Kage kiyoku	Glittering brightly–
Namiji harukeku	Boats far out at sea
Fune zo kogi yuku	Are being rowed away.[33]

A balance is struck by the concentration of landscape elements on the right and poem on the left, although in the center of the fan Gyokuran's calligraphy slightly overlaps some pine trees. Just to the left of center is the character for "moon"; from its placement above the pines it can be read as a pictorial image, showing that the poem and painting are inextricably woven together in terms of content and design. Gyokuran's impressionistic view of Akashi Bay at night is enhanced by her choice of paper treated with mica, which sparkles softly as though illuminated by moonlight.

Notes

1. Many of the most famous women *waka* poets of the eighteenth century came out of the townsmen (*chōnin*) class rather than the court nobility or upper-class samurai families. See Mori Keizō, "Tokugawa jidai no joryū kajin," in Miwata Gendō, ed., *Nihon josei bunka shi*, vol. 2, 565-566, 570.

2. Mori Keizō, *Kinsei joryū kajin no kenkyū*, 2.

3. For a list of women *waka* poets of this period, see Mori, *Kinsei joryū kajin no kenkyū*, 12-13.

4. A masterless samurai. The best sources for biographical information on Ōhashi are Mori Ōkyō, *Kinko zenrin sōdan*, 472-475, and Shimizu (Fueoka) Hōgan, *Bijin Zen*, 172-185. Unless otherwise noted, all of the information regarding Ōhashi's life was taken from these two books.

5. For further information in English regarding Kaji and her descendants, see Stephen Addiss, "The Three Women of Gion," *Women in the History of Chinese and Japanese Painting*.

6. Fukui Kyūzō, *Kinsei waka shi*, 229. The sources utilized for most of the biographical information on Kaji and her descendants in this chapter are: Fujita Tokutarō, "Gion no sansai jo," *Nihon joryū bungaku hyōron*; Nonomura Katsuhide, "Gion no sansai jo," *Nihon joryū bungaku shi*; Aida Hanji, *Kinsei joryū bunjin den*.

7. Nonomura Katsuhide gives the name of Nakanoin in his article "Gion no sansai jo," 56. Aida Hanji includes Reizei Tamemura in the *Kinsei joryū bunjin den*, 157.

8. Nonomura, "Gion no sansai jo." This document was discovered by Mori Senzō.

9. These series are: *Jikken onna ōgi* (Ten Fans of Wise Women, circa 1843); *Ken'yū fujo kagami* (Mirrors of Intelligent and Strong Women, circa 1843); and *Kenjo reppuden* (Stories of Wise and Strong Women, circa 1841-1842).

10. Kaji's granddaughter Gyokuran is also included in this parade, but not her adopted daughter Yuri.

11. Suzuki Susumu gives Yuri's dates as 1694-1764 in his article "Taiga to Gyokuran," *Kobijutsu*, no. 44, 49, as does Mori Senzō in *Mori Senzō chosaku shū*, vol. 3, 34. However, the biographical entries in the *Joryū chosaku kaidai* (p. 192), *Nyonin waka taikei* (p. 385), and *Kinsei joryū bunjin den* (p. 160) all record that she died in 1757, giving no age.

12. Joshi Gakushūin, *Joryū chosaku kaidai*, 192.

13. The poems in this volume have been republished in Tadamura Hatsu, ed., *Gion sanjo waka shū*; Furutani Chishin, ed., *Edo jidai joryū bungaku zenshū*, vol. 4, 83-101; Nagasawa Mitsu, ed., *Nyonin waka taikei*, 385-392.

14. Published in vol. 3 of the *San'yō ikō*. This biography has been translated by Burton Watson and appears in his book *Japanese Literature in Chinese* (New York: Columbia University Press, 1975), vol. 2, 162-167.

15. Quoted from Burton Watson, *Japanese Literature in Chinese*, 165.

16. Hitomi Shōka believes that she also may have studied with Nashinoki Suketami, a pupil of the Reizei school. See his article "Gyokuran" in *Nanga kenkyū*, vol. 2, nos. 9 and 10.

17. Suzuki Susumu, "Taiga to Gyokuran," 38.

18. She first wrote Gyokuran with characters meaning "jade orchid," but later changed the second character to read "wave."

19. The year of their marriage is uncertain, and there is some question as to whether or not they actually had a formal ceremony. There is a letter from Taiga mentioning Gyokuran which must date to the year 1752 or earlier that is used to support the 1751 date. See Matsushita Hidemaro, *Ike Taiga*, 77. Taiga's mother died in 1752; scholars have suggested that she may have been opposed to the marriage, hence Taiga's decision to wait. The fact that Gyokuran continued to use her surname Tokuyama, and that Taiga and Gyokuran are buried in different locations, has led to speculation that they may never have been officially married.

20. For a study of Taiga's life, see Melinda Takeuchi, "Ike Taiga: A Biographical Study," *Harvard Journal of Asiatic Studies*, vol. 43, no. 1 (June 1983), 141-186.

21. The *Heian jinbutsu shi* (Who's Who in Kyoto) lists separate addresses for Taiga and Gyokuran in 1768, but Suzuki Susumu believes that one was used as an atelier. See "Taiga to Gyokuran," 40. In the 1775 edition of the *Heian jinbutsu shi*, they are recorded as having the same address in Gion.

22. This volume contains a collection of poetry by forty-five Reizei pupils. Hitomi Shōka, "Taigadō fujin Gyokuran Joshi," 16.

23. Gyokuran's verses from the *Shirofuyō* were republished in Tadamura, *Gion sanjo waka shū*, and Nagasawa, *Nyonin waka taikei*, 102-103.

24. For further discussion of Gyokuran's unique combinations of painting and poetry, see Stephen Addiss, "The Three Women of Gion."

25. In his *Kiryo manroku*. Nonomura, "Gion no sansai jo," 63.

26. Several such handscrolls are extant in Japan; the Spencer Collection at the New York Public Library includes one example which has portraits of courtesans as well as their poems.

27. One of the few published examples of Kaji's calligraphy appears in Mori Keizō, *Kinsei joryū kajin no kenkyū*.

28. The title of the book contains a play on Kaji's name which is also the Japanese name for the paper mulberry.

29. The poems in the *Kaji no ha* have been republished in modern books, including Furutani, *Edo jidai joryū bungaku zenshū*, vol. 4, 61-101, and Nagasawa, *Nyonin waka taikei*, 377-384.

30. Translated by Stephen Addiss.

31. Stephen Addiss was the first to make this connection. There are other examples of Gyokuran's calligraphy which seem to follow the style of the poet Katō Chikage (1735-1808). See Komatsu Shigemi, ed., *Nihon shoseki taikan*, vol. 22, no. 24.

32. Gyokuran and Yuri sometimes combined their efforts, with Yuri inscribing *waka* on her daughter's paintings.

33. Translated by Stephen Addiss.

Chapter Six: *Bunjin* (Literati Artists)

By far the largest number of recognized and appreciated women painters in Japan emerged from the *bunjin* world. *Bunjin* (pronounced *wen-jen* in Chinese) literally means people who excel in literary works. The word originated in China where learning was venerated, and for centuries intellectuals trained in philosophy and classical literature filled the thousands of Chinese governmental posts. The ideal scholar was viewed as a sophisticated, cultured person, and hence aspiring young men were expected to master literati arts in their leisure time, especially poetry, painting, and calligraphy. The particular style of painting developed by scholar-artists is termed *wen-jen hua* or literati painting. In essence, this art form was created by scholar-amateurs who rejected "professionalism" and sought to remove painting from its associations with mere crafts. Whereas academic artists displayed representational fidelity and technical finesse, scholars emphasized personal expression and stressed the kinship between painting and calligraphy. Literati tended to limit themselves to certain subjects, with landscape being the dominant theme because it reflected their yearning to rise above the vicissitudes of the human world and to achieve a spiritual communion with nature.

Interest in the Chinese literati painting tradition was stimulated in Japan by the Tokugawa government's promotion of Confucianism, which led to the study of many facets of Chinese culture including literature, painting, and calligraphy. However, because the sociopolitical structure of Edo-period Japan was extremely different from that in China, the literati concept was considerably broadened. Although theoretically *bunjin* were people who emulated Chinese scholars by orienting their lives toward personal cultivation in many arts, in Japan *bunjin* painters were those artists who rejected the academic style of the Kano school and turned primarily to the Chinese literati painting tradition for inspiration. This tradition became known in Japan as *bunjinga* (literati painting) or *nanga* (southern painting).[1] Travel abroad was forbidden by the government, but Japanese artists learned to paint in the Chinese literati style by studying examples from imported woodblock-printed books and paintings, as well as by learning from the few Chinese painters who actually visited Japan.[2] Introduced in the late seventeenth century, literati painting rapidly progressed in Japan, and by the latter part of the eighteenth century it was beginning to enjoy widespread popularity, reaching a broad segment of the urban and rural populations.

The earliest known female practitioners of *bunjinga* were active in the second half of the eighteenth century, and they were primarily the wives, sisters, or daughters of well-known *bunjin* artists. Most prominent were Ike Gyokuran (1727 or 1728-1784), Kō Raikin (active late eighteenth century), and Tani Kankan (1770-1799), all of whom were married to artists working in the Chinese literati tradition. As for most women of the Edo period, their husband's occupation and his family's social position were the major factors in determining the direction of their lives. It might not seem unusual for these women to have become intensely interested in Chinese art and culture like their husbands. However, women were generally not encouraged to develop more than basic artistic skills. To spend their time painting was considered sinful in an age when a feudalistic society expected them to devote themselves to raising a family and managing a household. Thus, in order to mature as artists, Gyokuran, Raikin, and Kankan had to overcome the restraints of tradition and convention.

Women *bunjin* were aided by the fact that they lived and worked within small worlds of creative and unconventional intellectuals, who did not always support the standards adopted by the rest of Japanese society. Eccentric behavior seems to have been acceptable in certain coteries of Japanese *bunjin*. One might even say that it was invited, using as evidence two multivolume books that were published in the final decade of the eighteenth century. These were entitled the *Kinsei kijin den* (Lives of Eccentrics of Recent Times) and its sequel, *Zoku kinsei kijin den*; both provide biographical accounts of those men and women singled out as "eccentrics."[3] This immortalization of nonconformist figures might seem paradoxical in an age when Japanese society was beset by innumerable governmental regulations attempting to control and conventionalize lifestyles, yet it was precisely these conditions that may have incited so many Japanese to break free. There was also a Chinese precedent for eccentric behavior among artists, since Chinese accounts are abundant with legends about literati who clung to their individuality and unorthodox lifestyles. Japanese *bunjin* with creative inclinations followed suit, striving to achieve the lofty and untrammeled manner of their Chinese exemplars.

Gyokuran and Raikin had developed nominal skills in painting before getting married, but all three women proceeded to learn from their artist-husbands. In these cases, their husbands were atypical Japanese males with progressive attitudes. Not only did these men lead extraordinary lives modeled after Chinese *bunjin*, but from biographical accounts we learn that they were unusually affectionate, showing a devotion that went beyond mere loyalty between wife and husband. They urged their wives to cultivate artistic talents in much the same manner that they themselves did, perhaps realizing that by allowing their wives to develop personally, in return the women brought more happiness and companionship to the marriages. Nevertheless, the wives were not free to ignore traditional family and household duties, and certainly did not enjoy the liberty of their husbands, who traveled extensively. Kankan and Raikin both bore children, and they probably maintained a more or less traditional lifestyle with the exception that they were encouraged to paint in their free time.

Gyokuran was more offbeat in comparison, just as her husband Taiga's eccentric behavior stood out among other artists of the day. She and Taiga did not have children, instead dedicating their lives to painting, composing poetry, and making music. It was undoubtedly because Taiga was a free spirit himself that he permitted his wife to indulge in her own artistic fantasties. He was such a strong personality among artistic circles that one wonders if he did not also encourage the open-minded attitudes of other artists towards their wives by setting a precedent with Gyokuran. Taiga's artistically collegial relationship with Gyokuran was widely publicized, and it may have inspired other men with artistic inclinations to seek out lively, creative companions rather than meek, feudal wives.

From the extensive literature on the subject of *bunjin*, it is possible to reconstruct the type of environment in which Gyokuran, Raikin, Kankan, and their husbands might have lived. In general, Japanese *bunjin* were members of the samurai or townsmen classes. Many of the men were Confucian scholars, working in official posts for the shogun or daimyo. Others served as teachers, spending their days lecturing on the Chinese classics at one of the many clan schools. Some, like Taiga, are more difficult to categorize, for although they were men of arts and letters, they held no official position and were often members of the townsmen class. Background or social status, however, did not matter to these individuals, who were drawn together by their intense interest in Chinese literature, art, and culture. Gathering primarily in Kyoto, Osaka, and Edo, they formed Chinese language study groups, held meetings where they composed poetry and painted pictures, and even organized exhibitions of Chinese art. It is not known to what extent their wives were allowed to share in these gatherings. Women most likely did not participate, particularly if they had families, yet Gyokuran, Raikin, and Kankan vicariously developed an interest in the Chinese literati painting tradition which was then nurtured by their husbands.

Theoretically *bunjin* artists painted for pleasure and self-expression more than as a vocation. Nevertheless, many of them did earn a livelihood through selling their paintings. We know that Gyokuran joined Taiga in producing works for sale, but we cannot be sure in the cases of Raikin and Kankan. The artistic reputations of these women were so intertwined with those of their husbands that one wonders whether these women would be known today if it were not for their husbands' fame. This does not reflect on the quality of women's art, nor is it intended to undermine their accomplishments, but is merely a result of Japan's long-standing male-dominated society. As was noted in chapter five, more of Gyokuran's works have been preserved, in comparison with her mother and grandmother, primarily because she was the wife of Taiga. It was not until the nineteenth century that women came to be celebrated as artists in their own right and happily were no longer obliged to ride on the coattails of their artist-husbands.

Ike Gyokuran (1727 or 1728-1784)

Gyokuran's biography was given in chapter five, which emphasized her skills as a *waka* poet. This chapter will focus on Gyokuran's paintings in the Chinese literati manner, consisting primarily of landscapes and "four gentlemen" (plum, bamboo, orchid, and chrysanthemum) subjects. She is perhaps the most famous of the women *bunjin* artists, achieving widespread recognition in her own day. Gyokuran was selected for inclusion in lists of painters in the 1768, 1775, and 1782 issues of *Heian jinbutsu shi* (Who's Who in Kyoto), and was one of the few female painters singled out for praise by the important later artist-critic Tanomura Chikuden (1777-1835).[4] It is believed that her first training in *bunjinga* may have come from Yanagisawa Kien. However, Taiga quickly became the major influence upon the development of Gyokuran's painting style following their betrothal around 1750. Gyokuran's mature work shows traits of Taiga's style of his thirties, which is not surprising given the fact that they were probably married when he was in his late twenties. However, Gyokuran should not be viewed merely as an imitator of Taiga. Although she employed similar compositional designs as well as Taigaesque motifs and brush patterns, Gyokuran exercised her own imagination and created very personal variations of her husband's style. In particular, she had an eye for the fanciful, and experimented with exaggerating certain spatial effects. She also cultivated her own style of applying brushstrokes, resulting in paintings with rich textures resembling tapestry. Another one of her deviations from the Chinese *bunjin* tradition was the frequent addition of *waka* instead of Chinese poems. Taiga is usually given the credit for Japanizing the Chinese literati tradition, but there are some examples of Gyokuran's paintings which could be considered even more evocative of an indigenous spirit.

Kō (Ōshima) Raikin (active late eighteenth century)

Biographical material on Raikin is scarce; we do not even know her birth and death dates.[5] Her family name was Okuda, and as a child she lived in Kyoto. In her youth she served the Confucian scholar Itō Tōsho (1728-1804);[6] Raikin showed herself to be quite intelligent, and she became adept at Chinese poetry, calligraphy, and painting. She especially loved to paint bird-and-flower subjects, and her brushwork was admired as pure and elegant. While Raikin was in the service of the Itō family, she met the multitalented scholar Kō Fuyō (1722-1784). The date is not recorded, but they were married sometime before 1772.[7] The marriage was not arranged, but was a love match.

An intimate friend of Ike Taiga, Fuyō, too, was progressive enough not to force traditional roles on his wife. One must assume that Raikin knew Gyokuran, although no specific meetings between the two women are recorded.[8] Raikin developed her own style as an artist, and she and Fuyō even collaborated on some works together.[9] Fuyō was best known for his seal engraving, but he also painted and wrote poetry in the Chinese literati manner. Paintings by Raikin and Fuyō are rare, but extant works have shared stylistic characteristics, especially in their landscapes. Along with Gyokuran, Raikin was included in the list of artists in the 1782 issue of *Heian jinbutsu shi*. Her paintings feature exquisitely detailed brushwork and formal compositional beauty.

Tani Kankan (1770-1799)

Kankan was the first wife of Tani Bunchō (1763-1840), the most important *bunjin* painter active in Edo in his day.[10] She was born in Edo to a family having the surname of Hayashi.[11] At the age of sixteen (1785), Kankan became the wife of Bunchō. Since Bunchō's family were vassals to the second son of the eighth Tokugawa shogun, it can be assumed that Kankan was from an upper-class samurai family as well.[12] Kankan is described as having a retiring nature, but she was known to be talented and virtuous. She studied painting with Bunchō,[13] becoming skillful at landscapes and figures, as well as birds and flowers. As in the case of Gyokuran, Kankan did not merely mimic the style of

11. *Portrait of Kankan*
From her tombstone at
Genkūji in Tokyo

her husband, but after mastering the basic techniques she created her own unique manner, displaying preferences for certain types of compositions and brushstrokes. Her work reflects the eclectic tendencies of her husband, however, and hence Kankan's style is not as immediately recognizable as that of Gyokuran.

Four years before Kankan died she became a devoted follower of Buddhism, and as part of her discipline she painted an image of the bodhisattva Kannon every day. She produced over one thousand Kannon paintings; it has been suggested that Kankan may have started this practice upon discovering that she had contracted some incurable illness.[14] Kankan died in 1799 at the age of thirty.[15] Bunchō, deeply saddened by his wife's death, arranged for a special memorial print to be issued, as well as erecting a separate monument next to her grave the following year. On her gravestone he had engraved an image of a standing woman which is presumed to have been taken from a portrait of Kankan that Bunchō himself painted (Figure 11). In this way he preserved the memory of his artistic young wife not only for himself, but for future generations.

30. Ike Gyokuran (1727 or 1728-1784)

Spring Landscape
Hanging scroll, ink and colors on silk, 112.1 x 48.6 cm.
Signature: Gyokuran
Seals: Gyoku, ran; Shōfū
Asian Art Museum of San Francisco,
The Avery Brundage Collection
Published: Asian Art Museum of San Francisco, *A Decade of Collecting (1966-1976)* (San Francisco, California: 1976), no. 163.

This monumental landscape, with its fanciful construction and whimsical spatial ambiguities, well represents the imaginative spirit of Gyokuran. She usually has been categorized as one of Taiga's many followers, and indeed her husband's repertoire of styles and subjects formed the foundation for Gyokuran's painting. However, in Gyokuran's best works she displays a personal, often dreamlike, vision that distinguishes them from Taiga. Gyokuran and Taiga both loved to playfully manipulate space in order to create bold designs, but Gyokuran tended to dramatize certain features of Taiga's work in her own paintings, resulting in rather bizarre, fantastic fabrications of the natural world.

This landscape is the product of one of Gyokuran's extravagant flights of fancy. It depicts a tiny coastal village ringed in by strangely shaped rock forms and tall mountains. The season is spring, with peach blossoms in full bloom and hills rich in green foliage. The scene is heavily peopled: fishermen can be seen out on the bay, while figures on foot and on horseback perform their daily chores. This type of subject was painted by many *bunjin*, but Gyokuran's rendition is strangely unsettling for a number of reasons. She has employed a tilted ground plane in an effort to suggest spatial recession, yet she consistently negates space by her patterned arrangement of forms and the use of bold lineament in defining them. The broad path in the lower left foreground changes from solid to void like an optical illusion, causing the viewer to wonder about the safety of the two tiny travelers. Farther up in the composition, rice paddies resembling moon craters wiggle their way toward the village. The relationship of the paddies to the land around them is especially curious, for they appear more as holes in a mountainside than as fields on level ground. One presumes that Gyokuran was aware of the spatial contradictions in such works, but that she sought to achieve an otherworldly quality and enjoyed adding elements of surprise.

Gyokuran's brushwork, too, is distinctive; her areas of repeated texture strokes describing the rocks and trees resemble embroidery, due to the predominantly linear strokes which she so regularly and meticulously applied. Thus, although Gyokuran composed the landscape of

Taigaesque rock forms, trees, fields, and mountains, she transformed the motifs and brush methods so that they expressed her own vision. The box for this painting bears an inscription by Taigadō Teiryo, the fifth generation follower of Taiga, who once wrote that there were no women artists respected more than Gyokuran.[16]

31. Ike Gyokuran

Peony, Bamboo, and Rock
Hanging scroll, ink and colors on paper, 92.7 x 41.6 cm.
Signature: Gyokuran
Seal: Gyokuran
The Mary and Jackson Burke Collection

Few painters would dare to juxtapose eloquence with raw vitality in the manner that Gyokuran does in her paintings of certain plant subjects. Here she has presented us with a startling bold and eccentric conception of a rather standard subject–peony, bamboo, and rock. The jet black brushwork defining the bamboo leaves and rocky foreground immediately catches the eye. A large peony is thrust into the center of the composition, playfully painted with Gyokuran's characteristic curvilinear strokes which rhythmically undulate like billowing waves. The appearance of a solitary peony is a bit strange, since the flower grows on a bush rather than on a single stalk as shown here. However, Gyokuran was not interested in faithful renditions of nature, preferring a more abstract arrangement of forms. This distortion of nature can also be seen in her style of painting bamboo with plump, triangular leaves.

The peony is set off by the application of a pale blue wash around the flower; to help formally balance the composition, Gyokuran also added the same color of wash in the lower left foreground and in the sky directly surrounding the bamboo. In comparison with the rather graceful strokes describing the peony, the brushstrokes outlining the rock are untamed. Gyokuran was clearly influenced by Taiga, who loved to dazzle his viewers with dynamic brushwork and boldly conceived forms. Yet Taiga never depicted rocks quite as awkwardly flamboyant as these, once again reflecting Gyokuran's own creative spirit at work.

32. Ike Gyokuran

Chrysanthemums and Rock
Hanging scroll, ink on paper, 104.1 x 28.6 cm.
Signature: Gyokuran
Seals: Gyokuran; Gion fū ryū
The Mary and Jackson Burke Collection

Chrysanthemums are among the "four gentlemen" subjects favored by literati painters. By blooming late in the autumn, they symbolize fortitude and resoluteness. Chrysanthemums had also been the beloved flower of the Chinese poet T'ao Yüan-ming, who gave up his official position and retired to a life of simplicity and rustic poverty. T'ao wrote about raising chrysanthemums in his poems, and he served as inspiration for later literati who aspired to lead lives close to nature.

Numerous paintings of chrysanthemums are extant by Gyokuran as well as by Taiga, indicating that this subject was one that they both fancied. In terms of basic style and composition, Gyokuran seems to have followed her husband's lead; however, the Burke scroll displays many of the same personal characteristics of Gyokuran noted in Cat. 31. She has once again outlined the unusually shaped rock with thick, forceful strokes. Ink wash is combined with very dry strokes, evoking the rough, mottled texture of an old, eroded rock. Alongside the rock, Gyokuran added a chrysanthemum plant with three magnificent flowers. Her brushwork is full of life, animating the forms and expressing her own personal zeal. Gyokuran's preference for curvilinear shapes is evident in every brushstroke; the lines defining the flower petals show the refinement and joyful repetition that are the hallmarks of her style. As in Cat. 31, Gyokuran has taken care to formally balance her composition. Springing upward from the right, the plant bends leftward over the centrally positioned rock. In order to stabilize the composition and to maintain a lively rhythm, Gyokuran slightly tilted the two largest flowers so that they point in different directions. The uppermost chrysanthemum echoes the shape and direction of the one just below, offsetting the massive bloom closest to the ground.

33. Kō Raikin (active late 18th century)

Two Birds
Hanging scroll, ink and colors on silk, 92.6 x 33.3 cm.
Signature: Raikin
Seals: Geijo kai hitsu; Raikin
Private collection

Raikin was best known for her paintings following the Chinese decorative bird-and-flower tradition, which became extremely popular in Japan during the eighteenth and nineteenth centuries. This style was initially introduced through imported paintings from China, but more significantly through the activities of the Chinese artist Shen Nan-p'in (active circa 1725-1780). Shen accepted the invitation of a Nagasaki magistrate and came to Japan in 1731 in order to propagate Sung and Yüan painting styles. He stayed for two years, teaching eager Japanese pupils what essentially was a late Ming tradition rather than Sung or Yüan. The Japanese were highly impressed with the vivid coloring and the fresh, lifelike quality of Shen's compositions. As a result of his visit, an entire school devoted to this new Chinese bird-and-flower tradition sprang up in Japan, where it was called the Nagasaki school. From Nagasaki, the style quickly spread throughout Japan where it attracted artists working in other traditions. Because of its Chinese origins, it caught the attention of Japanese *bunjin* artists; Raikin is one of many who took up the Nagasaki style and achieved a high degree of skill.

Her painting of two colorful birds perched on a rock surrounded by peonies is typical of this genre. In designing the composition, Raikin followed Nagasaki school conventions and depicted a large, Chinese-style rock thrusting upward diagonally from one corner. This diagonal movement is carried further by a stalk of peony, which makes a sweeping curve and points upward to the right. The poses of the two birds respectively echo the diagonal lines of movement to the left and right; a subordinate oblique thrust downward, initiated by the red bird, is continued by the peony extending into the lower left corner.

Raikin focused a great deal of her attention on describing the brilliant plumage of the birds. To make them appear even more magnificent, she applied hair-fine lines of gold paint over certain areas. The peonies, too, were done with extraordinarily meticulous brushwork, and Raikin achieved a naturalistic touch by carefully shading the leaves and using a different tint of green to color their undersides. Like other Japanese artists who experimented with this Chinese style, Raikin was interested in recreating natural textures and representing her subject in a manner faithful to nature. Yet these desires were subordinated by a native tendency to embolden the painting through simplification of design and brushwork, so that the overall impression is more overtly decorative than her Chinese predecessors.

34. Kō Raikin

Landscape with Fisherman
Hanging scroll, ink and colors on paper, 20.3 x 14.5 cm.
Signature: Raikin
Seal: Rai, kin
Published: Aimi, "Kō Fuyō to Raikin," *Nanga kenkyū*,
no. 2:8-10, part 3, 8.
Marui Kenzaburō Collection

Most of Raikin's extant landscapes are small in size,
resembling album leaves. Because of their petiteness and
delicately rendered brushwork, her paintings have a
Sinophile, jewel-like nature distinguishing them from the
free, more boldly brushed paintings of fellow *bunjin* Taiga
and Gyokuran. Raikin's paintings are rarely dated, so it is
impossible to establish any sort of chronological
development in her style. Biographies relate that before
meeting Kō Fuyō she was skilled in painting, especially
birds and flowers. Raikin's landscape paintings on the
other hand, share many qualities with those by her
husband, leading to speculation that she learned that
particular subject from him, studied with him under the
same artist, or relied upon the same Chinese models. This
similitude between the work of husband and wife extends
to compositions, brushstroke methods, and strong use of
color. Raikin and Fuyō were not born with the inventive
genius of Taiga and Gyokuran, who quickly went beyond
their Sinophile models, Japanizing them in the process.
The former couple preferred instead to cultivate and
maintain a certain Chineseness in their paintings, resulting
in conservative works with a refined, quiet beauty.

This landscape is a gem among Raikin's paintings. Our
attention is invariably drawn to the empty space at the left,
where a tiny figure peacefully fishes from his boat. In true
Chinese fashion, he is dwarfed by the surrounding
mountains and their thick, luxuriant growth. Raikin has
depicted the mountains with dry, ravelly texture strokes,
over which she has laid light washes of blue, green, and
peach color. One of her special skills lay in blending the
different colors together to create subtly rich hues,
resulting in a refreshing coolness indicative of the lush
scenery she portrays.

35. Kō Raikin

Landscape
Hanging scroll, ink and colors on paper, 131.2 x 55.1 cm.
Signature: Raikin
Seals: Raikin; Geijo kai hitsu
Private collection

This landscape is one of Raikin's most ambitious works, rendered on a larger scale than she ordinarily attempted. The composition is a dramatic one, depicting a fishing boat passing through a strait which separates the towering cliff at the right from the sloping bank in the lower left. Flowering trees reach out from both land masses, intermingling with the variegated shades of verdant, spring foliage. Although the seated figure in the boat, shown playing the flute, adds an interesting genre element, the focus is really on the powerful landscape forms which embrace him. The trees and cliff are diagonally oriented, imparting a sense of vigor to the composition. The movement initiated by the two large trees thrusting upward from the lower left is skillfully counterbalanced by the angle of the cliff jutting across the water.

Despite the large size of this composition, Raikin's brushwork here shows her characteristic delicate linework and tiny dotting. The mountain forms are built up with sparingly applied thin, parallel strokes to represent the uneven surfaces. Clusters of "pepper dots" enliven the edges of the rocky forms. Raikin employed an almost identical type of dotting for the foliage of the tree leaning out over the boat. Her repertoire of brushstrokes was somewhat limited, yet Raikin compensated by underlaying and overlaying her lines and dots with skillfully blended color washes, imparting a fertile richness to her rather austere designs. Raikin's refined and precise brushwork, abundant use of color, and her use of archaic methods such as the fishnet water patterns seen in this landscape, culminate in creating the antique Chinese flavor she and many other *bunjin* artists enjoyed.

36. Tani Kankan (1770-1799)

Fishing in the Moonlight
Hanging scroll, ink and colors on paper, 80.6 x 31.8 cm.
Signature: Kankan
Seal: Suiran
Published: *The Register of the Spencer Museum of Art*,
vol. 5, no. 10 (1982), p. 113.
Spencer Museum of Art: Gift of the Richard and Patricia
Cotton Memorial Fund, 81.71

The majority of Kankan's extant paintings are landscapes.
She learned how to paint from Bunchō, and consequently
many of her works reflect his style of brushwork as well as
compositions. A few lingering Bunchōesque features are
still evident in this landscape, but Kankan transcended her
husband's influence, creating a personalized view of nature
with brushwork expressive of her own spirit.

Her basic composition is a conventional one: trees leaning
inward from a foreground bank at the left, a river with a
fishing boat in the middleground, and distant mountains
beyond. Unlike Raikin in the previous work, Kankan has
depicted the figure and boat in relatively large scale in
comparison with the other landscape elements, making
them a prominent part of the overall compositional design.
To further accentuate this portion of the composition, she
applied light washes of pink, peach, and blue color to the
figure and objects in the boat, as well as to the bamboo and
rocks around them. Washes of pale color appear in other
areas of the painting, but not in such concentrated fashion.
What is unique to Kankan is that the figure out fishing
appears to be a woman, not one of the generic Chinese
figures usually employed by Japanese *bunjin* artists. The
woman's hair is pulled back and secured in what looks like
a bun; the blue *haori* or jacket worn over her robe bulges in
the back where it overlays the heavy, padded *obi* (sash). It
is believed that certain Japanese painters communed with
nature by imagining themselves as inhabiting their
landscape paintings; such a practice may explain why
Kankan modified the traditional male figure type and
depicted a woman.

Moving away from the figure, we discover that the land
masses and river have been arranged along a zigzag line in
order to draw one back into the picture. In the distance,
our gaze is halted by a towering mountain peak rising out
of the mist, composed entirely of light gray wash. One of
the most striking features of the landscape is the freedom
and vitality of Kankan's brushwork, especially the heavy,
wet strokes describing the twisted trees. She was clearly
influenced by Bunchō's work of the late 1780s and 1790s.
Unlike Bunchō, however, Kankan paid little attention to
structuring the mountain and rock forms, preferring instead
to concentrate her energy on the trees and their foliage.
One old leafless tree looms over the fishing boat; above it,
echoing much the same angle, is another tree extending out
over the river. Kankan employed some of her blackest

brushwork to describe the branches, highlighting them as important elements in the painting. One of the most outstanding features of this landscape is the balance Kankan has skillfully maintained between the dramatic and gentle elements of nature.

37. Tani Kankan

Kannon, 1795
Hanging scroll, ink on paper, 135 x 30 cm.
Signature: Kankan
Seal: Itsuka issan tōka issui (five days to paint one mountain, ten days to paint water)[17]
Private collection

Beginning in 1795, Kankan painted an image of Kannon every day in order to demonstrate her devotion to Buddhism. After her death, Bunchō had the design of one of these paintings engraved into wood, printed, and distributed to friends and family as a kind of memorial. This scroll, too, stands as a tribute to Kankan's artistry and Bunchō's dedication to his deceased wife.[18] One of Kankan's paintings of Kannon, dated the eleventh day of the twelfth month of 1795, is mounted at the bottom. The bodhisattva, seated in a three-quarter view pose, was simply depicted with thin lines of gray and black ink.[19] More precise brushwork was used to render the abbreviated facial features, crown, and necklace. Although her portrayal was limited in numbers of strokes, Kankan captured a sense of the deity's inner peace, something for which she herself may have been striving.

Above the painting are mounted woodblock-printed inscriptions composed by five of Bunchō's friends. From top to bottom, right to left, the inscriptions are by: Sō Rikunyo (1737-1803), Nakada Sandō (dates unknown),[20] Kimura Kenkadō (1736-1802), Hamada Kyōdo (dates unknown), and Nozawa Suiseki (1781-1841).[21] In general, the texts are commemorative in nature, praising Kankan's art and mourning her early death. Suiseki gives us the most information, for he describes the events leading up to the memorial print. After narrating a few brief facts about Kankan's biography, Suiseki wrote that Bunchō was extremely saddened by Kankan's death. To console himself, Bunchō searched for an example of her painting and found a portrait of Kannon which she had done the day before she died. Full of admiration, Bunchō decided to have it made into a woodblock print, and Suiseki undertook the task of having it engraved.

The uppermost inscription by Rikunyo bears a date–the

seventh month of 1800–exactly one year after Kankan died. It is likely that all of the other inscriptions were written during the year after Kankan died, and that this collective work was put together by Bunchō's friends and perhaps presented to him on the first anniversary of Kankan's death.

Notes

1. *Nanga* is an abbreviation for "Southern school painting," referring to the Chinese scholar-artist Tung Ch'i-ch'ang's (1555-1636) theory of the Northern and Southern schools, in which the Southern school represents the literati or scholar-amateurs.

2. For more information on visiting Chinese painters, see Stephen Addiss, ed., *Japanese Quest for a New Vision: The Impact of Visiting Chinese Painters, 1600-1900* (Lawrence, Kansas: Spencer Museum of Art, 1986).

3. Several women artists in this exhibition appear in these books, including Sasaki Shōgen, Kaji, Yuri, Gyokuran, Ōhashi, and Chiyo.

4. In his *Sanchūjin jozetsu* (Osaka, 1834), 2.

5. Most biographies of Raikin consist of one or two simple sentences. The longest entry appears in the *Kangakusha denki shūsei* written by Chikurin Kan'ichi in the late Edo period. For this text, see Aimi Kōu, "Kō Fuyō to Raikin," part 3, 10. This article is the best source of information on Raikin.

6. Tōsho was the eldest son of the distinguished scholar Itō Tōgai.

7. Fuyō's grave inscription records that he had one daughter (age thirteen) and one son (age six). If his daughter was thirteen when he died in 1784, she must have been born in 1772. Therefore, he and Raikin must have married by 1771.

8. Both women contributed designs to a woodblock-printed volume entitled *Kishunhō* (Noble Spring Fragrance) published in 1777 which contains paintings and calligraphy by a host of artists. There is a copy of this book in the New York Public Library; Raikin did a magnolia, and Gyokuran a branch of plum.

9. In the Yabumoto Collection, Hyōgo, there is a bird-and-flower painting by Raikin with a poetic inscription by Fuyō. For an illustration, see Kobayashi Tadashi, *Bunjin no hana to tori* (Kyoto: Fuji Art, 1979), no. 59.

10. Bunchō was an eclectic painter with a tremendous range of styles and techniques. Nevertheless, he is usually classified as a *nanga* or *bunjin* artist.

11. The best source of information on Kankan's life is an inscription on her gravestone at Genkūji in the Asakusa district of Tokyo, which Mori Senzō found recorded in the *Akanuma sōbo sōsho*. For the text, see *Mori Senzō chosaku shū*, vol. 3, 200-201. Kankan's original surname frequently appears in both seals and signatures reading "Hayashi-shi Kankan."

12. Satake Eiryō says in his article "Bunchō fujin Kankan Joshi" that Kankan was the daughter of a shogunal vassal named Wada Tameuemon, but this information is not verified.

13. Bunchō was hailed as the great champion of painting teachers, having more than two thousand pupils. His teaching mania obviously extended to his home, for in addition to Kankan, he taught his two younger sisters, Tani Shun'ei and Tani Kōran, as well as a daughter named Yao by his second wife.

14. Satake, 20.

15. During her fourteen-year marriage to Bunchō, Kankan bore only one child, a daughter. Bunchō later had six children by his second wife.

16. Hitomi Shōka, "Taigadō fujin Gyokuran Joshi," 14.

17. Kankan's seal bears the same legend appearing on seals of both the visiting Chinese painter I Fukyū and Ike Taiga. See Addiss, *Japanese Quest for a New Vision*, 17 and 29. The legend probably derives from a couplet written by the Chinese eighth-century poet, Tu Fu, in a eulogy on the painter Wang Tsai: "Ten days to paint one stream, five days to paint one stone–an accomplished artist cannot be hurried."

18. This scroll was studied many years ago by the noted Japanese scholar Mori Senzō. See *Mori Senzō chosaku shū*, vol. 3, 300-301.

19. An almost identical Kannon, painted in the fifth month of 1796, is published in Kanagawa Kenritsu Hakubutsukan, *Edo ha no kaiga* (Yokohama: Kanagawa Ken Bunkazai Kyōkai, 1979), no. 4.

20. The husband of Bunchō's sister Shun'ei. Sandō wrote that he was sojourning in the Kansai area when he received the announcement of Kankan's death, which arrived in the form of a letter containing the memorial woodblock print of Kankan's last Kannon painting. His inscription is dated 1799.

21. Two of the authors had their inscriptions written out by professional calligraphers. Rikunyo's was done by Oe Sebi and Nakada Sandō's by Morikawa Chikusō.

Nineteenth-Century Women Artists
Chapter Seven: ## Late Edo-period *Bunjin*

As noted, the largest percentage of women artists in Japan were practitioners of the Chinese literati painting tradition known as *bunjinga* or *nanga*. In the previous essay, Ike Gyokuran, Kō Raikin, and Tani Kankan were discussed as the eighteenth-century forerunners. The nineteenth century saw a dramatic increase in the number of women *bunjin*, and active female members were not uncommon in the major artistic and literary circles. This chapter will focus on five representative women *bunjin* of the late Edo period: Tachihara Shunsa (1814-1855), Ema Saikō (1787-1861), Yoshida Shūran (1797-1866), Chō Kōran (1804-1879), and Tōkai Okon (1816-1888).

One of the primary reasons for the increase in the number of female *bunjin* was that many scholars encouraged talented women to join their ranks. Their motivation in this regard was stimulated by Chinese precedents: the Ch'ing-dynasty poet Yuan Mei (Sui-yüan) was known to have had many female pupils, and in 1796 he published their poetry in a volume entitled *Sui-yüan nü-ti-tzu hsüan* (Selections from Sui-yüan's Women Pupils). This book was subsequently republished by the poet Ōkubo Shibutsu (1766-1837) in Japan[1] where it had a catalytic effect on Japanese scholars of Chinese studies, who soon began to cultivate women pupils. Women *bunjin* were so much in vogue that the poet-scholar Kikuchi Gozan (1772-1855) included a section with biographical information on them in his 1807 *Gozandō shiwa*. One of the most important leaders in this movement was Rai San'yō (1780-1832), an extremely influential historian and scholar of Chinese-style prose and poetry in early nineteenth-century Japan. San'yō in particular is well-known for promoting his female proteges; four of the women artists included in this chapter received his encouragement.

The growing number of women *bunjin* coincided with the rise in literacy among both men and women. There would seem to be a definite correlation between the broadening range of roles for women and the vast expansion of the educational system. Although moral doctrines were still a large part of the standard education for women during the nineteenth century, lifestyles were less rigidly defined than before and women gradually came to enjoy more freedom. More young women attended schools, receiving a more extensive education than had previously been the case.

What types of families were likely to send their daughters to school? What kind of education did they receive? It seems that merchants were most inclined to spend money educating their girls, since shopkeepers' wives needed to read and write in order to mind the family business.[2] Doctors and samurai with good educations were also apt to send their daughters to school or to provide for their education in another way. Of the five nineteenth-century women *bunjin* included in this chapter, Ema Saikō, Yoshida Shūran, and Tōkai Okon were all daughters of physicians; Tachihara Shunsa and Chō Kōran came from samurai families. Kōran is the only one for whom there is evidence that she formally attended a school. The others most likely had private tutoring. In either case, the education they received was the same. All went beyond merely learning to read the Japanese *kana* syllabary and were tutored in Chinese studies, beginning with the *Four Books*,[3] and moving on to the more recondite prose and poetry.

Prior to the introduction of Western learning, the Chinese language was considered the road to serious scholarship in Japan: philosophy, ethics, and history were all written in Chinese. So, too, were books on medicine, astronomy, mathematics, and the law. Children were usually introduced to Chinese studies between the ages of eight and ten, whereupon they learned passages in this difficult language through rote memorization. Kōran once astonished her teacher (who was also her husband) by memorizing an entire book of 494 Chinese T'ang-dynasty poems while he was away on a journey.[4]

Encouragement from family and friends was the crucial factor in motivating women to rise above what was ordinarily expected of them. The Japanese women *bunjin* in this chapter were daughters or wives of artists or scholars, or had close personal connections with important cultural figures such as Rai San'yō. Furthermore, Kōran's and Saikō's natural mothers both died when they were young, which may have led to their adopting more independent, masculine lifestyles. Fathers served as role models, exemplified in this touching poem by Saikō who emulated her father's zeal for learning:

A Winter Night

My father deciphers and studies Dutch books;
His daughter reads Chinese poetry.
Divided by a single lamp,
We each follow our own course.
I read on without stopping,
But become tired, letting my mind wander to chestnuts and sweet potatoes,
Ashamed that I cannot attain the spirit
Of my eighty-year-old father whose eyes are not yet cloudy.[5]

Like their male colleagues, women *bunjin* became well-versed in Chinese poetry and calligraphy, as well as in painting. Many were members of informal literary societies. Saikō and Kōran both belonged to a group called the Hakuōsha (White Sea Gull Society) which met monthly at a local temple in their hometown of Ōgaki. Ten regular members belonged to this group which was led by Kōran's husband Yanagawa Seigan (1789-1858).

12. *Hakuōsha* (detail), 1822
Ema Shōjirō Collection

At their meetings members would discuss cultural issues, compose poems, and paint for one another, while enjoying the comraderie they shared with like-minded friends. A portrait of the Hakuōsha society survives which was painted in 1822 (Figure 12); in the lower right is Saikō with Kōran seated just behind her.

Societies like this one were plentiful in nineteenth-century Japan; Saikō and Kōran were also members of a diverse circle of poets and artists centering around Rai San'yō in Kyoto which included their female friend Shūran. Although Saikō was older than the other two, these women had a great deal in common: they were all poet-artists who felt at ease in a masculine society and who did not hesitate to work in a primarily masculine tradition. Good friends, they often wrote poems and letters to each other, and occasionally they went on pleasure trips together.

The subject matter painted by women *bunjin* was predominantly landscape and nature studies of the "four gentlemen" (bamboo, plum, orchid, and chrysanthemum). This was in keeping with the traditional Chinese models favored by Japanese literati artists. Saikō, Kōran, Shūran, and Shunsa each received instruction in painting and calligraphy from their fathers, local priests, or artists in the circles they associated with. In many cases their brushwork is strong and confident, far from the so-called "feminine" manner which one might expect. This is not surprising, since these women patterned their styles after works by their male teachers. Japanese art historians are fond of using the term *joseiteki* or "feminine" to describe the painting and calligraphy styles of women artists. This adjective is often inappropriate, because the style in which these women painted is essentially no different from that of their male counterparts. Of course, works by women artists exist in which delicate brushwork prevails, but this is also true for works by contemporary male painters such as Tanomura Chikuden and his followers.

Compared with most women of the day, the lives of these women were unconventional, but it would be incorrect to view them as early advocates of women's liberation in Japan. We learn from Kōran's poems that she did not turn her back on the household chores expected of a Japanese wife; in this respect she conformed to the traditional role of women. Moreover, it is clear that she wholeheartedly embraced this domestic aspect of her life. As she wrote in a poem when she was around thirty-nine:

> I look for thread ends on the tattered silk of my torn winter clothes,
> And add fallen leaves to the firewood which furnishes fuel for cooking lunch.
> Do not laugh at my trifling mind inclined toward hard work and frugality–
> What is the merit of being a wife besides this?[6]

Outside their immediate circle of friends, how were these extraordinary women looked upon by their contemporaries? That they earned the respect of their peers is indicated by the fact that the names of Kōran, Saikō, Shūran, and Okon were listed alongside men in the *Heian jinbutsu shi* (Who's Who in Kyoto) in sections devoted to painters, poets, calligraphers, and musicians.[7] However, some men were still unable to accept women into the scholarly world. For example, Kōran was referred to as a "lewd woman" in the 1847 *Tosei meika kidan*, a book of parodies of well-known Kyoto Confucian scholars and poets.[8] This criticism was purportedly written by the *bunjin* artist Oda Kaisen (1785-1862), who obviously held conservative views about the proper behavior of women; he was doubtless uncomfortable with Kōran's active role in Kyoto *bunjin* circles. The following anecdote suggests that even her husband Seigan sometimes felt embarrassed about being accompanied by Kōran.[9] According to one of his pupils, Seigan frequently accepted invitations to visit a certain feudal lord. Because he could not bring himself to admit that his wife had come with him, he left her in a waiting room. The lord's attendants, believing that Kōran's presence indicated a jealous nature, would tease her while she waited. One time Seigan stayed inside very late; he had given a lecture after which he was purposely detained by the ladies-in-waiting. When Kōran learned of this, she became so upset that she jumped into the garden well. Fortunately, the well was dry and she was not injured, but the disturbance was brought to the attention of the lord, who said that he did not mind if Kōran visited him with Seigan. From that time on, Kōran always accompanied Seigan, and the lord came to recognize her literary merits as well.

From stories such as this, we can see that nineteenth-century women entered into the male *bunjin* world only with some difficulty and under certain conditions. They had to have a Chinese education, which was largely determined by family background. The women who were accepted into the literati world were expected to maintain dual roles; that of poet-artists and that of wives (if they were married) or daughters. Their situation was not unlike the dilemma faced by many career women today; the women *bunjin* discussed here seemed to have accepted the situation and performed both roles as required. Even then they were not immune to criticism from those with old-fashioned attitudes. Life as a female *bunjin* was thus not an easy one, and none of these women would have matured as artists or poets without complete dedication. With the change of government in the succeeding era, women were given more opportunities; the artists represented here are to be recognized for blossoming early.

Tachihara Shunsa (1814-1855)

Shunsa was the eldest daughter of Tachihara Kyōsho (1785-1840), a noted Confucian scholar-artist from Mito (Ibaragi prefecture). She followed her father's footsteps by learning Chinese poetry, painting, and calligraphy from him. Around the age of fourteen or fifteen, Shunsa is believed to have also begun studying painting with Watanabe Kazan (1793-1841).[10] Both *bunjin* artists exerted a strong influence on the development of her painting style. Shunsa concentrated on bird-and-flower subjects, which she rendered in precise, detailed brushwork. Ten years later, in 1839, Shunsa became a lady-in-waiting to the wife[11] of the Maeda daimyo who ruled Kaga fief (Ishikawa prefecture). This was one of the highest-ranking positions that a daughter of a samurai family could obtain; Shunsa lived and worked in the inner quarters of the Maeda castle. For reasons unknown she remained single, diligently serving the Maeda family for the last fifteen years of her life.

Whether her death was the result of natural causes is open to question. Ōhashi Bishō relates two different stories in which Shunsa tragically committed suicide.[12] According to one, Shunsa was beautiful and talented, and thus gained the affection of her lord master. She was so thrilled that she announced her love in a letter to her father. Kyōsho was indignant, for instead of refining her skills in the literary and military arts in true samurai fashion, his daughter had become a warrior's plaything. With his return letter to Shunsa, he sent a short sword; Shunsa was so overcome by grief that she killed herself. In the second story, when Shunsa went to serve in the castle, she outshone the other attendants, making them jealous. One day some money disappeared from the master's purse, and the servants blamed it on Shunsa. When an investigation took place, the money was found in Shunsa's room. Even though she was innocent, she was so mortified that she committed suicide. Neither of these two stories can be verified, and are not repeated in other articles discussing Shunsa.

Ema Saikō (1787-1861)

Saikō was the eldest daughter of Ema Ransai (1747-1838), a doctor of medicine and avid scholar of both Confucianism and Rangaku (Dutch studies). They lived in the village of Ōgaki in Mino province (Gifu prefecture).[13] Both her mother and older brother died when Saikō was only three, the same year in which her younger sister was born. Ransai remarried soon after, but the early death of Saikō's natural mother may have resulted in the stronger than usual bond between father and daughter. The fact that Ransai no longer had a son may also have caused him to lavish more attention on Saikō. Ransai taught her Chinese, as well as the basic skills of calligraphy and painting. In the Ema Shōjirō Collection there is a painting done by Saikō at age five, and a calligraphy of a Chinese-style poem which she wrote at age nine.[14] When she reached the age of thirteen, Saikō became a painting student of the Kyoto monk Gyokurin (1751-1814), who specialized in bamboo.

Because the Ema family no longer had a male heir, Ransai decided to adopt a son-in-law. He first tried to arrange a marriage between Saikō and a young man named Shōsai in 1804, but Saikō refused on the grounds that she was too deeply involved in her studies of painting. Ransai then arranged for Shōsai to marry Saikō's younger sister. Three years later Ransai retired and Shōsai inherited Ransai's position as doctor to the daimyo of Ōgaki.

In 1813, Rai San'yō paid a visit to the Ema household, an event that was to have a major impact on Saikō's life. As a distinguished poet and scholar, San'yō spent a great deal of his time traveling around Japan meeting with other *bunjin*, including journeys to Mino to visit the large number of scholars, poets, and artists who lived there. San'yō had been urged by one of his friends to meet Ransai, prompting this trip to Ōgaki. Upon visiting the Ema family, San'yō was charmed by Saikō's beauty and talents, and he agreed to become her teacher. In the following year (1814), San'yō informed Ransai of his wish to marry Saikō, but Ransai refused. There are many tales regarding San'yō's marriage proposal, but the facts are not clear. Saikō was supposedly absent at the time this occurred. It is generally believed that Ransai was oblivious to Saikō's warm feelings for San'yō, and rejected the proposal out of respect for her previously stated desire to devote her life to artistic pursuits. Ransai was probably also aware of San'yō's history of dissipation, and may not have been eager to have his daughter marry a man of that character. Upon Saikō's return home, Ransai told her what had transpired and she was visibly shaken. When he found out that she favored the marriage, he sent someone to Kyoto to negotiate with San'yō. However, in the meantime San'yō had arranged through one of his friends to marry a woman named Rie.

Distressed by the turn of events, Saikō never married. Many exaggerated stories have been passed down over the years regarding her relationship with San'yō after his marriage to Rie.[15] The letters and poetry written by San'yō and Saikō to each other tell us that Saikō remained one of his favorite pupils up until the time of his death. They carried on a spirited correspondence, with Saikō sending San'yō poems she had written; in return he sent her corrections.[16] Beginning in 1814, Saikō traveled to Kyoto once every two or three years, usually in the spring or autumn.[17] The length of her stays ranged from two weeks to one month. The main purpose of her visits was to meet and study with San'yō, as well as to view the lovely Kyoto scenery.

During these trips to Kyoto, Saikō frequently visited San'yō's home, where she formed a sisterly relationship with Rie. From the diary of San'yō's mother Baishi, we know that Saikō accompanied San'yō and members of his family on many journeys, and that on several occasions she stayed overnight at his home. It is clear that they remained devoted to one another, and that their relationship went beyond that of teacher and pupil. They had a special friendship which blossomed over the years, and one could even surmise that a form of love existed between the two. However, rumors that San'yō and Saikō carried on a romantic affair after his marriage would seem to be unfounded. Saikō had been raised in a very strict and proper family, and it is unlikely that she would act in such a way as to offend the moral standards of her day. The fact that she was welcomed by San'yō's family and colleagues, and that she was frequently praised for her quiet, gentle, and virtuous nature, suggests that she and San'yō were not lusting after one another in secluded inns as some writers would lead us to believe.[18]

San'yō introduced Saikō to many Kyoto *bunjin*, including Uragami Shunkin (1779-1846),[19] Nakabayashi Chikutō (1776-1853), Ōkura Ryūzan (1785-1850) and his wife, Yoshida Shūran, Koishi Teien (Genzui, 1784-1849), Unge (1783-1850), and Yamamoto Baiitsu (1783-1856). Upon her first visit to Kyoto in 1814, the monk Unge composed the following poem about Saikō.[20]

Presented to Saikō Joshi from Mino while at a Teahouse:
This elegant, refined lady's brush has the spirit of the wind.
A delicately scented fragrance is emitted from her green sleeves.
One flourish of ink results in bamboo on a round fan;
Untainted by cosmetics, she is unsurpassed.

San'yō made sure that Saikō was included in any *bunjin* gatherings that occurred while she was visiting, and over the years she made many group excursions with other *bunjin* to beauty spots all over Kyoto and Nara. San'yō urged her to consider moving to Kyoto, but any hopes she might have entertained were dashed when her brother-in-law died in 1820, for she then was expected to remain home and to help with the family.

In addition to studying Chinese poetry with San'yō, Saikō continued to refine her skills in calligraphy. From 1814 on, San'yō sent her modelbooks filled with characters he had brushed which she would then copy. As a result of this practice, Saikō's calligraphy shows her teacher's distinctive influence. Saikō had initially studied painting with Gyokurin, but through San'yō's guidance she became a pupil of Uragami Shunkin around 1817. Saikō continued to focus on the "four gentlemen" (especially bamboo), but expanded her repertoire to include other bird-and-flower subjects as well. Her handling of the brush was cool and crisp; this and the fact that she used ink, and only occasional pale colors, resulted in images that have the lofty and austere qualities praised by *bunjin*. San'yō was proud of the progress his pupil made, and took examples of Saikō's painting with him when he traveled in order to promote her talents. The following letter was written by San'yō to his friend and patron Chikka.

> I am sending you one ink bamboo painting by my female student, Saikō. Recently, you have been careful not to spend money, and have not bought Ming paintings. Luckily this bamboo painting has been mounted and I send it to you because I thought you might find pleasure in this sort of painting as well... P.S.: I would like to add that, although this lady's painting is famous, it used to be of a vulgar kind, similar to the paintings by Gyokurin and that after becoming my student, she corrected these vulgar aspects, so that now this painting looks like a genuine Chinese painting by a Ming painter, with many of the Southern School characteristics: notice, for example, the texture strokes in the rocks around the lower part of the painting.[21]

San'yō not only introduced Saikō to fellow *bunjin* and patrons, but also spoke highly of her to the visiting Chinese painter, Chiang Yün-ko (J: Kō Unkaku, dates unknown), whom San'yō had met in Nagasaki. Chiang sent a poem to Saikō in 1819, and thereafter through the auspices of San'yō they carried on a correspondence in which Chiang advised Saikō on Chinese poetry.

In addition to making a name for herself in Kyoto, Saikō also became a major cultural figure in her hometown of Ōgaki. Around the year 1820, Yanagawa Seigan formed the Hakuōsha poetry society in Ōgaki; Saikō was one of ten members who also included Seigan's wife, Kōran. The following year, several of Saikō's poems were published in the *Mino fūga*, a compilation of verses by *bunjin* living in the Mino area. San'yō, who was actively involved in the publishing world, later tried to persuade Saikō to allow a collection of her verses to be published. As fuel for his argument, he gave to Saikō a copy of the *Zuien jodaiko shisensen* filled with poems by the women pupils of Yuan Mei. However, she refused out of modesty.[22] Nevertheless, some of her verses were published in collections of other poets, and Saikō became so famous that traveling *bunjin* made a special point of stopping in Ōgaki to visit her.

The years 1831-1832 were unlucky for Saikō. Both her stepmother and Rai San'yō died, and her father Ransai became quite ill. San'yō's death must have been quite a blow to the poetess. However, it did not dampen her enthusiasm for composing verse and painting. She turned to San'yō's pupil Gotō Shōin (1797-1864) for instruction in poetry, periodically visiting him in Osaka, and maintaining an active correspondence. Saikō also continued to journey to Kyoto with more or less the same frequency as before. During these trips, she would visit with San'yō's family and other Kyoto *bunjin*, participating in banquets and excursions like those that had taken place when San'yō was still alive.[23]

Saikō's father Ransai died in 1838, but due to the energies of Saikō and other *bunjin*, Ōgaki continued to flourish as a cultural center. In the 1840s and 1850s she was a member of two poetry societies there, the Reiki Ginsha and Kōsaisha; she became the leader of the latter group. The 1850s saw the rise of loyalist factions in Japan, which proposed that the Tokugawa shogunate be overthrown and rule restored to the emperor. San'yō had supported this cause; his son, Rai Mikisaburō (1825-1859), and several other *bunjin* with whom Saikō associated, such as Yanagawa Seigan and Kohara Tesshin (1817-1872), were avid loyalists. From Saikō's letters we know that she, too, was sympathetic to the loyalist movement, but there is no evidence that she participated. She kept abreast of their activities through letters from Ema Tenkō (1825-1901), with whom she had formed a fast friendship. In 1856 Saikō suffered a cerebral hemorrhage; although she recovered, she never fully regained her health. In the same year, she began to receive the patronage of the wife of the Toda daimyo. Saikō was invited to Ōgaki Castle where she was given gifts in return for her paintings. She had another stroke in 1861, however, and died in the ninth month at the age of seventy-five. One of the first women *bunjin* to gain complete recognition in a male-dominated world, Saikō owed her fame in part to Rai San'yō. Yet, fame did not fully satisfy her. Throughout her life Saikō wrote poetry suggesting that she would have preferred a normal married life to that of a spinster. The following poems were included in the *Shōmu ikō*.

The peaceful night gets quieter and I am slow to go to bed.
Trimming the wick of the lamp, I leisurely read books written by women.
Why should it be the lot of talented women to end up like this?
Most of them in empty boudoirs, writing poems of sorrow.
(written in 1815)

To inscribe on my portrait (1831):

Lonely room, fiddling with a brush as the years go by;
One mistake in a lifetime; not the kind to be mended.
This chaste purity to rejoice in–what do I resemble?
A hidden orchid, a rare bamboo–sketch me in some cold form.[24]

By one mistake, I have no family to serve;
Aimlessly, I have indulged in writing amidst the rivers and lakes.[25]
But I am shamed by your verse coming from far away
In which I am praised as the outstanding woman of the literary world.
(written in 1851)

Despite the melancholic nature of such poems, Saikō did not go through life as the morose and grieving woman that some scholars have suggested. Much of her poetry is bright-spirited, drawing heavily upon nature imagery through which she expressed her own feelings. Although she supposedly tried to discourage the young women who idolized her from imitating her lifestyle, she was proud of the accomplishments of her female colleagues. Evidence for this is a handscroll owned by Saikō which contains paintings and calligraphy by twenty-two women artists.[26] Over the years, Saikō must have collected examples from female artists whom she met. She then had the works mounted together in a handscroll which stands as a rare testament to the artistry of women active in nineteenth-century *bunjin* circles.

Yoshida Shūran (1797-1866)

In comparison with Saikō, far less is known about Shūran. The daughter of the Kyoto doctor Yoshida Nangai, Shūran married the painter Ōkura Ryūzan. Like Saikō, Shūran and her husband studied poetry and calligraphy with Rai San'yō, and they were part of San'yō's immediate circle of *bunjin* friends. Shūran learned to paint from her husband's teacher, Nakabayashi Chikutō. Unlike Ryūzan, who painted primarily landscapes, Shūran seems to have restricted her output to "four gentlemen" and other plant subjects rendered in monochrome ink, being particularly skilled at painting orchids. She was among the most multitalented of women *bunjin*, for she was also adept at playing the seven-stringed *ch'in* which she had studied with Uragami Gyokudō (1745-1820), the most highly regarded Japanese master of the instrument in his day.[27] Shūran even learned Gyokudō's compositions based upon the ancient Japanese *saibara* music, rather than only the Chinese pieces more often studied.[28]

Shūran's recognition in the arts began when she was around sixteen, for in that year she was listed in the *Heian jinbutsu shi*. Thereafter, she appeared in almost every issue, often in more than one category: 1822 (calligraphy, *bunjinga*, *ch'in*); 1830 (calligraphy, *bunjinga*, *ch'in*); 1838 (*bunjinga*, *ch'in*); 1852 (calligraphy, *ch'in*).[29]

There is no mention of children in any of the existing short biographies of Shūran. We know that she and her husband regularly attended *bunjin* gatherings in Kyoto. Through these events, she came to know Saikō and Kōran. One spring, Kōran met Shūran and went to admire the cherry blossoms, afterwards composing a poem with the concluding couplet:

Last night the spring wind wove a brocade of flowers–
I welcome my female friend, and we celebrate by drinking *sake*
while viewing the blossoms.[30]

Following *bunjin* tradition, these women even collaborated on paintings.[31] Shūran was especially close to Saikō; they had the shared experience of being pupils of San'yō, who nurtured their aspirations to excell in *bunjin* arts. Nothing is known of Shūran's later years, except that she died in 1866, sixteen years after her husband Ryūzan.

Chō (Yanagawa) Kōran (1804-1879)

Kōran, the daughter of a samurai, was born in the village of Sone in Mino province; as a child she learned to read and write Chinese from her great-uncle who served as a priest at the temple Kakeiji.[32] Her mother died when she was only thirteen, and a year later she was permitted to enroll at a private village school, the Rikasonsō (Pear Flower Villa) established by Yanagawa Seigan. Three years later, at the age of seventeen, Kōran married Seigan. Her husband continued to play a significant role in fostering Kōran's studies in Chinese poetry, literature, and painting. He was the central figure in the Hakuōsha literary society which met monthly in Ōgaki.

Intrigued with the idea of meeting poets and scholars in other parts of Japan, Kōran and Seigan embarked in 1822 on a long journey west. They were encouraged by their friend Rai San'yō who had returned from Kyūshū a few years earlier. Traveling to the other end of Japan was no easy undertaking; since they had little money, they went most of the way on foot and enjoyed the hospitality of other scholars.[33] Seigan was viewed by many as eccentric because he took his young wife along with him; women traditionally remained at home while their husbands traveled. They went as far as Nagasaki, sojourning in the bustling port city for three months. There they became friends with a Chinese merchant from Suchou, Chiang Yün-ko, who was adept at painting and poetry. The opportunities to visit directly with a Chinese painter, and to associate with Japanese *bunjin* artists from all over Japan, stimulated Kōran's interest in painting; several of her earliest extant works date from these years of travel. At this stage of her life she created primarily decorative depictions of birds and flowers.

Kōran and Seigan returned to their hometown in 1826, four years after their departure. However, the long journey to Kyūshū had whetted their appetite for a more intellectually cosmopolitan lifestyle, and in the following year they went to live in Kyoto. Throughout their lives they moved countless times, later living for some years in Edo and Hikone before eventually returning to Kyoto. They seemed to have taken literally the advice of the Chinese scholar-artist Tung Ch'i-ch'ang (1555-1636), who wrote that in order to be truly cultivated, one should travel ten thousand miles and read ten thousand books.[34] The couple made a meager living through lectures, calligraphy and poetry lessons, and selling paintings. Although Kōran experienced difficulty at first, she gradually adapted to a bohemian lifestyle, and as the years went on devoted more and more of her time to reading and composing poetry, painting, and playing the Chinese seven-stringed *ch'in*.[35]

Kōran received her first formal instruction in painting around the years 1827-1828 when she became a student of Nakabayashi Chikutō in Kyoto. Under Chikutō's direction she learned to paint bird-and-flower subjects and landscapes in the Chinese manner. Eventually she rejected the more decorative themes and turned wholeheartedly to the Chinese literati tradition of ink monochrome painting. Kōran gradually began to add poetic inscriptions to her works, enhancing their *bunjin* spirit. She made rapid progress as a painter, and by 1830 she was listed with *bunjinga* artists in the *Heian jinbutsu shi*.[36] Her talents were also recognized in Edo during the thirteen years she and Seigan lived there (1832-1845). One of her bamboo paintings was reproduced in the woodblock-printed book *Hyaku meika gafu* (Album of Calligraphy and Paintings by One Hundred Artists, 1837). This was followed by a collection of 130 of her poems entitled the *Kōran koshū* printed in Edo in 1841.

Kōran never bore any children, probably due to infertility rather than by choice. At age forty she wrote a poem lamenting her life without children, indicating her compliance with the customary role of women. Other poems tell us that Kōran strove to conform to tradition, despite the fact that she was known for her strong-minded and severe personality. From the anecdotes that have been passed down, it is obvious that her relationship with Seigan was not always a peaceful one. In Edo, they were unable to keep servants because she was so difficult, and the couple argued endlessly. Once Seigan even threatened to send Kōran back home, but in the end they were inseparable.

While living in Edo, Kōran and Seigan became involved in the heated politics of the day, which centered around the question of opening the country versus an exclusionary policy. Both harbored anti-shogunate sentiments and participated in the loyalist movement to restore power to the emperor. After returning to Kyoto in 1846, Seigan acted as an elder advisor to the patriots gathering there, and the Yanagawa home became a meeting place for those seeking reform. In 1858 Seigan was implicated in a plot to assassinate a shogunal official who had been sent to Kyoto to stamp out loyalist factions, but Seigan died of cholera three days before government officals came to arrest him. The officials thereupon took Kōran captive. She was imprisoned in Kyoto for half a year, but refused to answer questions regarding loyalist activities. While in jail, Kōran allegedly chanted poetry and painted on wooden boards. Upon her release, she moved back to her old home and opened a private school for women, where she taught Chinese-style poetry. The women studying at her school found it extremely arduous because Kōran was so strict and demanding. Normally, a widow would have gone to live with her children or family; it is significant that Kōran did not return to her hometown, instead choosing to live independently in Kyoto.

Kōran remained active in Kyoto literary and artistic circles until her death at the age of seventy-seven. From a collection of her poetry called the *Kōran ikō*[37] we learn about the people and places she visited and the activities in which she participated during the second half of her life. She continued to associate with many of Seigan's pupils, including Ema Tenkō, Okamoto Kōseki (1811-1898), Ono Kozan (1814-1910), and Yamanaka Shinten'ō (1822-1885). In some ways Kōran as a widow was even more prominent than before. While her husband was alive she had remained somewhat in his shadow, but now she blossomed artistically and the unwavering strength of her character manifested itself more freely in her artworks. She became more prolific in painting, in part because she had no children to rely upon and producing scrolls was one way to help support herself.[38] Her unrelenting devotion to the scholarly arts must have helped to overcome the hardships which she faced. She continued to write poetry, with the subjects of her verses frequently drawn from nature. As to the recognition accorded to her as a poet, the scholar Okazaki Shunseki observed that although some people believed that Seigan had assisted her in writing, the poems Kōran composed after his death were in many ways superior to her earlier ones![39]

Tōkai Okon (1816-1888)

Unlike the other women discussed in this chapter whose artistic talents evolved over long years of practice and dedication, Okon was a child prodigy who reached the height of her fame around the age of nine. She was born in a small mountain village in the Iwafune district of Niigata prefecture.[40] Her father was a physician and seems to have been the major figure in promoting Okon's studies. She was introduced to Chinese literature when she was just a few years old, and it is said that she did not play like ordinary children, instead spending her days and nights memorizing Chinese poetry and practicing calligraphy. When Okon was five years old, she wrote out the name of a Shinto deity in large characters: this calligraphy was presented to a shrine on Mount Takao. In 1822 Okon was taken by her parents to Edo, where she further refined her brushwork by becoming a pupil of the monk Dokuhon (died 1857).

Okon moved to Kyoto in 1825 with her parents, and her precocious brushwork quickly captured the attention of several leading poets and scholars. A year later she was honored by an invitation to appear at the imperial court. After writing out several examples of calligraphy before an audience in the palace, Okon was personally presented with gifts by the emperor—one of the highest honors in Japan. Rai San'yō took a special interest in the unusually gifted girl, and in 1826 composed the following poem extolling Okon's brushwork and commemorating her visit to the imperial palace.[41]

> Okon is a genius at grass script;
> Raising and waving her youthful hand she creates billowing ocean waves.
> In her previous life she learned the secrets of a drunken priest;
> She derived her style of flying ink from Huai-su.
>
> Who named this lovely girl "Kon"?[42]
> As expected, she grows wings and ascends to the gates of the immortals.
> The energy in her brushwork is like that of wild horses.
> The ink that she grinds in her inkstone leaves heavenly traces.

She was surrounded by rows of court ladies,
Struggling to see her jadelike wrist as it swept thousands of troops away.
When she started to write she won the smile of the emperor–
Among the billowing clouds of colorful robes, a special being had appeared.

After her five fingers moved delicately like serpents,
A perfect jade cup was given to her by the emperor.
Inside the cup were painted sixteen yellow chrysanthemums;
This divine gift, white like frost, was her worthy reward.

When her young hand grasped the brush, she was filled with ecstasy;
The movement of her writing astonished everyone who was present.
After she finished she called out gently for more paper–
She completed her calligraphy with hands as fresh as springtime.

San'yō's colleague, the Confucian scholar and poet Shinozaki Shōchiku (1781-1851), in turn wrote a prose verse about Okon which he presented to her family in 1827.[43] Okon also became acquainted with the scholar-official from Akita, Sukegawa Rokudō (dates unknown), who also dedicated a poem to her.[44] Okon's brushwork so astonished the capital that in 1830, at the age of fourteen, she was listed alongside other famous calligraphers in the *Heian jinbutsu shi*.

Okon continued to travel to various places with her father who wanted to proclaim her talents. However, he was warned by Shōchiku that if he persisted in allowing Okon to indulge herself in calligraphy, her chances of securing a good husband and living a normal life would be ruined. When her father became ill in Osaka around 1831, Sukegawa Rokudō came to Okon's aid and helped to provide household expenses.

In 1832 Okon married a government official from Akita named Okamura Yoshichirō, probably through the introduction of Rokudō or Shōchiku. Okon then lived with her husband's family in Osaka and relinquished any hopes of an artistic career. That she still continued to develop her artistic skills, however, is evident from a calligraphy handscroll brushed forty-six years later in 1878 (Cat. 55). At this time in her life Okon was forced to call upon her calligraphic skills in order to make a living. After the beginning of the Meiji period in 1868, when the feudal government was abolished and her husband lost his official position, Okon sold her calligraphy in order to help with the family finances. It is likely that she continued to support herself by this means after her husband's death. Nevertheless, examples of her later work are exceedingly rare. The few pieces of Okon's calligraphy which survive are almost all from her childhood, when for a few years she was allowed to blossom as an artist before withdrawing to the life of a proper Japanese wife.

38. Tachihara Shunsa (1814-1855)

Bamboo and Plum
Hanging scroll, ink and colors on paper, 22.2 x 15.4 cm.
Signature: Tachihara-shi Shunsa
Seal: Koame (Shōu)
Private collection

Shunsa's delicate brushwork was perfectly suited to the small format in which she frequently chose to paint. After studying with both her father and Watanabe Kazan, she concentrated on depicting the "four gentlemen" as well as bird-and-flower themes. Here she has created a simple yet striking design featuring bamboo and plum. Branches of both plants spring inward from the right, thrusting diagonally into the lower left and upper right. Shunsa has masterfully positioned the forms so that they counterbalance one another. Although the painting itself is small, through the liberal use of empty space she has created a feeling of expansiveness.

The clarity of compositional forms is also echoed in Shunsa's brushwork: the slender lines defining the bamboo and plum are crisp and precise. She contributed to the purity of the design by using color sparingly. Shunsa added white pigment to the budding plum blossoms, with pale yellow dots representing the stamens. To the interior of the bamboo leaves and stems she applied varied shades of green color washes. Shunsa deliberately chose not to fill in the outlined forms completely with color, in order to retain the feeling of openness. The overriding mood of cool austerity is appropriate to her *bunjin* subject celebrating endurance and fortitude.

39. Tachihara Shunsa

Chrysanthemums and Rock
Hanging scroll, ink and colors on silk, 87.8 x 36.4 cm.
Signature: Tachihara-shi jo Shunsa shiga
Seals: undecipherable; Koame (Shōu); Safu
Ibaragi Kenritsu Rekishikan
Published: Ibaragi Kenritsu Rekishikan, *Ibaragi no meihō*,
no. 108 (1985); Ibaragi Kenritsu Rekishikan, *Muromachi
suibokuga-Kinsei kaiga*, no. 94 (1983); *Kobijutsu*, no. 61, p.
68; Ibaragi Kenritsu Rekishikan, *Mito no nanga*, no. 128;
Kokka, no. 588, p. 353.

This painting is considered to be Shunsa's masterpiece, depicting large, pink chrysanthemums rising majestically alongside an eroded Chinese rock. Chrysanthemums are one of the "four gentlemen" and therefore represent certain *bunjin* ideals (see Cat. 32). Shunsa's version of this subject is more elaborately painted and embodies more color than some *bunjinga*. However, it is far from ostentatious. The gentle lyricism of her brushwork and subdued application of pale color washes imbue this "gentleman" with the mild yet firm spirit long admired by literati.

Shunsa's predilection towards plant subjects was abetted by the surge in interest in plant life by both the intelligentsia and general public at this time. This was in part a response to the earlier introduction of traditional Chinese pharmacology called *honzōgaku* which entailed a precise study of the medicinal properties of animal, vegetable, and mineral substances. During the late eighteenth and early nineteenth centuries, numerous botanical studies were published in Japan, with new varieties imported from abroad, and plant-viewing gardens established. There is a letter stating that Shunsa received a sample of a special species of flower along with some notes from the *honzōgaku* scholar Satō Chūryō.[45] The interest in *honzōgaku* led many artists to specialize in flowers and grasses, and in some cases inspired them to practice methods of realistic depiction.

Shunsa structured her compositions with great sensitivity, compressing the painted motifs into limited areas in order to control the lines of movement. Here the main thrust is vertical, with a subordinate one leftward. The growth of the chrysanthemums follows the movement initiated by the shape of the rock. Shunsa left almost half of the silk unpainted, creating the feeling of spaciousness that she seems to have sought. The composition is balanced asymmetrically, with the painted forms consolidated in the right half offsetting the poetic inscription at the left. In calligraphy recalling that of her father, with slender, sharp lines tapering in thickness, Shunsa wrote the following quatrain in Chinese characters:

In the pure wind and white dew floats a solitary fragrance.
Only the chrysanthemums can be seen on this cold evening,
Whereupon I recall the poetry of the ancients,
And in these surroundings forget all of my worldly ambitions.

Shunsa undoubtedly learned her sophisticated coloring techniques from Watanabe Kazan, whose naturalistic manner of painting birds and flowers evolved from his studies of Chinese and Western arts and sciences. Kazan was adept at using variegated colored washes to represent the three dimensionality of nature's forms. The leaves and flowers of Shunsa's plants display a more patterned arrangement than one finds in nature, but her use of gradated color washes to suggest volume shows Kazan's influence. One of the most outstanding features of this work is the striking juxtaposition of the soft, almost nebulous brushwork describing the plant forms against the bold, rough strokes outlining the rock, demonstrating Shunsa's genius at balance and contrast.

40. Tachihara Shunsa

Yellow Bird on a Branch
Folding fan, ink and colors on paper, 30 x 44 cm.
Signature: Shunsa-jo gisaku
Seal: Saren
Spencer Museum of Art: Gift of Mr. and Mrs. William F. Bond in appreciation of Harry Packard, 85.314
Published: *The Register of the Spencer Museum of Art*, vol. 6, no. 3 (1986), p. 84.

Shunsa signed this fan "Playfully painted by Shunsa," and indeed it has a light-hearted touch not always apparent in her work. In particular, the brushwork displays a looseness and freedom quite different from the polished, restrained nature of the previous two paintings. It is likely that Shunsa painted the design on this fan extemporaneously in response to a request from a friend or patron.

The composition is typical of Shunsa, with the main branch entering from the lower right and extending diagonally to the left. A smaller twig shoots upward, providing a perch for the yellow bird which is positioned so that its tail points obliquely to the upper right, counterbalancing the leftward diagonal thrust. The design is simple, yet works effectively within the fan shape. As always, the painted forms are given more impact through the ample use of blank space around them.

Shunsa refrained from using ink outlines and employed pale color washes to describe the forms. Slight changes in hue within the leaves hint at light and shade, but the hard-surfaced paper commonly used for folding fans did not allow for her usual subtle gradations. Color was obviously of primary concern to her, judging from the rich range of greens, browns, and blues found in the tree leaves. The bright yellow of the bird's feathers causes it to project vividly from its resting place, inspiring the viewer to conjure up its spring melody.

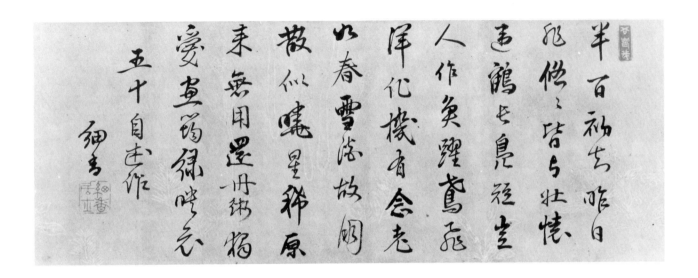

41. Ema Saikō (1787-1861)

Poem at Age Fifty
Hanging scroll, ink on colored paper, 17.3 x 45.9 cm.
Signature: Saikō
Seals: Gosōga; Saikō koji
Private collection

Saikō refined her skills in calligraphy as well as in poetry and painting, studying from modelbooks prepared for her by Rai San'yō. Her writing shows the strong influence of her teacher, featuring smooth, rounded characters brushed with an even, stately rhythm. This poem, in the format of eight lines of seven characters each, was written by Saikō in a form of running script at the age of fifty. The paper is pale blue with printed designs of fern shoots and other plants, and may well be a special Chinese paper which she received as a gift. Her richly inked poem is autobiographical in nature: looking back over the first half century of her life, Saikō expresses melancholic feelings about the course her life has taken.

As I reach fifty, I begin to understand the mistakes of the past.
As the years slowly pass, they have gone against my ambition.
Cranes are tall, ducks short–it is not men who made them thus.
Fish leap, hawks soar–all follow the course of nature.
My intentions have melted like the snow in springtime.
Old friends have vanished like stars in the morning brightness.
In the end there is no use in Taoist practices for longevity–
I only love to paint bamboo, its greenness reflected on my garment.

One of the "mistakes" that Saikō refers to in her first line must be the early misunderstanding with Rai San'yō. By this time he had been dead for four years and thus he is surely one of the old friends who Saikō notes have "vanished." Consequently this poem is one of her most personal expressions within the scholarly calligraphic tradition.

42. Ema Saikō

Bamboo and Rock, 1852
Hanging scroll, ink on satin, 132 x 58 cm.
Signature: Saikō
Seals: Suiboku; Ejo jōjō; Saikō koshi
Ema Shōjirō Collection
Published: Tsubota, *Nihon josei no rekishi*, no. 6, p. 10;
Sōga, *Zusetsu jinbutsu Nihon no josei shi*, vol. 7, p. 78;
Kado, *Ema Saikō*; Ōgaki Shi Bunka Kaikan, *Ōgaki no
senken ten: Ransai to Saikō*, p. 24.

Saikō is most famous for her depictions of bamboo. She
began her study of painting as a young child, and in her
early teens received lessons from Gyokurin, a Kyoto monk
who specialized in bamboo. Gyokurin died in 1814, and
under San'yō's guidance, Saikō began to study painting
with Uragami Shunkin around 1817. She met with
Shunkin directly on her periodic visits to Kyoto; when she
was in Ōgaki, she sent paintings to him and he returned
them with corrections marked in red coupled with long
explanations.[46] According to San'yō, her style changed
dramatically under the direction of her new teacher,
becoming more refined and closer to Chinese *bunjin*
models.

Saikō never tired of bamboo; half of her extant paintings
depict this subject, and she mastered a variety of
techniques. This bamboo painting, done when she was
sixty-five years old, is a magnificent example of Saikō's
mature style. Typical of her bamboo are the tall, thin
culms, from which spring slender, sharply pointed leaves.
This painting recalls the works of famous Ming painters of
bamboo such as Hsia Ch'ang (1388-1470). Saikō's
brushwork is crisp and deliberate, imbued with the strength
which connoisseurs have long referred to as "bone."
Although many leaves overlap one another, Saikō
preserved their clarity of structure. She varied the tonality
of her ink, presenting the bamboo closest to us in rich
black and gradually lightening the tones to create the
illusion of receding planes. Overall, the ink has a dry,
dessicated quality; this effect resulted from painting on
satin fabric which absorbed the ink more readily than
paper. Saikō described the painting process in her quatrain
in the upper right, comparing her bamboo to "azure
dragons" emerging from misty clouds.

> I have filled this scroll with misty clouds of ink:
> Azure dragons, halted by the wall of rocks,
> Snake forth their claws in the lower foreground,
> Seeming to drink the inkstone until it is dry.

43. Ema Saikō

Chrysanthemums
Hanging scroll, ink and colors on paper, 122 x 27.3 cm.
Seal: Saikō
Ema Shōjirō Collection
Published: Sōga, *Zusetsu jinbutsu Nihon no josei shi*, vol. 7,
p. 49; Ōgaki Shi Bunka Kaikan, *Ōgaki no senken ten:*
Ransai to Saikō, p. 23.

Although bamboo was Saikō's forte, her second favorite
"gentleman" was the chrysanthemum, a symbol of
fortitude and the scholar-recluse T'ao Yüan-ming (see Cat.
32 and 39). This scroll is undated, but the lack of a poetic
inscription as well as a signature may indicate that it was
done early in her career. She learned to paint this subject
from Shunkin, who advocated the use of proper Chinese
"Southern school" models as prototypes. Consequently,
his paintings and those of his pupils like Saikō exhibit
structural clarity and continental modes of brushwork,
giving their works a conservative flavor in comparison to
those by earlier *nanga* masters. This generation gap is
obvious when Saikō's chrysanthemums are contrasted with
Ike Gyokuran's (Cat. 32). Not only is Saikō's composition
more Chinese in spirit, but her brushwork has the restraint
and blandness sought by Chinese *bunjin*.

Saikō's compositional design is rather subdued; the
movement of the Chinese rock jutting at an angle from the
lower left is suspended by the vertical growth of the
chrysanthemums. After defining the shape of the rock
with dry, medium gray ink, Saikō filled in the interior with
a light ink wash. The resulting texture has the rough,
mottled quality associated with this highly admired type of
rock. The forms of the chrysanthemum stems, leaves, and
petals were also defined with ink line and wash, but Saikō
enlivened the plants by adding light washes of yellow,
green, and blue. Although following literati conventions,
she has succeeded in expressing both the genteel nature
and the vitality of her subject.

44. Ema Saikō

Landscape, 1856
Hanging scroll, ink on silk, 118.5 x 43.2 cm.
Signature: Saikō jinen nanajū
Seals: Ketsuen kanboku; Ema jōjō; Saikō Joshi
Spencer Museum of Art: Jennifer Lyn De Gasperi Memorial
Fund, 86.55

Extant landscape paintings by Saikō are rare: this example
is inscribed as painted at age seventy. It is believed that
she turned to this subject late in her life, after she had
thoroughly mastered the "four gentlemen." Landscape
required a more sophisticated understanding of Chinese
brush methods, a challenge that Saikō was prepared to face
only after she had reached an advanced age.

Although Shunkin had died in 1846, Saikō probably
received her initial training in this subject from him. The
standard Chinese compositional designs and mild-
mannered brushwork reflect the ideals of Shunkin and
other *bunjin* painters with whom Saikō associated in
Kyoto, such as San'yō, Chikutō, Ryūzan, and Baiitsu.
However, Saikō developed an individualistic manner of
applying brushstrokes which distinguishes her landscapes
from those by her colleagues.

She has constructed her mountain view by arranging the
landscape elements into diagonal planes which move
upward in a zigzag pattern. The path which begins in the
lower right invites us to enter; through the shifting
diagonal orientation of the footpath, we are led deeper into
the woods until we encounter an open pavilion situated on
a small plateau. From that point, the trail is obscured by
mist, but our imagination allows us to climb higher and
higher until we reach the uppermost peaks.

The tranquil, mysterious forces of nature are evoked
through the use of soft, gray washes and texture strokes
which build up the mountain forms. Saikō avoided color,
using only ink; her manner of texturing is unusual and
reveals a personal touch in the way she overlays wet areas
of wash with dry, scumbled strokes. Black accents in the
form of clusters of dots are sparsely scattered throughout,
animating the mountain forms. The complex interplay
between her arid brushstrokes and moist washes enriches
the surface texture of Saikō's painting, providing the subtle
excitement that literati looked for in each other's works.
The quiescent mood is further conveyed in Saikō's quatrain
in the upper right, which reads:

How many places have I once traveled,
Where pure streams rushed between white rocks?
As I grow old, I can no longer freely roam,
So I pick up the brush to depict those hills and mountains.

45. Yoshida Shūran (1797-1866)

Orchid
Hanging scroll, ink on paper, 21.6 x 33 cm.
Signature: Shūran Joshi utsusu
Seal: Sa, to
Private collection

Shūran's favorite themes for pictorial expression were the "four gentlemen." Many of her extant works depict orchids, a well-known literati subject that had acquired many layers of meaning in China. As early as the poetry of Ch'ü Yüan (circa 340-circa 280 B.C.), the orchid had been associated with the virtues of the high-principled gentleman scholar. The Oriental species of this plant is quite different from the showy plants of the West: the Chinese orchid is tiny and delicate in comparison. "Fragile and unassertive, blooming modestly and spreading its delicate fragrance in hidden places, it was a particularly suitable image for a sensitive man who had withdrawn from the world."[47]

The orchid became a popular subject among *bunjin*, partly because of its traditional symbolism, but also because the form of this plant lent itself beautifully to calligraphic brushwork. A poet like Shūran, skilled in handling the brush through writing, could master the subject without difficulty. This painting is typical of Shūran's orchids; she preferred simple compositions and usually chose to depict one plant. Here she began just to the left of center in order to allow space at the right for the long leaves. One of the most striking features of the Oriental orchid is the graceful sweep of its leaves; *bunjin* artists enjoyed the free-flowing movement of the hand and brush that was required.

Shūran brushed her orchids spontaneously, with fluid gestures communicating the svelte nature of the plant. Each stroke is firm yet pliant, an indication of her skill in brushwork. She has deliberately utilized a variety of ink tones to enliven the composition, reserving black for the flower stamens and for one of the leaves extending upward to the right. Through the rhythmic movements of her supple brush, she has given the impression that her orchids are swaying in a gentle breeze.

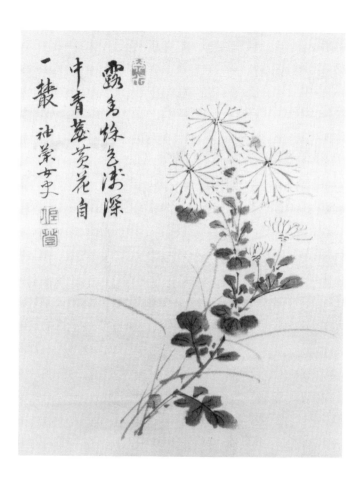

46. Yoshida Shūran

Chrysanthemums
Album leaf, ink on satin, 10 x 16.3 cm.
Signature: Shūran Joshi
Seals: Kinsui; Sato
Nagoya City Museum
Published: Kamiya Hiroshi, "Shūenjō," *Nagoya Shi Hakubutsukan kenkyū kiyō*, vol. 6 (1982), p. 80.

This leaf is from an album titled the "Shūenjō" which was compiled for the scholar Murase Sekkyō (1827-1879) in the middle of the nineteenth century. The album contains paintings and poetry by fifty-two *bunjin*, many of whom were followers of Rai San'yō.[48] Shūran was one of three female contributors to the album, the other two being Saikō and Kōran.

Shūran painted the branch of chrysanthemums in moist gray ink, arranging it so that it has a slight diagonal orientation. Leaves and grasses curve elegantly to the right and left, displaying some of the same graceful linear rhythms apparent in her orchid paintings. Vitality emanates from each brushstroke, imbuing the forms with the "spirit resonance" so important to literati painting. Shūran balanced the chrysanthemums with her couplet at the left, bringing this quiet ink painting to life through her evocative use of Chinese-style poetry.

> Its dewy fragrance lies amidst a full range of autumnal colors–
> Blue stamens and amber petals are united in a single blossom.

47. Yoshida Shūran (with Ōkura Ryūzan)

Peony and Orchid
Framed panel, ink on paper, 25.1 x 80.3 cm.
Signature: Shūran Joshi
Seals: Jo Sato no in; Jōbun
Private collection

This painting is the combined effort of husband and wife: Shūran brushed the peony to the right, and Ryūzan painted the orchid to its left. Such joint endeavors were common in *bunjin* circles, where individuals with shared sentiments about art and poetry liked nothing better than to cooperate in producing collaborative works called *gassaku*. Having both studied painting with Chikutō, Shūran and Ryūzan were extraordinarily compatible in style. Both brushed the plants using wet ink, varying the amount of water in order to create contrasts in tonality. Shūran's brushwork forming the peony is especially succulent. Not only are the orchid and peony consistent in style, but they are also skillfully integrated in terms of placement within the overall compositional design. It is difficult to say which part was painted first; the second artist deserves special credit for uniting the two through the judicious placement of his or her portion.

48. Chō Kōran (1804-1879)

Butterflies, 1824
Hanging scroll, ink and colors on silk, 123 x 41 cm.
Signature: Chō-shi Keien
Hirose Chōji Collection
Published: Nagoya Shi Hakubutsukan, *Owari no kaiga shi: Nanga* (Nagoya: 1981), no. 149. Ōgaki Shi Bunka Kaikan, *Ishin kaiten no senku ningen: Seigan--sono kiseki*, p. 37.

This is one of Kōran's earliest dated works, painted in 1824 when she and Seigan were on their western journey. In addition to inscribing the date, she recorded that it was done at the terrace of Chōmu Rōkei, and afterwards presented to him as a gift. Since butterflies were a popular subject in Chinese painting, we might assume that Kōran followed Chinese models;[49] however, the range of species in this painting, coupled with the blank background, suggests that she may also have been inspired by botanical texts. Western scientific books were imported to Japan in large numbers from the eighteenth century on, responding to the burgeoning interest among Japanese intellectuals eager to acquire knowledge from the West. Botanical studies were subsequently published in Japan, exposing Japanese artists of various schools to Western artistic styles and techniques.

Kōran does not seem to have employed any naturalistic mode of expression here, but the fact that she depicted twenty different species of butterflies demonstrates a kind of scientific approach to her subject matter. She seems to have been especially enamored with these insects, perhaps because their multicolored wings are so visually appealing and an artistic challenge to recreate.[50] Kōran painted the butterflies with a combination of ink, pigments, and gold paint so that their jewel-like wings form intricate patterns against the amber silk background. Her sense of design is already apparent in the asymmetrical arrangement of the butterflies along diagonally oriented lines. Kōran's long poetic inscription in the upper right reads:

> In the gentle wind, among the hundred grasses, they are
>   equal to flowers,
> Each one as vivid as cut-out rosy clouds.
> I know that the spring god cherishes them very much
> And especially sends spring to the domain of the lord of
>   pollen.
> Low they fly and gently dance to and fro,
> I sigh over such a vast expanse of springtime scenery.
> Which family has a refined daughter to prepare the brush?
> She should paint these browlike moths as they are.
> Plants on the old terrace are covered with mist;
> Green mounds of a thousand ages are things of the past.
> I love their pure spirit that cannot be scattered
>   by the breeze–
> They fly everywhere together in the spring wind.

49. Chō Kōran

Landscape in the Style of Mi Fu
Hanging scroll, ink on paper, 193 x 39 cm.
Signature: Chō-shi Kōran utsusu
Seal: Shinsen yoji
Hakutakuan Collection

After Kōran became a pupil of Nakabayashi Chikutō in Kyoto in 1828, although she continued to paint bird-and-flower subjects, she began to shift her attention to landscape and the "four gentlemen." This landscape is not dated, but on the basis of style and signature it must be a work of her early years with Chikutō. It was obviously intended as an essay in the style associated with the Chinese Sung-dynasty master Mi Fu, featuring mountains composed of layers of repeated horizontal dots. By the nineteenth century, a larger number and wider range of Chinese paintings than before were available to Japanese artists for study. As *bunjin* like San'yō, Shunkin, and Chikutō acquired a deeper understanding of Chinese styles, they began to direct themselves toward capturing the proprieties of the orthodox literati tradition. Consequently, a trend toward conservatism was initiated in *bunjinga*; paintings of this era are characterized by conventional, tightly organized compositional schemes, systematic building up of forms, and restrained brushwork.

Kōran's *Landscape in the Style of Mi Fu* is exceptionally close to Chikutō's works following the Sung master.[51] Beginning at the bottom with a foreground bank and grove of trees, Kōran layered the mountains along a vertical axis, occasionally interspersing plateaus and areas of mist-shrouded houses and trees. By using a range of ink tones from light gray to black, she created a feeling of moist atmosphere and lush foliage. Like Chikutō, Kōran applied her brush very systematically, the primary stroke being the oval-shaped "Mi dot" made by laying the brush tip down horizontally. Her brushwork is restrained, exhibiting an allover consistency: the repetition of similarly shaped mountain forms and brushstrokes establishes a sense of unity and stability. At the same time, the build-up of short horizontal strokes creates a shimmering surface pattern. Despite her efforts to evoke the spirit of original Chinese works, Kōran's paintings, like those of her teacher, exhibit the Japanese sensitivity to scintillating surface effects.

50. Chō Kōran

Winter Landscape, 1855
Hanging scroll, ink and colors on satin, 157.8 x 66.7 cm.
Signature: Kōran Chō-shi
Seals: Chō-shi Keien; Dōka; Hi ji yū kei shin ji kichi
Spencer Museum of Art, 86.51

Over the years, Kōran deepened her understanding of
Chinese literati painting. The compositional structure and
brushwork of this landscape recall paintings by the late
Ming artist Lan Ying done in the manner of the Yüan-
dynasty master Huang Kung-wang (1269-1354). Numerous
paintings by Lan Ying were brought to Japan, and they
were instrumental in the formulation of the styles of
Chikutō and other artists of the nineteenth century
including Kōran. In particular, the squared-off shape of
the mountain forms and clustering of rocks in this work
suggest the influence of Lan Ying filtered through the
brush of Chikutō.

Kōran's composition is carefully structured; beginning in
the lower right, she organized the bridges and slopes along
powerful diagonal lines, enticing the viewer to penetrate
deeper into the mountains. We can imagine ourselves as
the tiny figure riding his horse across the bridge in the
bottom left. Although Chikutō's influence is evident, once
Kōran learned his basic principles of painting she no
longer felt bound to imitate his style, and began to produce
more sophisticated and personal works. The use of steep
diagonals and the cloudlike rock formation in the center
left all seem to reflect her own tastes and inclinations.
Kōran defined the forms with a combination of both dry
and wet brushstrokes in gray tonalities. In order to create
the effect of a wintry scene, she left the interior of the
rocks and mountains unpainted, allowing the white satin to
represent snow. Darker lines of ink were employed as
accents along the edges of the rocks and trees, and pale
washes of tan and green color for the trees and architecture.
Kōran further dramatized the snow-covered forms by
surrounding them with dark wash. The theme of a snowy
landscape was initiated in China by the eighth-century
literatus Wang Wei, and it became especially popular
among Japanese *bunjinga* artists in the late nineteenth
century. Kōran alludes to Wang Wei in her quatrain at the
upper left:

> Wind cuts through the jade forests and silvery peaks,
> Rich lustre shines to the limits of nature's beauty.
> [Wang] Tzu-yu turning back his boat and [Meng] Huo-jan
>   on his travels–
> Together they enter a scene worthy of the poet-painter
>   Wang Wei.

Kōran's landscape forms half of a pair of scrolls, the other
being a calligraphy by her husband Seigan.

51. Chō Kōran

Bamboo and Rock
Hanging scroll, ink and light colors on silk,
125.7 x 31.7 cm.
Signature: Chō-shi Kōran shiga
Seals: Chō-shi Keien; Dōka
Private collection

As Kōran matured as an artist, she turned more and more to "four gentlemen" themes. Perhaps because she had been forced to suffer on account of poverty or political convictions, or had lacked acceptance because she was a woman, these subjects came to have special meaning for her. This is evident in *Bamboo and Rock* on which she inscribed a poem alluding to the endurance of bamboo and its ability to rejuvenate.

> The town is filled with peach and plum blossoms,
>   competing in springtime.
> They resemble, in their profusion, frivolous people.
> Who notices that this "gentleman" can be strong and
>   upright,
> Creating spring amidst the hills even in the eighth month.

From the 1840s on, Kōran almost always added verses to her paintings. Here poem and painting are powerfully united, a feature frequently apparent in her work. Rich black ink was used in the writing as well as in the bamboo leaves in the center and lower left, underscoring the close relationship between painting and calligraphy. Kōran introduced tonal variation through the use of wet, gray ink to form the remaining bamboo and the eroded garden rock, and through the soft modulation of ink and light color within the rock which contrasts with the sharp, crisp leaves of the plants.

52. Chō Kōran

Plum Blossoms
Hanging scroll, ink on paper, 134.9 x 47.6 cm.
Signature: Nanajūsan Chō Kōran
Seals: Chō-shi Keien; Dōka; Kōshō
Private collection

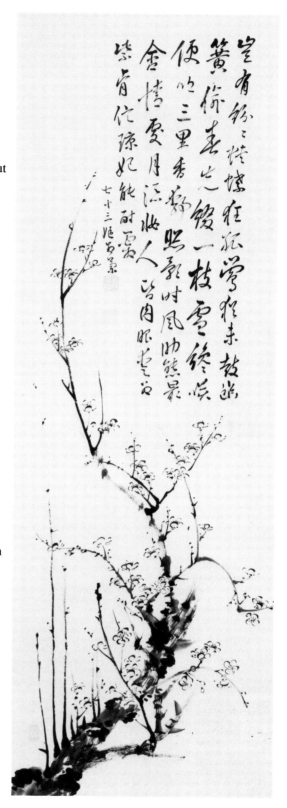

In Chinese poetry there is a long tradition of poems about women in which the plum is used allegorically to express distress at the passage of time and loss of youth.[52] Plum trees were especially appropriate symbols for women *bunjin* since "they share a delicate and understated elegance that sets them apart from the ostentation and overt sensuality of colorful flowers and voluptuous women."[53] By the Sung dynasty, the flowering plum had become identified with women who lived in solitude and who had suffered bitter hardships. Kōran was aware of the hidden meaning of this subject, and she employed the plum time and time again as a metaphor for herself. Her poem on this painting eschews the butterflies of her youth and praises the plum tree: through inference Kōran compares herself to this harbinger of spring which survives the snow and cold.

> Where are the butterflies, madly flying to and fro?
> The lonely nightingale has not yet begun to sing.
> Before the arrival of spring, one snowy branch
> Blossoms a little, sending forth its fragrance three *li*.
> Silently its shadow moves with the help of the wind;
> Its most cherished moment comes when whitened by the
>   moon.
> Most people have eyes for only bright reds and purples–
> Who can believe that this jade lady endures the frost?

The vigorous quality of Kōran's brushwork is apparent in this work, particularly in the dry, rough strokes forming some of the branches. The painting harmonizes with the calligraphy: one forked branch even reaches upwards as though to embrace it. Furthermore, the vertical columns of writing are echoed in the lower left by the rows of twigs springing upward from the main branch. As Kōran grew older, she wrote the poems on her paintings in larger characters than before, giving them a more prominent role in the overall design. Her calligraphy exhibits the same raw power as does her painting. Kōran's inner strength at age seventy-three is fully displayed in this scroll; the idea communicated in painting, poem, and calligraphy is that while blossoms may last only a moment, the tree endures.

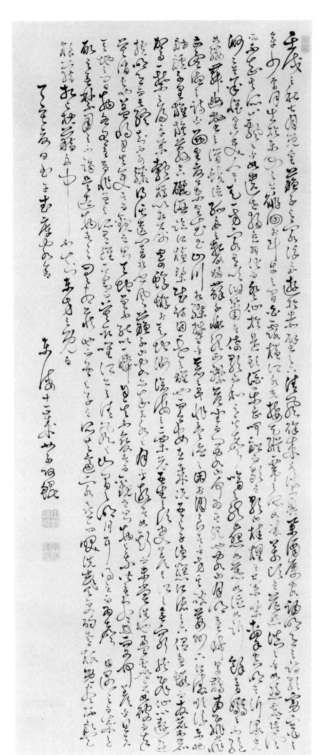

53. Tōkai Okon (1816-1888)

Red Cliff
Hanging scroll, ink on paper, 135.6 x 57.5 cm.
Signature: Tōkai jūissai joshi Okon
Seals: So(no) kao etsujin; Sanno hen Kon; Tōkai ryōha
Shōka Collection
Published: Fister, "Tōkai Okon," *Calligraphy Idea Exchange*, vol. 3, no. 4, p. 27.

Okon was taken by her parents to Kyoto in 1825; she soon succeeded in making a name for herself and was invited to demonstrate her calligraphy skills for the imperial court at the youthful age of nine. San'yō enthusiastically supported Okon, describing her brushwork as resembling billowing ocean waves. We can glean some idea of Okon's proficiency through an example of grass script inscribed by her as having been written at age eleven, two years after her visit to the court. Because of the extreme speed and abbreviation in writing, grass or cursive script most dramatically conveys the essence of calligraphy as an art form. Perhaps no other traditional visual art of the world is so kinesthetically exciting. The fundamental principle underlying this script is to write each character as quickly and simply as possible while still conveying the structural essence of its form.

In order to allow for expression of the greatest possible creative freedom, calligraphers frequently chose to write standard texts from the classics which they had memorized. Okon's text here is the Chinese poet Su Shih's (1037-1101) first essay on the Red Cliff, which is considered to be one of the classics of Chinese literature.[54] The lively rhythm of her brushwork reveals the speed with which she wrote. Nevertheless, she maintained a formal balance within each character and in the relationships between them. The descending linear rhythm within the columns is continually varied, occasionally being interspersed with dramatic flourishes of the brush or characters exaggerated in size for accent. Her brushlines display great freedom of movement, yet they have a structural integrity reflecting the control of the calligrapher's hand, a remarkable feat considering the tender age of the artist.

54. Tōkai Okon

Poem about Huai-su, 1831
Hanging scroll, ink on silk, 84.5 x 39.1 cm.
Signature: Tōto Joshi Kon sho
Seals: So(no) kao etsujin; Tōkai; Kon Joshi
Private collection
Published: Fister, "Tōkai Okon," *Calligraphy Idea Exchange*, vol. 3, no. 4, p. 31.

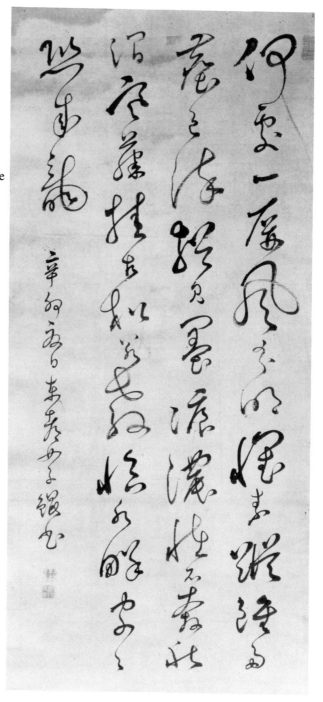

In his poem dedicated to Okon, San'yō observed that she derived her style of writing from the Chinese monk Huai-su (circa 735-800), who was noted for practicing a form of cursive script described as "wild" or "mad." In comparison to more orthodox cursive styles, "wild" script had more connections between characters in a column. The resultant shapes were often extreme and exaggerated and appear to have been written in a state of exhilaration. Freest and most eccentric of all writing styles, "wild" cursive script was developed for purely artistic reasons and represents the ultimate calligraphic self-expression.

Okon herself acknowledged her debt to Huai-su. At the age of fourteen she wrote out this poem, in which she described his calligraphy as running down the paper like a river over strange rocks, creating dragonlike images.

> Where did this screen come from?
> It is unmistakably the brushwork of Huai-su.
> Although covered with dust,
> One can still see the saturated ink traces
> Running like a river in autumn over strange rocks,
> Or like winter vines suspended from ancient pines.
> If placed next to the water-filled paddies,
> You might be afraid the characters will join to become a
>   dragon.

Her own writing in this example resembles closely the Red Cliff essay done three years earlier, but here there are fewer characters and they have been written with a fuller brush. This allowed Okon to exploit the contrast of thickening and thinning linework, and the characters seem to have more three-dimensional space. One can follow each turn of the brush as it went through the motion of its silent dance.

55. Tōkai Okon

Calligraphy at Age Sixty-four
Handscroll, ink on silk, 20.2 x 150 cm.
Signature: Rokujūyon ō Sanno hen Kon
Seals: So(no) kao etsujin; Sanno hen Kon; Shū hen yon kai
Spencer Museum of Art, 85.197
Published: Fister, "Tōkai Okon," *Calligraphy Idea Exchange*, vol. 3, no. 4.

This handscroll is one of the rare examples of Okon's calligraphy dating from her later life; the content of its text is autobiographical and is important as Okon's artistic testament.

> When this old woman was young, I wrote calligraphy in grass script. Following my father, I traveled all over the country and even to the capital, insulting the glory of the emperor by appearing before him. My three teachers–Rai San'yō, Shinozaki Shōchiku, and Sukegawa Rokudō– recorded this honor for my father and each presented poems to him on several occasions. They told my father that because his young daughter was so unusually talented in calligraphy, in the future she would be certain to suffer adversity. Therefore, they taught me the principles of a happy marriage with many children, and moreover that I should not devote my life to calligraphy. Accordingly I was married to Mr. Okamura. I had my teachers' poems and essays mounted and often hung them on the wall, remembering my father and the kindness of my three teachers fifty years ago. Nowadays misfortune has fallen; my husband has died and I have run out of money; only these three scrolls remain.[55] A friend has asked for them, but I am unable to endure exchanging them for money. Instead I will keep them at home in memory of my late father and my three teachers. As I record this I cannot help wiping away the tears.

The strength, control, and endless variation exhibited by Okon in this handscroll make it clear that she did not put away her brush upon becoming married. Her writing at age sixty-four expresses the maturity and controlled vitality, not present in her childhood work, that can only come with age and experience. The freedom of her early writing is still apparent, but the forms are more integrated and the handling of the brush is more naturally controlled. Her brushwork displays a wider range in the tonality and character of the ink (wet, dry, dark, light), and the composition of groups of characters is more varied. There is a balance between powerfully expressive strokes and those showing restraint; the overall impression is one of confident rhythm and natural harmony.

The function of this calligraphy was to communciate a personal message. It was not a flashy display of skill as were the works of her youth. Yet artistically the later handscroll has more merit in terms of balance and inventiveness of shapes and linear rhythms, indicating that at this point in her life calligraphic artistry flowed forth intuitively from Okon's hand, springing directly from her emotions.

Notes

1. In 1820 and again in 1830. Shibutsu slightly altered the characters in the title, which in Japanese became *Zuien jodaiko shisensen*.

2. Dore, *Education in Tokugawa Japan*, 254.

3. *Analects* (Lun Yü), *Mencius* (Meng Tzu), *Great Learning* (Ta Hsüeh), and *Golden Mean* (Chung Yung).

4. Itō Shin, *Yanagawa Seigan Ō*, 65-66.

5. This poem is included in vol. 2 of Saikō's poetry collection entitled *Shōmu ikō*.

6. From the *Kōran ikō*.

7. Shunsa was not included because she spent her life in the provinces of Mito and Kaga, and was unknown in Kyoto.

8. Soeda Tatsumine, "Ema Saikō to Yanagawa Kōran," 24.

9. Soeda Tatsumine, "Yanagawa Seigan to Kōran Joshi," 150-151.

10. Kazan also had another female pupil named Saitō Kōgyoku (1814-1870).

11. Yohime; a daughter of the eleventh Tokugawa shogun, Ienari.

12. See his "Geien zatsuwa," *Kaiga sōshi*.

13. The most accurate source of information on Saikō is Itō Shin's book entitled *Saikō to Kōran*. Unless otherwise noted, the biographical information supplied in this chapter comes from this volume.

14. For illustrations, see Ōgaki Shi Bunka Kaikan, *Ōgaki no senken ten: Ransai to Saikō*, 14-15.

15. Many of these slanderous stories were written in the Meiji and Taishō periods. Certain authors felt free to fictionalize and obviously had not read the actual letters of Saikō and San'yō. Accounts of Saikō written in her own time are all favorable.

16. Many examples of Saikō's poems with San'yō's corrections in red ink are preserved in the collection of Ema Shōjirō. San'yō also served as a poetry teacher to Saikō's brother-in-law, Shōsai.

17. Before San'yō's death, Saikō made seven trips to Kyoto: in 1814, 1817, 1819, 1822, 1824, 1827, and 1830.

18. For example, Sakamoto Kizan's *Rai San'yō* and Ichiyama Shunjō's *Zuihitsu Rai San'yō*. See Itō, *Saikō to Kōran*, 174.

19. A momento from Saikō's first visit to Kyoto in 1814, documenting her association with Shunkin and his father Gyokudō, is a collaborative painting produced by the three *bunjin*. For an illustration, see Hiroshima Kenritsu Bijutsukan, *Rai San'yō o chūshin to shita nanga ten*, no. 85. In that year, Saikō also contributed a painting to an album which was compiled and presented to Gyokudō on his seventieth birthday. See Mori Senzō, *Mori Senzō chosaku shū*, vol. 3, 407. A woodblock illustration of one of her bamboo paintings was also included in the 1814 *Meika gafu* (A Book of Paintings by Famous Masters).

20. Over the years, Unge dedicated several poems to Saikō, and he was clearly one of her many admirers. They became close friends and he visited her in Ōgaki in 1827. For Unge's poems, see Akamatsu Bunjirō, ed., *Unge Shōnin ikō*.

21. Quoted from Yoko Woodson, *Traveling Bunjin Painters and Their Patrons: Economic Life Style and Art of Rai San'yō and Tanomura Chikuden* (Ann Arbor: University Microfilms, 1983), 42.

22. Ten years after her death, in 1871, a two-volume collection with three hundred of Saikō's verses was published by her nephew and niece, entitled the *Shōmu ikō*. Later, twenty-six of Saikō's poems were also included in vol. 40 of the *Tung-yang shih hsüan* (J: *Tōei shisen*), an anthology of Edo-period *kanshi* compiled by the Chinese scholar Yü Ch'ü-yüan and published in China in 1882. See Sano Masami (annotator), *Tōei shisen* (Tokyo: Fukko Shoin, 1981).

23. She became such a distinguished figure that in 1852 her name was listed in the *Heian jinbutsu shi* in the section on well-known people from other provinces. Earlier, she had been noted as a skilled poet, calligrapher, and painter in the *Sanno jinbutsu kō*.

24. Translated by Burton Watson.

25. By referring to rivers and lakes, Saikō alludes to the fact that she has not mingled with the rest of the world.

26. In the Ema Shōjirō Collection in Ōgaki. The women included in this handscroll are: Hirata Gyokuon, Kobayashi Haihō, Chō Kōran, Shōkō, Teitei, Baien, Renzan Joshi, Sennanseihō, Gyokue-jo, Tōshi (wife of Uragami Shunkin), Yoshida Shūran, Rie (wife of Rai San'yō), Shidō (wife of Okada Hankō), Fusen-jo (wife of Yokoi Kinkoku), Sennanhōmei, Kan-shi me Yao, Hara Saihin, Ryūtai Joshi, Shinoda Bunpō, Mankō-jo, Oda Shitsushitsu, and Ran-jo.

27. Mori Senzō, *Mori Senzō chosaku shū*, vol. 3, 412-413.

28. For further information on Gyokudō's *ch'in* music, see Stephen Addiss, *Tall Mountains and Flowing Waters* (Honolulu: University of Hawaii Press, 1987).

29. Shūran's name also appears in the 1847 *Kōto shoga jinmei roku* (Record of Calligraphers and Painters in the Imperial Capital), with a note that she was a painting pupil of Chikutō, and that she was also skilled in calligraphy, poetry, and the seven-stringed *ch'in*.

30. From the *Kōran ikō*.

31. When Saikō visited Kyoto in 1841, it is recorded that at a banquet, she, Shūran, and Shunkin shared in the creation of a painting. Saikō painted bamboo, Shunkin a rock, and Shūran added an orchid. Itō, *Saikō to Kōran*, 194.

32. The information about Kōran's life that follows was drawn largely from Itō Shin, *Yanagawa Seigan Ō*. For a biographical study in English, see Fister, "The Life and Art of Chō Kōran."

33. Among the notable *bunjin* they visited were Kan Chazan (1748-1827) in Kannabe, Rai Kyōhei (1756-1834) and Rai Itsuan (1800-1856) in Hiroshima, Kamei Shōyō (1773-1836) in Chikuzen, and Hirose Tansō (1782-1756) in Hida.

34. For Tung's text, see Susan Bush, *Chinese Literati on Painting* (Cambridge, Massachusetts: Harvard University Press, 1971), 191.

35. Kōran did not begin to play the *ch'in* until 1846, when she became a pupil of a man named Ogata living in Tsu.

36. Kōran's name appeared in successive issues of the *Heian jinbutsu shi*, including 1838, 1852, and 1867.

37. This collection of 450 verses was never published during Kōran's own lifetime, but survived into this century in the form of a handwritten manuscript by Ono Kozan. It was later published by Tominaga Chōjo in his *Seigan zenshū*, vol. 4.

38. From Kōran's letters, we know that she was patronized by Kumagai Naotaka, the owner of the famous paper store, Kyūkyodō. Ninchōji, "Kōran mibojin no shokan," 139.

39. Tōkari Soshinan, "Seigan fusai no tegami," 27.

40. The biographical information on Okon in this section has been adapted from Mimura Seizaburō, "Tōkai Kon-jo."

41. This poem appears in vol. 1 of the *San'yō ikō* (1826), but was also written out by him in scroll format. One version is in the collection of the Spencer Museum of Art.

42. Kon is the literal pronunciation of her name, but Japanese often add an honorific *o* as a prefix, and consequently she is usually referred to as Okon. The character *Kon* refers to a large, mythical fish mentioned in Chuang Tzu.

43. For an illustration of Shōchiku's text and an English translation, see Fister, "Tōkai Okon," 29 (Figure 2b).

44. Ibid., 30 (Figure 2c).

45. See Ibaragi Kenritsu Rekishikan, *Mito no nanga*.

46. In the Ema Shōjirō Collection there is a handscroll of bamboo done by Saikō with corrections and notations by Shunkin. For an illustration of one segment, see Ōgaki Shi Bunka Kaikan, *Ōgaki no senken ten: Ransai to Saikō*, 21.

47. Quoted from James Cahill, *Hills Beyond a River* (New York and Tokyo: Weatherhill, 1976), 17.

48. For more information on this album, see Kamiya Hiroshi, "Shūenjō," *Nagoya Shi Hakubutsukan kenkyū kiyō*, vol. 6 (1983), 69-80.

49. Butterflies and other insects can be found in the works of Nagasaki school followers of Shen Nan-p'in, but they are depicted in a more fully developed setting with flowers, plants, and rocks.

50. Kōran did an almost identical painting in 1823, as well as other renditions of butterflies. For an illustration of the former, see Itō Shin, *Saikō to Kōran*.

51. For a similar painting by Chikutō, see Nagoya Shi Hakubutsukan, *Owari no kaiga shi: Nanga* (Nagoya, 1981), pl. 86.

52. For a thorough study of the plum motif in Chinese art and literature, see Maggie Bickford, *Bones of Jade, Soul of Ice* (New Haven, Conn.: Yale University Art Gallery, 1985).

53. Ibid., 19.

54. For an English translation of the Red Cliff essay, see Cyril Birch, ed., *Anthology of Chinese Literature* (New York: Grove Press, Inc., 1965), 381-382.

55. The three scrolls referred to by Okon are now in the collection of the Spencer Museum of Art.

Chapter Eight: Ukiyo-e Painters and Printmakers

In the nineteenth century a surprising number of women painted professionally outside of *bunjin* circles. As was the case in the eighteenth century, these women were most often part of the mercantile ukiyo-e world. Earlier women ukiyo-e artists did only paintings; now they were involved in producing prints as well.

Japanese prints were, from the beginning, products of teamwork. The process involved artists, engravers, and printers, all of whom were coordinated and paid by publishers. Competing with one another in commissioning designs from the leading artists, publishers continually searched for new talent. Achieving success may have been a mixed blessing, for those who did were called upon by publishers to pour forth an incredible number of designs. As a result, all of the major artists had workshops where they trained apprentices in the art of designing prints. Apprentices learned and mastered the subjects and style of their teacher; the more advanced pupils were permitted to assist him (more rarely her) in fulfilling commissions. The pupils who excelled might be retained by a publisher, and if their designs proved popular, they moved on to establish their own studios. However, success in the print world was potentially as fleeting as the "floating world" they depicted; if an artist's prints did not sell, he or she would soon be out of work. Artists contended with one another to stay in public favor, catering to current tastes and fads.

Women with artistic interests were somewhat at an advantage in the nineteenth-century ukiyo-e world, for suddenly they seemed to be in fashion. Several of the leading ukiyo-e artists readily accepted women into their studios, including Katsushika Hokusai (1760-1849), Utagawa Toyokuni I (1769-1825), Utagawa Toyokuni II (1777-1835), Tsunoda Kunisada (1786-1864), and Utagawa Kuniyoshi (1797-1861). Whereas Kitagawa Utamaro (1753-1806) had designed a diptych (*Edo meibutsu nishiki-e kōsaku*) around 1804 depicting the making of multicolored prints in Edo,[1] in which he cleverly substituted beautiful women for the less attractive real craftsmen, as the nineteenth century progressed, women working in ukiyo-e ateliers became a reality.[2]

Not only did ukiyo-e artists take in women apprentices, but there was a growing interest in female historical figures as subject matter for prints. Kuniyoshi seems to have initiated this trend, doing numerous series memorializing heroines, dutiful wives, and other virtuous women. Among them were his *Kenjo reppuden* (Stories of Wise and Strong Women), *Kenjo hakkei* (Eight Views of Wise and Strong Women), *Jikken onna ōgi* (Ten Fans of Wise Women), *Ken'yū fujo kagami* (Mirrors of Intelligent and Strong Women), *Kokon honchō meijo hyaku den* (One Hundred Stories of Famous Women of Our Country, Ancient and Modern), and *Honchō taoyame soroi* (Delicate Ladies of Our Country). Kuniyoshi even included several women poets in these series; notable Edo-period figures he portrayed were Chiyo (see chapter four) and Kaji (see chapter five). The attitude of ukiyo-e artists toward women surely paralleled society's changing views and acceptance of women into the art world; whereas previous prints had depicted women as graceful beings whose duties lay in pleasing men, now women were portrayed as having vigorous, sophisticated personalities.

Hokusai was without a doubt the most prolific artist in Edo during his time. Two of his daughters, Ōi (active Bunsei-Kaei eras, 1818-1854) and Tatsu (active Bunka and Bunsei eras, 1804-1830), achieved a respectable degree of fame as painters, generally following the style of their father. They did primarily figure paintings in the bold and colorful tradition favored by Edo townspeople. Hokusai also seems to have accepted other women pupils outside of his own family. These include Hokumei (active Bunka and Bunsei eras, 1804-1830), who in addition to illustrating books specialized in *bijinga* (paintings of beautiful women),[3] and a lesser known figure called Hokuei.[4]

Toyokuni I had a daughter named Kunika-me (1810-1871) whom he encouraged to paint; however, her work does not survive.[5] His other women pupils included Kunito-me (active Bunsei era, 1818-1830), the wife of a samurai serving the Tokugawa shogun, and

Kunihisa I (active Kyōwa and Bunka eras, 1801-1818). Kunihisa is probably the most well-known of Toyokuni's female pupils; both prints and paintings by her have been preserved.[6] Toyokuni II had a woman pupil whose name was written with similar characters, Kuniku-me (active Bunsei and Tenpō eras, 1818-1844).

Kunisada is only known to have had one female pupil, Sadaka-me (active Bunsei era, 1818-1830), who in turn tutored another woman named Kakuju-jo (active Bunkyū era, 1861-1864), the designer of a small number of fine actor prints which earned her fame. Kuniyoshi also instructed some important women pupils. Under his guidance, his first and second daughters Yoshitori (active mid-nineteenth century) and Yoshi-jo (active Kaiei-Bunkyū eras, 1848-1864)[7] took up the brush. Yoshitori died young, but is the better known of the two because of the *Sankai medetai zue* series on which she collaborated with her father (Cat. 64-66). Yoshitama (1836-1870) was a third female student of Kuniyoshi, although she later studied with the artist Shibata Zeshin (1807-1891). The daughter of a barber, she assisted in applying the colors to Kuniyoshi's prints, occasionally producing paintings and prints under her own name as well.[8]

There are a host of other women ukiyo-e artists of the nineteenth century whose names and works have come to light: Fuki (active Bunka and Bunsei eras, 1804-1830);[9] Hirai Renzan and Nagahara Baien;[10] Ikutoshi;[11] Mizuno Shuho (born 1875);[12] Otowako (active Bunsei era, 1818-1830); Ryūko (active Bunsei era, 1818-1830); Hō-shi Shunei-jo; and Yanagita Sai-jo. In many cases we know very little about these women, and can only speculate who their teachers might have been from the style of their paintings and prints. As more attention is directed toward female ukiyo-e artists in the years to come, it should be possible to piece together a more comprehensive study of their art and lineages. Nevertheless, a few generalities can be made.

Works by all ukiyo-e artists of the nineteenth century, including women, fall into a category which has long been termed "decadent" because of the growing trend toward dramatic and often violent compositions, vivid and contrasting colors, and a greater degree of stylization. It is a fact that ukiyo-e artists were always attracted to what was novel; seeking to titillate and please their ever restless patrons, they moved away from the classical compositions and idealized figures of the previous generation and developed an art that was more in tune with the tastes and desires of their nineteenth-century audience. Shocking tales of revenge and murder as well as ghost stories captivated the Edo public, who sought in prints the sensational stories which they read about or witnessed on stage. In order to communicate these stories more directly, ukiyo-e designers replaced the early idealism with a more mannered treatment; dynamic, often contorted movements superseded the relaxed, graceful atmosphere. Designed to appeal to a sophisticated, art conscious audience, woodblock prints became more richly colored and elaborate than ever before. In particular, engraving details reached an astonishing level of technical brilliance. Scholars have now begun to study and admire the achievements of later prints, looking at them with aesthetic values derived from a greater understanding of the society for which they were produced.

Because of the widespread enthusiasm for prints in Japan's urban centers, publishers and artists catered to a wider public than ever before. Prints were mass-produced at an astounding rate in the nineteenth century, and overproduction inevitably brought about a decline in quality at times which has led to criticism. Nevertheless, it was still a period of exciting activity in ukiyo-e, and is particularly interesting because of the work by women artists at this time. Because paintings and prints by others are scarce, only four women ukiyo-e masters are included here: Ōi, Tatsu, Kakuju-jo, and Yoshitori.

Katsushika Ōi (active Bunsei-Kaei eras, 1818-1854)

Scholars seem to agree that Ōi was the third daughter of Hokusai, the first to be born to his second wife, but beyond that the facts about his children are confused.[13] Of all his offspring, the most has been written about Ōi.[14] She married the son of an oil seller around the year 1820;[15] her husband, Minamizawa Tōmei,[16] was a pupil of Tsutsumi Tōrin III (circa 1743-1820). Ōi also studied with Tōrin; painting apparently came naturally to her and it is said that she poked fun at her husband's work. Perhaps because of her uncompromising character, what started out as a marriage of companionship eventually

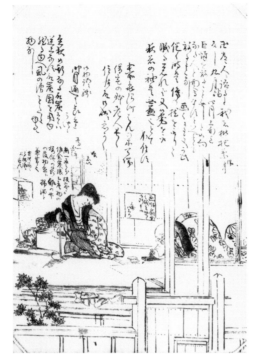

soured, and they were divorced. Ōi then seems to have returned home to live with her father.[17] She did not remarry and there is evidence that she assisted Hokusai in his workshop until his death. The year of her divorce is not known, but Eisen (1790-1848) wrote in 1833 that Ōi had taken over certain responsibilities in her father's studio, indicating that by that year she had moved back home.[18]

Ōi and Hokusai were apparently two of a kind: free spirits, neither one cared about material wealth or household cleanliness. They lived in relative poverty, purportedly moving constantly because they would leave one place after it became too unbearable to stay. Ōi found cooking tiresome, so she would buy prepared food at the local market. After eating, she did not bother to clean up, leaving the food wrappings scattered around the room. There is a sketch by one of Hokusai's pupils, Tsuyuki Iitsu (died 1869), depicting Hokusai and Ōi in one of their residences (Figure 13). At the right is Hokusai, painting on the floor, and to his left is Ōi. She has her head cocked to one side as she watches her father paint, but her expression is not the look of fascination one might expect. Instead she appears somewhat bored and lethargic, which fits with the description we have of her slovenly lifestyle. She was homely, and Hokusai called her "Ago-ago" because of her protruding chin (the Japanese word for chin is *ago*). Ōi apparently drank like a man and smoked tobacco (she holds a long pipe in Figure 13). She developed an interest in divination, and took doses of medicinal herbs in an attempt to achieve immortality. In her later years she turned to Buddhism, becoming devoutly religious.

Hokusai and Ōi were devoted to one another. At some point, Ōi, whose given name was originally Ei (or Oei), adopted an artistic name written with characters that were pronounced Ōi. It is said that she did this in response to her father's frequent summons for her, "Ōi, ōi."[19] When Hokusai traveled to Shinshū (Nagano prefecture) in 1845, he told his host-patron Takai Kōzan (1805-1883) that he could not bear being parted from Ōi whom he had left in Edo. Takai encouraged Hokusai to return and fetch her, which Hokusai promptly did.[20] Ōi became friendly with many of Hokusai's friends and pupils. The novelist Shikitei Sanba (1776-1822) inscribed at least one of her paintings (Cat. 56), and Ōi collaborated on works with Hokusai's pupils Hokuba (1771-1844), Sekkōtei, Hokuga, Tokutokusai (Sekkō, active 1830-1840), and Hokuju (active 1789-1818).

In addition to helping her father, Ōi produced formal and informal paintings as well as book illustrations. No single sheet prints with her name have yet been discovered, but she designed the illustrations for the 1847 *E-iri nichiyō onna chōhō-ki* (Cat. 59) and the dictionary of Chinese-style tea, *Sencha jibiki no shu* (1848). Like other ukiyo-e artists in her time, Ōi experimented with Western perspective and chiaroscuro in her painting.[21] In addition to paintings and book illustrations, she also made a type of doll called *keshi ningyō* which she sold to help earn a living.

After Hokusai's death in 1849, Ōi's whereabouts are unclear. Sources differ as to what she did; she may have drifted from place to place to stay with pupils or friends. According to one story, she left the home of her brother's family (Kase) in 1857 and went to Kanazawa, where she died at the age of sixty-seven. Another story says that she died near Kanazawa in the land of a samurai vassal of the Tokugawa family. Still another story relates that she died at the home of Takai Sankurō in Shinshū.

Katsushika Tatsu (active Bunka and Bunsei eras, 1804-1830)

There is a small corpus of paintings by the woman artist Tatsu which continues to puzzle art historians. One example, in the Los Angeles County Museum of Art (Cat. 60), is signed "Painted by Hokusai's daughter, Tatsu." However, the standard biographies of Hokusai do not list Tatsu among his daughters. She may have been another child who was not recorded, or Tatsu could be an alternate name for one of his known daughters. Some scholars believe that Tatsu was Hokusai's second daughter (recorded as Otetsu),[22] while others insist that Tatsu was a sobriquet used by Ōi, perhaps during the period she was married.[23] It is also possible that Tatsu could be another name for Hokusai's first daughter, Omiyo, or his fourth, Nao.

Because of her ambiguous identity, nothing is known about Tatsu's life except that she seems to have worked in the early nineteenth century. The three known paintings with her signature all depict seated *bijin* in similar pose, rendered in a style modeled after that of Hokusai.

Kakuju-jo (active Bunkyū era, 1861-1864)

Kakuju-jo is one of the rare female artists who actually had a woman for a teacher; she is recorded as having studied with Kunisada's pupil Sadaka-me. Unfortunately, no works by Sadaka-me are known, making it impossible to determine how much influence she had on the development of Kakuju-jo's style. Since Kakuju-jo's prints show an obvious debt to Kunisada, it is likely that Sadaka-me closely adhered to the style of her master. Judging from existing works, Kakuju-jo was a print-designer and not a painter. Prints with her signature are few in number, and all seem to depict scenes from kabuki plays.

Yoshitori (active mid-nineteenth century)

The eldest daughter of Kuniyoshi, Yoshitori made a name for herself through a series of seventy prints published in 1852 entitled *Sankai medetai zue*; she designed the landscape insets, and her father the figures of women in the foreground. It is obvious from Kuniyoshi's own prints that he recognized the contributions women had made in both the past and present. Moreover, he supported the idea of women taking active roles in society, and taught both of his daughters artistic skills. Although the younger daughter does not seem to have designed prints, Yoshitori did for several years.[24] Little is known of her life, though we can surmise that she had a son by the year 1840. In a print from the series *Yōdō shogei kyōsō* (Instruction for Children in the Accomplishments) done close to that time, Kuniyoshi depicted a mother showing her child how to draw (Figure 14); beside her lies a sketch bearing the signature Yoshitori-jo, revealing that this is a portrait of Kuniyoshi's talented daughter and grandson.

56. Katsushika Ōi
(active Bunsei-Kaei eras, 1818-1854)

Courtesan at the New Year
Hanging scroll, ink and light colors on paper,
24.5 x 36.7 cm.
Signature: Gidō Ōi ga
Seal: Ōi?
Prof. Dr. Med. Gerhard Pulverer Collection
Published: *Ukiyo-e*, vol. 52 (1972), pl. 370.

This work is a collaboration between Ōi and the popular writer Shikitei Sanba: Ōi did the painting of the *oiran* or high-ranking courtesan, and Sanba wrote the long inscription which begins in the upper right and ends in the lower left. Sanba associated with a number of ukiyo-e designers, and was a welcome guest at gatherings of artists and poets in Edo because of his ability to compose witty, spontaneous verses.[25] The theme of this painting and accompanying prose suggests that it was created at the start of a new year, perhaps as a gift for a mutual friend. Sanba's rather rambunctious inscription says:

> Make your plans for the year in the spring, the season for the "first purchase" of a courtesan. Make your plans for the day in the morning, the time of the client who has stayed all night. An *oiran* always has a New Year's feeling in her heart, but her client never realizes that there is a final day of reckoning.[26] If one realizes how quickly pass the endless cycles of birth and reincarnation, the "first apparel" of the

second day [soon becomes] the plain white robes of the first day of the eighth month.[27] As Ikkyū[28] said, "Take care, take care!"[29]

Ōi's depiction of the courtesan has all of the nonchalance and uninhibited spirit of Sanba's mocking prose. Seated so that she faces away from the viewer, the courtesan bides her time by reading a book. Hairpins protrude from her elaborate coiffure, giving her the appearance of a cat seen from behind, with ears pricked and whiskers bristling. Her voluminous outer robe flows around her, the folds splayed adroitly at the right. At the bottom of her garment is a design of pine boughs, perhaps alluding to the new year.

Although rendering the painting almost entirely in ink, Ōi employed a faint pink wash to portions of the clothing. Her brushwork is free and spontaneous, imbued with the light-hearted quality one finds in *haiga* (see chapter four). She achieved artistic variety through contrasting gray washes with dry, rough outlines; Ōi employed darker ink as accents, drawing attention to the courtesan's head and the pine design. Usually celebrated for her more formal, detailed paintings, Ōi was obviously a master at conveying the essence of her subject in this sort of informal, abbreviated work. She undoubtedly learned this style from Hokusai; several sketchlike works of courtesans by him remain which are very similar in nature.[30] The spontaneous mode was practiced by Hokusai's other pupils as well; in another cooperative work in which Ōi participated with five other Hokusai followers, all six artists rendered their figures in this abbreviated manner.[31]

57. Katsushika Ōi

Courtesan Writing a Letter
Hanging scroll, ink on paper, 26.2 x 28 cm.
Signature: Gidō Ōi giga
Seal: Shigenaga no in
Dr. and Mrs. George A. Colom Collection
Published: *Ukiyo-e*, vol. 72, pl. 649.

Pausing with brush in hand, a slender courtesan
intently fills a long paper scroll with her elegant
calligraphy. She is most likely writing a love letter. This
painting was done in Ōi's informal style also seen in Cat.
56. The pose of the woman is almost identical, though
here she faces the viewer. The textile design on her
garment is likewise the same, featuring a pine bough
springing from the lower hem. Ōi defined both the figure
and her outer robe with dry brush lines, filling in some of
the interior portions with wet ink washes. Although the
conception is simple, Ōi has employed a diversity of brush
techniques and ink tonalities in order to create a visually
rich design.

The subject of courtesans had enjoyed long-lasting
popularity in ukiyo-e, due to the unflagging demand of
urban patrons. Ōi was obviously familiar with the
contemporary Yoshiwara scene; judging from her extant
works, she chose to paint courtesans more often than any
other subject. This is in marked contrast to her father, who
painted everything under the sun. In her informal
paintings, Ōi seems to have been most influenced by the
style Hokusai practiced from 1795-1805. Hokusai's
paintings of courtesans from this period are
characteristically portrayed with long, thin faces. Some
scholars have attempted to assign dates to Ōi's works by
associating them stylistically with Hokusai's various
periods; however, Ōi may well have painted in 1820 in a
style that Hokusai had utilized in 1800. It is virtually
impossible to recreate a chronology for Ōi's artistic
development, since she did not date any of her paintings,
and we are not even certain of her birth and death dates.
Her skill as an artist, however, is evident in all of her
works.

58. Katsushika Ōi

Three Musicians
Hanging scroll, ink and colors on silk, 47 x 67.3 cm.
Signature: Ōi suijo hitsu
Seal: Ō
Museum of Fine Arts, Boston,
Courtesy William Sturgis Bigelow Collection
Published: Akai, *Nikuhitsu ukiyo-e*, vol. 7, no. 48; Narazaki
Muneshige, ed., *Zaigai hihō* (Tokyo: Gakushū Kenkyūsha
1969), vol. 4, no. 94.
(not in exhibition)

This scroll exemplifies the formal beauty of Ōi's more colorful, detailed painting style. Three women kneel in a circle facing one another, each concentrating intensely on the stringed instrument she is playing.[32] In comparison with Ōi's two casually brushed paintings (Cat. 56 and 57), the coloring here is opaque, displaying the bold and vivid hues characteristic of nineteenth-century ukiyo-e. Ōi has clothed two of the women in rather flamboyant *kosode*,

contrasting their garments with the subdued brown robe of the older woman at the right.

The poses of the figures and brush manner recall Hokusai's works of his middle years. Hokusai's influence is especially notable in the jagged brushwork defining the neckbands and sleeve openings. However, Ōi has not exploited as much the thickening and thinning of lines, and her strokes lack the nervous animated brushwork of her father. Instead she devoted her attention to recreating the textures and sumptuous designs of the fabrics; the color combinations are electric at times. Traces of shading are apparent in the checkered *kosode* of the woman at the far left, hinting at Ōi's interest in Western artistic techniques. By utilizing a concentration of black and rich hues, she invites attention to the milk-white faces and agile hands of the women, consciously positioned to evoke rhythmic interplay among them. The circular arrangement of the figures and the movement implied through their fingers and heads creates a musical rhythm of its own, evocative of the piece that the women are playing. The masterful design and exquisite detail combine to make the Boston scroll one of Ōi's most outstanding paintings.

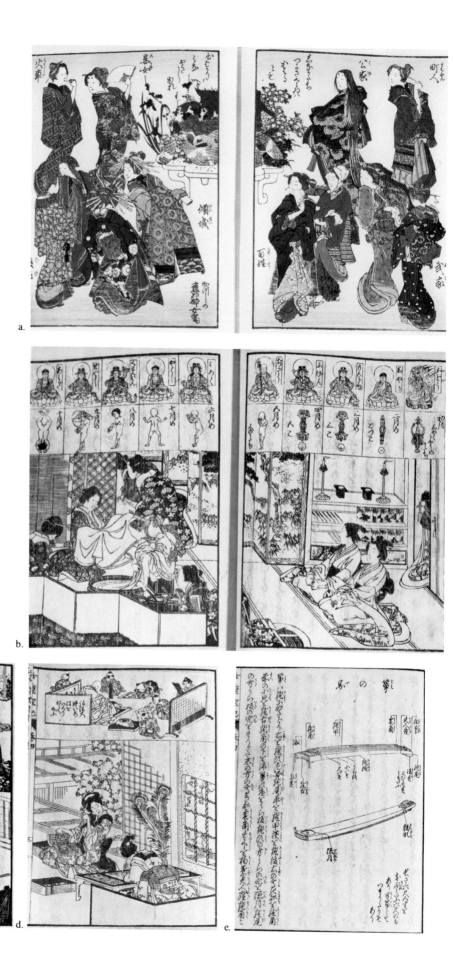

a.

b.

c.

d.

e.

59. Katsushika Ōi

E-iri nichiyō onna chōhō-ki
(Illustrated Handbook for Women), 1847
Woodblock-printed book, 25.4 x 17.3 cm.
Signature: Ōiei-jo hitsu
Ravicz Collection

f.

The *E-iri nichiyō onna chōhō-ki* is one of two woodblock-printed books known to have been illustrated by Ōi. This particular volume was edited by Takai Ranzan (1762-1838) and published in Edo in 1847. An earlier edition by him was printed in 1829, but the first version of this book was written (and possibly illustrated) by Naemura Jōhaku, appearing in Kyoto in 1692; several editions were published in the Edo period in different cities under different titles.[33]

An encyclopedia for women, the *Onna chōhō-ki* exemplifies the moral instruction books that were extremely popular in the Edo period. Most of them stressed the cultivation of traditional values which were considered of utmost importance for the proper functioning of women in Japanese society. Although the early editions were written for the women of the samurai and wealthy townsmen classes, by the nineteenth century such books were reaching a wider audience. Near the beginning of the *Onna chōhō-ki* there is a double page illustration depicting women from various walks of life (Cat. 59a). Top to bottom, right to left, they are labeled: townsperson, samurai class, imperial court, commoner, concubine, courtesan, prostitute, and widow. The *Onna chōhō-ki* is distinctive because, in addition to moral instruction, it contains a good deal of practical advice for women on day-to-day living. There is a plethora of medical information—how to detect the symptoms of tuberculosis, how to diagnose a pregnancy, foods to avoid during pregnancy (crabs, or the child will come out sideways, etc.), lucky directions in which a pregnant woman should contrive to face on various days of the zodiac, charms to secure an easy delivery, and herbs to improve the flow of milk. The section on pregnancy is especially interesting because of the detailed illustrations meant to show what the fetus looks like at each stage of its life in the womb (Cat. 59b). Underneath, an actual birth is depicted; this section is followed by advice on the care of infants and raising of children.

Long passages on etiquette and personal deportment are included, and on the correct forms for various ceremonies, especially weddings. The author made clear distinctions in the behavior and rituals for women of different classes. One illustration contrasts an elaborate samurai wedding above with the simple ceremony observed by the lower classes below (Cat. 59c). There are also detailed explanations and illustrations showing how to serve and eat various foods. Cosmetic tips include how to

clean and arrange one's hair, the application of powder, and tooth blackening. A great deal of attention is paid to the cultivation of feminine talents and activities deemed appropriate for women. There are sections on sewing, weaving, writing poetry and calligraphy (Cat. 59d), musical instruments (*koto* and *shamisen*) (Cat. 59e), as well as explanations of the games of incense identification (Cat. 59f) and poem cards.

Ōi's illustrations are quite different in style from those of the original seventeenth-century edition. Although she designed almost the same number of illustrations (there are thirty-eight pages with pictures) and depicted the same subjects, Ōi's figures are larger and better integrated into their settings. In addition, she rendered them in a contemporary style different from the earlier editions which had designs in the manner of Hishikawa Moronobu or Yoshida Hanbei; Ōi's figures are clearly patterned after Hokusai's works of his forties. She tends to include more detail, and the proportions of her figures and objects are more natural. At times she even employs a semi-Western perspective, with distant figures depicted on a smaller scale and lines receding along diagonals.

It is believed that some handbooks for women were authored by females, but this edition of the *Onna chōhō-ki* may be the only example which was actually illustrated by a woman. The editor or publisher may have felt that having a woman design the pictures would be a novel and saleable idea. With the publication of this book and a dictionary of tea with her designs in 1849, Ōi achieved a certain degree of fame in Edo two years before her father's death. Unfortunately, she seems to have faded into obscurity after Hokusai died.

60. Katsushika Tatsu
(active Bunka and Bunsei eras, 1804-1830)

Courtesan with Fan
Hanging scroll, ink and colors on silk, 44.6 x 34.4 cm.
Signature: Katsushika musume Tatsu-jo hitsu
Seal: Yoshinoyama
Los Angeles County Museum of Art, Ernest Larsen
Blanck Memorial Gift, 58.26.1
Published: Akai, *Nikuhitsu ukiyo-e*, vol. 7, no. 51;
Narazaki Muneshige, *Zaigai hihō* (Tokyo: Gakushū
Kenkyūsha, 1969), vol. 3, no. 95; *Ukiyo-e taisei*, vol. 9,
no. 28.

This depiction of a seated courtesan is celebrated as
one of the rare scrolls by Hokusai's enigmatic daughter
Tatsu.[34] It is exquisitely painted, with the courtesan's
garment rendered in rich, opaque pigments. The woman
looks downward, her face partially hidden in the wide
collar of her robe; deep in thought, her expression is one of
melancholy. Her right hand gracefully holds a flat, round
fan, indicating that the season is summer. Her gaze seems
to be directed toward the lacquer tray at the left which
contains a blue-and-white porcelain bowl filled with
morning glories. Perhaps they are a gift from a lover or
admirer.

The form and proportions of the figure, along with the
style of brushwork, resemble Hokusai's paintings dated
1807-1815. This is especially apparent in the brushlines
defining the courtesan's robes, which fluctuate dramatically
in thickness. While lacking Hokusai's personal dynamism
of brushwork, Tatsu has further animated the pictorial
surface by playing off darker areas against lighter ones.
The white face and hands of the courtesan, along with her
white undergarment decorated with cherry blossoms,
provide a welcome contrast to the somber darkness of her
outer robe; a similar contrast was achieved by the porcelain
bowl and black lacquer tray.

One assumes that Tatsu learned to paint from her
father; the seal she used on her paintings reading
"Yoshinoyama" seems to be identical to a seal Hokusai
used around 1815. Hokusai was known to bequeath names
and seals to favored pupils, and this is likely the case with
Tatsu. As to the problem of whether or not Tatsu is merely
an earlier name used by Ōi, stylistic differences in their
paintings and calligraphy seem to indicate that they were
not the same person. However, the situation cannot be
clarified until more works by both artists are brought to
light.

Two Edo *kyōka* poets added verses to Tatsu's painting,
associating the beauty of the courtesan with the morning
glories.

Oki ideshi	More than the silk
Tsubomi no imo ga	The awakening budding beauty
Kinu yori mo	Appears as fresh
Kasuri ni sakeru	As the morning glories
Asagao no hana	Blooming in the *kasuri* patterns.
(by Nanakyōkutei Gyokugi)	

Kaki ho yori	The morning glories which
Torieshimama no	I have just picked
Asagao ni	From the fence are
Tsuyu mo taruka to	Dripping with dew
Omou taoyame	As fresh as the maiden.
(by Chōkōtei Undō)	

61. Kakuju-jo (active Bunkyū era, 1861-1864)

Kanadehon Chūshingura, 1862
Woodblock prints, diptych, each 35.8 x 24.5 cm.
Signature: Meirindō Kakuko-me hitsu
Spencer Museum of Art: Weare-West Fund, 84.167

Kakuju-jo's known prints were all published in Edo in the year 1862, indicating that she enjoyed only a brief period of success. Without exception they depict episodes from the popular kabuki drama. This diptych represents a scene from the third act of *Chūshingura*, the famous tale of the revenge of the forty-seven samurai. Okaru (played by Sawamura Tanosuke) has been pushed away by her husband, the samurai Hayano Kanpei (here played by Bandō Hikisaburō). He has learned that his master attacked another feudal lord and as a result has been confined to his house. Kanpei believes that he should have been at his master's side, instead of enjoying the company of Okaru. He feels dishonor, knowing that his master will be asked to commit *seppuku*. Kakuju-jo has represented the moment just after the distressed Kanpei has had a violent fight with the henchmen of his master's enemy. Kanpei was preparing to kill one of them with his sword, but Okaru pulled him away. The couple stands in a state of shock, in front of a wooden gateway built into the stone wall surrounding the mansion. Black crows fly through the indigo blue sky above the pine trees, symbols of impending doom.

Kakuju-jo's stylized treatment of the figures, with their long oval-shaped faces and pointed chins, is clearly within the Kunisada tradition which she learned from Sadaka-me. The angular, stiff depiction of the clothing also recalls the style of Kunisada. Inspired by the bold color contrasts of the master, Kakuju-jo chose to emphasize the strident red, yellow, and green colors, along with blue and black. This vivid coloring gives the pair of prints much of its impact. The dramatic moment is also heightened by the diagonal lines of the fences and walls which converge in the center, leading the eye directly to the two figures.

62. Kakuju-jo

Sukeroku yukari no Edo zakura
Woodblock print, 32.4 x 24.1 cm.
Signature: Meirindō Kakuju-jo ga
Mary Baskett Gallery, Cincinnati, Ohio

Acting out an episode from the first scene of *Sukeroku yukari no Edo zakura* (Sukeroku: Flower of Edo) are the kabuki actors Kawarazaki Gonjūrō (Danjurō IX) and Nakamura Shikan; respectively they are playing the roles of the hero Sukeroku (right) and his brother Shinbei, the latter disguised as a *sake* merchant. Sukeroku, actually Soga no Gorō, is searching for his family's treasured sword; his strategy is to frequent the Yoshiwara pleasure district and to provoke quarrels in order to cause samurai to draw their swords. Oblivious to the missing sword and Sukeroku's plan, Sukeroku's mother has become troubled by her son's brawls and asks his brother Shinbei to speak

with him. Shinbei confronts Sukeroku and reprimands him for upsetting their mother, whereupon Sukeroku confesses the reasoning behind his madness. Shinbei is immediately sympathetic and wishes to join forces with Sukeroku. Sukeroku proceeds to try to teach him how to fight. Kakuju-jo has depicted the scene in front of a Yoshiwara teahouse where Sukeroku adopts various fighting stances which his brother then clumsily tries to imitate. The results are quite comical because Shinbei is by nature gentle and delicate and does not have his brother's masculine build.

As can be seen in the previous diptych, Kakuju-jo relied upon a small range of colors, with blue, red, green, yellow, and black predominant. The limited polychromy and comparatively unadorned design work together to achieve a direct impact on the viewer. Forceful action is suggested by the pose of both actors, whose legs extend at sharp diagonals; this movement is counterbalanced by the horizontal gestures of their arms and the strong vertical of Shinbei's halberd.

63. Kakuju-jo

Sukeroku yukari no Edo zakura, 1862
Woodblock print, one sheet from a triptych, 32.4 x 24.1 cm.
Signature: Meirindō Kakuju-jo ga
Mary Baskett Gallery, Cincinnati, Ohio

This print originally formed the right sheet of a triptych which has since been separated.[35] It depicts the actor Kawarazaki Gonjūrō playing the role of Sukeroku in the kabuki play *Sukeroku yukari no Edo zakura*. The pose of the figure is strikingly close to that of the same actor (playing the same role) depicted in Cat. 62, showing how print designers habitually drew from a repertoire of designs. In both, Sukeroku has assumed a pose of strength and vigor called a *mie*. This is a moment in kabuki when the hero takes a dramatic stance, pauses, and crosses one eye, usually to tumultuous applause. Here Sukeroku has freed his right arm from his black outer robe, an indication that he is prepared to fight. In the opening of the second scene, Sukeroku has discovered that a wealthy samurai named Ikyū, who frequents the establishment of his courtesan mistress, possesses the sword he seeks. Kakuju-jo shows Sukeroku luring his adversary into combat. The color range is even more limited than usual for Kakuju-jo, with black prevailing. Nevertheless, the actor's diagonal stance, together with the crossed eyes of his *mie*, convey the dynamic spirit of the hero.

139

64. Utagawa Kuniyoshi (1797-1861) and Yoshitori (active mid-19th century)

Sankai medetai zue, no. 2: *Whales from Hirado*, 1852
Woodblock print, 37.5 x 25.4 cm.
Signature on inset: Yoshitori ga
Museum of Fine Arts, Springfield, Massachusetts:
The Raymond A. Bidwell Collection, 60.DO5.522

65. Utagawa Kuniyoshi and Yoshitori

Sankai medetai zue, no. 65: *Lime from Kawochi*, 1852
Woodblock print, 38.1 x 25.4 cm.
Signature on inset: Yoshitori ga
Museum of Fine Arts, Springfield, Massachusetts:
The Raymond A. Bidwell Collection, 60.D05.925

Yoshitori collaborated with her father on a series of seventy prints entitled *Sankai medetai zue* (Propitious Products of Mountains and Seas). Kuniyoshi designed the large bust portraits of attractive women in the foreground, and Yoshitori depicted the scenes within the rectangular insets in the upper left.

Yoshitori's views are labeled with the name of each location and its special products, scenes, or activities. Here a group of men are pulling in a huge black whale off the coast of Hirado in Kyūshū. There seems to be an implied relationship between the activity of the female figures and the scenes in the insets. Here the woman looks up from the theatrical program she is reading and says "Hayaku mitai"[36] (I want to see it soon), perhaps referring to a kabuki performance. Her wish obviously parallels the desire of the men pulling in the whale as it slowly comes into view.

Here Yoshitori has depicted four men gathering lime from the hillsides of Kawochi. Down below, a young mother is nursing an overly energetic child. The woman looks exhausted and says "Hayaku nekashitai" (I'd like to put him to bed early). The connection between the female figure and the lime gatherers may involve a play on the verb *nekaseru*, which in addition to meaning "to put to sleep" can mean "to complete a task." The men, too, are eager to finish their chore.

66. Utagawa Kuniyoshi and Yoshitori

Sankai medetai zue, no. 41: *Mackerel from Nōtō*, 1852
Woodblock print, 37.5 x 25.4 cm.
Museum of Fine Arts, Springfield, Massachusetts:
The Raymond A. Bidwell Collection, 60.D05.527

In the upper left, Yoshitori's workers strain to turn the pulley which hauls in the fishing boats; the woman below is biting her sleeve in a display of anger or jealousy. The caption reads "Harebottai" (swollen face or puffy eyes); in Japanese, puffiness is used as an expression of unhappy emotion. While the fishermen arrive at this peculiar look through their hard, thankless task, the woman's frustration may be dissatisfaction with an ill-fated love relationship.

In all three prints, the style of Yoshitori's landscapes and figures recalls that of Andō Hiroshige (1797-1858). Landscape forms are outlined with little interior texturing; they are given substance through the graduated color printing technique which became highly developed during the second quarter of the nineteenth century. Within these settings, the lively actions of the figures become the crucial element in creating successful designs. Rendering them with great brevity, Yoshitori is able to evoke the mood and excitement of the workers' labor through their bending, pulling, leaning, activated poses.

Notes

1. For a reproduction, see R. A. Crighton, *The Floating World: Japanese Popular Prints 1700-1900* (London: Victoria and Albert Museum, 1973), pl. 1169.

2. The best sources for biographical information on women ukiyo-e artists are Inoue Kazuo, ed., *Ukiyo-e shi den*; Nihon Ukiyo-e Kyōkai, *Genshoku ukiyo-e dai hyakka jiten*; and Yoshida Teruji, *Ukiyo-e jiten*.

3. For an illustration of one of Hokumei's paintings, see Hayashi Yoshikazu, *Enpon kenkyū: Oei to Eisen*, 66.

4. Hokuei's name does not appear in the standard ukiyo-e biographical dictionaries, but a painting by her signed Katsushika Hokuei is in a 1976 catalogue published by the Tokyo ukiyo-e dealer, Hakurodō, pl. 196. It bears an inscription by Shokusanjin. The female artist Hokuei is not to be confused with the Osaka ukiyo-e artist of the same name.

5. Her name was originally Kin, but later it was changed to Kokin. She was given the art name Itchōsai Kunika-me by her father, who began to teach her how to paint when she was around ten. In 1826, one year after her father died, she was married to Watanabe Ihei, a proprietor of a confectionary in Ichigaya. By 1828 she had discontinued painting, for there is a memorial marker where she buried her brushes dated that year. According to Inoue's *Ukiyo-e shi den*, she quit of her own free will, but one wonders if she was not pressured to do so by her husband's family.

6. For illustrations, see Yoshida, *Ukiyo-e jiten*, vol. 1, 327, and Nihon Ukiyo-e Kyōkai, *Genshoku ukiyo-e dai hyakka jiten*, vol. 2, 36.

7. For an illustration of a triptych by Yoshi-jo, see Nihon Ukiyo-e Kyōkai, *Genshoku ukiyo-e dai hyakka jiten*, vol. 2, 102. Most biographies state that she was married to her father's adopted heir, Taguchi Kiei; however, some say that she became the wife of Eiki, a pupil of the artist Satake Eikai (1803-1874), and after Eiki's death married Washizu Ikkaku.

8. Yoshitama appears at work in Kuniyoshi's workshop in a sketch from a woodblock book entitled *Gyōsai gadan* by Kawanabe Gyōsai (1831-1889). For an example of one of Yoshitama's own prints, see Nihon Ukiyo-e Kyōkai, *Genshoku ukiyo-e dai hyakka jiten*, vol. 2, 102. Yoshitama eventually retired from the art world and became a nun, traveled for two years, and died upon returning to Edo.

9. Daughter and pupil of Tsutsumi Tōrin III (circa 1743-1820). For an illustration of one of her prints, see *Genshoku ukiyo-e dai hyakka jiten*, vol. 2, 86.

10. Renzan and Baien were sisters; they often collaborated on paintings, with Baien doing the figures and Renzan the backgrounds.

11. Pupil of Utagawa Yoshiiku (1833-1904).

12. Pupil and wife of Mizuno Toshikata (1866-1908).

13. The *Katsushika Hokusai den* by Iijima Hanjūrō (Tokyo: Kobayashi Bunshichi, 1893) is the source on which everyone relies. According to this account, Hokusai had one son and two daughters by his first wife; the eldest daughter named Omiyo was married to the print designer Yanagawa Shigenobu (1787-1832), who became Hokusai's adopted son. The second daughter's name is not certain, but may have been Otetsu. Ōi was Hokusai's daughter by his second wife, who also bore him a son; Hokusai may have had a fourth daughter named Nao (by his second wife) who died young. Other nineteenth-century records are not as complete: Eisen's 1833 *Mumeiō zuihitsu* records Hokusai as having three daughters, but does not mention any sons. Kyokutei Bakin, in his 1835 *Ato no Tame no ki*, wrote that Hokusai had one son and one daughter. For a discussion of this problem, see Hayashi, *Oei to Eisen*, 51-52.

14. In addition to a long entry in Sekine Shisei's *Ukiyo-e hyakka den*, several articles have been written about Ōi (see the bibliography). Most of the information they quote is from the *Katsushika Hokusai den*.

15. This date is purely conjecture; Yasuda Gōzō concocted an elaborate chronology of Ōi's life which he sets forth in his article "Hokusai no musume: Oiei-jo." Although I believe that he is not far off the mark, most of it is speculative and should not be taken as fact.

16. His given name was Kichinosuke.

17. Hokusai's eldest daughter Omiyo also divorced her husband and returned home to live; however, she died young.

18. Yasuda, "Hokusai no musume," 33.

19. She may also have taken this name from the popular Ōtsu-e phrase "Ōi-ōi oyaji dono." The characters which she chose for the name Ōi literally mean "obedient to Tame"; the character *tame* was used by Hokusai in one of his names, Tamekazu, and therefore Ōi's selection of characters for her new name shows her filial respect for her father.

20. Takai said that he guessed Ōi to be around sixty at this time. This event is recorded in Iwasaki Chōshi, ed., *Takai Kōzan den*. See Hayashi, *Oei to Eisen*, 62-63.

21. For an illustration of one of her paintings featuring a dramatic use of chiaroscuro, see Akai Tatsurō, ed., *Nikuhitsu ukiyo-e*, vol. 7, no. 50.

22. Narazaki Muneshige in his entry on Ōi in *Zaigai hihō*, wrote that Tatsu was Hokusai's second daughter. This second daughter married, but died young.

23. Hayashi Yoshikazu, Yamaguchi Genshu, and Yasuda Gōzō all subscribe to this theory. Yasuda attempts to prove this through comparison of Tatsu's and Ōi's signatures, but his findings are unconvincing.

24. Yoshitori later married a fishmonger named Inosuke and together they lived in the Nihonbashi area of Edo.

25. For further information about Shikitei Sanba and his writings, see Robert W. Leutner, *Shikitei Sanba and the Comic Tradition in Edo Fiction* (Cambridge, Massachusetts: Harvard-Yenching Institute, 1985).

26. Traditionally, outstanding bills are paid on the last day of the year.

27. The courtesans' changes of robes for special spring and fall festivals suggest the rapid passage of time–in place of the seasonal changes that are usually used.

28. Ikkyū (1394-1481) was a famous Zen monk who broke tradition by patronizing courtesans.

29. I am indebted to Andrew Markus for his help in translating and interpreting this passage.

30. For reproductions of two examples, see Ozaki Shūdō, *Katsushika Hokusai* (Tokyo: Nihon Keizai Shinbun, 1967), no. 55 and *Hokusai nikuhitsu ga meihin ten* (Tokyo: Nihon Keizai Shinbunsha Bunka Jigyōbu, 1972), no. 83.

31. The other five artists were Hokuba, Sekkōtei, Hokuga, Tokutokusai, and Hokuju. For an illustration, see *Ukiyo-e*, vol. 52 (1972), 21 (pl. 369).

32. From right to left, the musical instruments represented are *shamisen*, *koto*, and *kokyū*.

33. It was published later in Edo with the title *Onna takara-gura*, and in Osaka with the title *Onna chōhō-ki taisei*. For further information, see Tanaka Chitako and Tanaka Hatsuo, eds., "E-iri onna chōhō-ki," *Kaseigaku bunken shūsei* (Tokyo: Watanabe Shoten, 1970), vol. 3, 10-14. A copy of the 1692 edition is in the Ryerson Collection at the Chicago Art Institute.

34. Two other paintings believed to be by Tatsu are known, both depicting courtesans in similar poses. One is published in Narazaki Muneshige, *Hokusai ron* (Tokyo: Atorie Sha, 1944), 9; it is signed "Tatsu-jo hitsu" and was stamped with the same "Yoshinoyama" seal as the Los Angeles painting. The other painting appeared in an exhibition catalogue published by the Tokyo dealer Hakurodō; it was not impressed with a seal, but the character "Tatsu" was cleverly painted on the fan held by the courtesan.

35. The central print portrays Sukeroku's courtesan mistress, Agemaki, and the left print a rich samurai named Ikyū.

36. These words appear just to the left of the series title.

Chapter Nine: *Waka* Poet-Painters in Kyoto

During the nineteenth century, there continued to be women who distinguished themselves in *waka* poetry. The Ansei era (1854-1859) represented the second crest of women's activities in *waka* circles, the first having formed in the Hōreki era (1751-1763–see chapter five).[1] The reasons behind the upsurge of women *waka* poets during the latter part of the nineteenth century are manifold. Not only were more women receiving literary educations by the second half of the century, but attitudes toward women among male *waka* poets were changing, paralleling a similar movement within Chinese poetry societies (see chapter seven). Kagawa Kageki (1768-1843) was the central figure in Kyoto poetic circles in the first half of the nineteenth century and maintained a major influence until the close of the century. He had many female pupils, including Takabatake Shikibu (1785-1881) and Ōtagaki Rengetsu (1791-1875). These two women are notable for their painting and calligraphy as well as *waka*.

The women *waka* poets who achieved notoriety at this time were not members of the Kyoto nobility or upper samurai class; instead they came from the townsmen class or from lower-ranking samurai families. Although women of the upper strata continued to learn *waka* as one of the feminine accomplishments, it is generally felt that their poems are undistinguished and lacking in creativity. This is also true of the immense quantity of *waka* composed by orthodox male court poets, who took their inspiration and vocabulary from classic anthologies such as the *Man'yōshū*, *Kokinshū*, and *Shin Kokinshū*. As previously in the eighteenth century, it was men and women from the middle class who breathed new life into the age-old *waka* tradition. Within this segment of society, only those women who were fortunate to be born to parents with good educations and literary interests were likely to be given special training in *waka*. In studying the background of the women in this exhibition, it has become clear that conditions had to be right in order for women to develop as poets and artists, the impetus frequently coming from artistic parents or spouses.

Takabatake Shikibu (1785-1881)

Takabatake Shikibu was perhaps fated to become an important figure in the Kyoto literary world; her given name, Shikibu, is written with the same characters as Murasaki Shikibu, who centuries earlier had dazzled the Japanese court (and later the world) with her memorable novel, *Genji monogatari*. The later Shikibu was the daughter of an Osaka physician. She loved *waka* as a child and became a pupil of Kagawa Kageki. Shikibu was permitted to continue her studies even after her marriage to the Kyoto acupuncturist Takabatake Kiyone.[2] Her husband had studied *waka*[3] and was supportive of his new wife's interests. In addition to *waka*, Shikibu took lessons in painting, calligraphy, and sculpture, and also learned to play two musical instruments, the lute (*biwa*) and a reed instrument (*shō*).[4] Her extant artworks include many delightful combinations of simplified paintings and *waka*, the subject most often being scenes from nature.

Shikibu seems to have shared a blissful life with her husband until his death in 1841. Her *waka* teacher, Kageki, died two years later, whereupon she became a pupil of Chigusa Arikoto (1797-1854). Biographies of Shikibu do not mention any children; as a widow she was now independent, and she responded by traveling to various provinces in Japan. By her sixties, Shikibu had become recognized as a multitalented woman. In 1847 she was noted for her calligraphy, painting, and *waka* in the *Kōto shoga jinmei roku* (Record of Famous Poets and Painters in the Imperial Capital).[5] Shikibu lived an unusually long life, reaching the venerable age of ninety-seven. Two collections of her poetry were published during her lifetime, and a third on the seventeenth anniversary of her death.[6]

Ōtagaki Rengetsu (1791-1875)

Like Shikibu, Rengetsu was a gifted individual whose skills in *waka*, calligraphy, and painting have long been recognized. She is perhaps most well known for her unique pottery on which she inscribed her poems. She was foremost a poet, but the elegant style of calligraphy which she developed has led her to be highly appreciated as an artist. In recent years, many examples of her calligraphy and pottery have appeared in exhibitions and on the art market, and Japanese today frequently refer to the "Rengetsu boom" which is taking place. In actuality, the current "boom" was preceded by one occurring over one hundred years ago, in her own lifetime. Rengetsu was one of the few women artists who attracted a sizable number of patrons, to the extent that she found it difficult to fulfill all of their requests.

Why is it that people both then and now have found Rengetsu so compelling? The fascination appears to stem from her extraordinary life and personality which found subtle expression in her poetry and art.[7] Born in Kyoto in 1791, within a few days of her birth she was given up by her natural parents and adopted by the Ōtagaki family, headed by a samurai[8] serving at Chion'in temple. The circumstances of her adoption and the identity of her biological parents are unclear; there is evidence that her father may have been a samurai of the Tōdō[9] family serving in the domain of Ueno in Iga province (Mie prefecture). Various opinions exist regarding her mother's station in life, ranging from a courtesan to the daughter of a merchant or low-ranking noble.[10] In 1798 the young Rengetsu (whose childhood name was Nobu), went off to serve the Matsudaira family at Kameoka Castle in Tanba.[11] As noted earlier, a position as lady-in-waiting at one of the many castles in Japan was considered very prestigious for samurai women. One of the beneficial aspects of such a post for Rengetsu was that she was surrounded by other cultivated women who devoted some of their time to artistic pursuits such as poetry and calligraphy. In addition, she received training in the martial arts of swordsmanship and *jujutsu*.[12]

While Rengetsu was in service at Kameoka Castle, both her stepmother and stepbrother died, leaving the family with no male heir. Her stepfather thereby followed customary practice and adopted a son who could later inherit his official post. Rengetsu returned home to her family in Kyoto in 1807, and in that year at the age of seventeen she was married to Mochihisa, the young samurai whom her stepfather had adopted.[13] In the eight years following her marriage, Rengetsu bore three children, all of whom died shortly after birth.[14] She and her husband were separated in 1815, possibly because he was not living up to her stepfather's expectations in performing official duties at Chion'in.[15] Mochihisa died later that year at the age of twenty-six.

Rengetsu's family again searched for an heir. In 1819, four years after her first husband's death, Rengetsu entered into another marriage arranged by her stepfather.[16] However, her second husband died an untimely death in the year 1823. Although Rengetsu was only thirty-three years old, she renounced the world, cut her hair, and became a nun. At this time she adopted the name Rengetsu which means "lotus moon." Rengetsu's stepfather also took Buddhist vows, and together they retired to live in a small building called Makuzuan within the Chion'in temple complex. They were accompanied by Rengetsu's daughter from her second marriage, who died two years later at the age of seven.[17] Even in an age of many infant deaths, to lose two husbands and all of one's children at such a young age was unusually tragic.

Rengetsu and her stepfather lived a quiet, secluded life at the Makuzuan. Since her stepfather had adopted a third son to assume his position, he no longer had to concern himself with official duties. In addition to participating in some Buddhist services, he and Rengetsu passed their time composing *waka* and playing the board game of *go*. Obviously, taking the tonsure did not necessarily imply a life devoted solely to religious duties. Paradoxically, it allowed Rengetsu the freedom to pursue a life devoted to many arts, and she followed a path similar to earlier poet-painters such as Chiyo and Kikusha (see chapter four). When her stepfather died in 1832, Rengetsu was left without financial support[18] so she moved to the area of Kyoto known as Okazaki, then a famous center for scholars, poets, and artists. From Rengetsu's choice of this location we may infer that she was drawn to a lifestyle allied to the arts.

Rengetsu's training in *waka* began in her childhood when she served as an attendant at Kameoka Castle. She also learned from her stepfather, who was quite skillful in composing poetry. There is evidence that Rengetsu may have studied briefly with Ueda Akinari (1734-1809) while living at Chion'in,[19] but it was not until she moved to Okazaki that she began to study *waka* intensively. In 1838 she became a pupil of Kagawa Kageki. After his death, she studied with Mutobe Yoshika (1806-1863) and remained his pupil for fourteen years. Rengetsu was also influenced by Kageki's teacher Ozawa Roan (1723-1801).[20] She never studied with Roan directly since he died when she was a child; however, Rengetsu revered him and sought out examples of his poetry to study.[21]

Rengetsu's *waka* is usually described by critics as displaying features of the Keien school founded by Kageki. Advocating the classical verses from the tenth-century *Kokinshū* as models, Kageki also stressed the importance of clear, ordinary language (as opposed to archaisms). Many of Rengetsu's *waka* are improvised scenery descriptions, containing plays on words and word associations typical of Heian-period poetry. On a cursory reading her poems may seem conventional, but upon deeper analysis Rengetsu's personal character shines through.

Upon moving to Okazaki, Rengetsu may have first tried to make her living as a teacher of poetry or *go*, but her reclusive nature forced her to abandon this occupation. She was apparently a woman of striking physical beauty, and the fact that she was a nun did not discourage men from making advances toward her. In order to make herself unattractive so that men would leave her alone, Rengetsu pulled out all of her teeth when she was in her forties, an example of her great determination and inner strength.

Rengetsu then turned to making pottery to support herself, especially creating utensils for use in the Chinese-style form of tea drinking known as *sencha* (Cat. 72 and 73). She seems to have been self-taught, crafting her pots by hand and adding a personal touch by incising or inscribing her own *waka*. The unique quality of her hand-modeled forms and their union of poetry, calligraphy, and pottery made her wares especially appealing to scholars and poets. The popularity of Rengetsu's pottery gradually extended to include clientele from all walks of life, and avid collectors began to seek her out. As a result of this unwanted attention, during her forties, fifties, and sixties Rengetsu moved more than thirty times, reportedly to escape the hoards of customers who beat a path to her door.[22] However, she never strayed too far from the Okazaki area, living also near Shōgoin, Kumano Shrine, and in the areas of Nagagyō-ku and Kitashirakawa.

Louise Cort has pointed out that Rengetsu's popularity was linked in part to her identity–the fact that she was a woman rather than one of the countless male potters.[23] The success of her pottery also depended heavily on her reputation as a poet. Evidence of the acclaim which Rengetsu received are the two books of her verse published in her lifetime. *Rengetsu Shikibu nijo waka shū* (1868), a compilation of verses by Rengetsu and her poetess friend Takabatake Shikibu, was followed in 1870 by *Ama no karumo*, devoted entirely to *waka* by Rengetsu, containing more than 300 verses.[24] Another indication of the esteem in which Rengetsu was held is the fact that her name appeared alongside other distinguished personalities in the *Heian jinbutsu shi* (Who's Who in Kyoto) in the years 1838, 1852, and 1867.[25] Rengetsu's poetry is still honored among present-day Japanese; her verses have even been included in high school textbooks.[26]

Shikibu and Rengetsu not only joined forces in the book of poetry mentioned above, but they also did collective artworks on occasion. Several examples remain in which Rengetsu added a poetic inscription to a painting by Shikibu.[27] Since Shikibu lived near Kumano Shrine,[28] they may have first met when Rengetsu was living in that area. Since both were pupils of Kageki and also calligraphers as well as painters, the two women shared many interests. Their painting styles are somewhat similar, suggesting that they may have influenced each other. Rengetsu also associated with other female poets of the day, including the nun Nomura Bōtō (1806-1867) and the Kyoto courtesans Ueda Chikako and Sakuragi.

Another relationship that Rengetsu treasured throughout her life was her friendship with the young painter Tomioka Tessai (1836-1924). She first came into contact with his family while living in Shōgoin-mura. She grew to love Tessai as though he were her own son, and even tried to adopt him at one point, but his family declined. Around 1850 Tessai became Rengetsu's live-in helper, assisting her by transporting clay and taking her ceramics to kilns to be fired. He accompanied her on some of her moves, watching over Rengetsu like a son during the last twenty-five years of her life. Tessai later became extremely famous as a painter, but in these early years he was virtually unknown. He and Rengetsu collaborated on a number of works, with Tessai doing the painting and Rengetsu adding poetic inscriptions. Since Rengetsu was a famous personality, his paintings with her poems suddenly became marketable commodities.[29] Rengetsu herself increased her output of simplified paintings, with Tessai perhaps serving as a stimulus.

Rengetsu discontinued her unsettled lifestyle in 1865 when she moved into a tea hut at the temple Jinkōin. She had been invited to live there by the abbot Wada Gesshin (also known as Gōzan, 1800-1870), who was a close friend of her brother-in-law Tenmin. Rengetsu had originally become a nun of Pure Land Buddhism at Chion'in. In her middle years she lived for a time at various Kyoto temples, but was not connected with them in a formal way. She associated with Tendai as well as Zen monks, indicating that she did not exclusively adhere to only one form of Buddhism.[30] In her later years at Jinkōin, Rengetsu entered into Shingon practices and for the first time deeply immersed herself in the study of Buddhism. Nevertheless, she continued to be prolific in painting, calligraphy, and pottery until her death.

Throughout her life, Rengetsu cared little about money and sold her calligraphy and pottery very cheaply. She wore plain clothes and ate simple foods, avoiding meat. Having compassion for those less fortunate, she gave untiringly of her time and money.[31] Tessai painted an evocative portrait of her in her later years, with Rengetsu seated in her studio, writing out a poem on a *tanzaku* (Figure 15). To her left are an inkstone, water dropper, and wooden stand for making pottery. Tessai's tenuous yet delicate brushwork defining Rengetsu's withered form conveys the fragility of her advanced years. Yet the intensity of Rengetsu's gaze and the confident way she grasps her brush expresses what has been described as an "indisputable quality of wizened toughness."[32] This same combination of delicacy and strength is present in her unique style of calligraphy.

Even if there had not been a surge in interest among art collectors, Rengetsu would still be remembered in Japan, for she is honored every year during the "Jidai Matsuri." One of the highlights of this festival is the parade with people dressed in costumes representing famous Kyoto personalities, one of whom is Rengetsu. The extraordinary strength and grace of her personality, which can be seen in the most modest of her artworks, made her one of the outstanding women in Japanese history.

15. Tessai, *Rengetsu* (detail)
   Jinkōin Collection, Kyoto

67. Takabatake Shikibu (1785-1881)

Autumn Waka
Hanging scroll, ink on paper, 34 x 49 cm.
Signature: Nanajūnana ō Shikibu
Mubōan Collection

Uraraka ni	In the calm weather
Kasumu koharu no	Of a hazy autumn,
Yū hikage	In the evening light,
Hana ni wakareshi	The geese, who left with [spring]
Kari wa ki ni keri	blossoms,
	Have once again returned.

Shikibu brought visual life to this poignant, autumnal verse by adding a sketchlike, suggestive painting to the left of her calligraphy. A flock of geese descends over the water and hills, its diagonal flying formation counterbalancing the oblique orientation of the staggered lines of writing. A peaceful, flowing movement predominates; the smooth curves of the birds' wings are echoed in both the rippling water and the fluid calligraphy. Shikibu rendered both image and poem primarily with dry, gray ink, employing darker ink sparingly for accents. Her poem-painting, done at age seventy-seven, has an astringent quality which masterfully evokes the dessicated scenery of autumn.

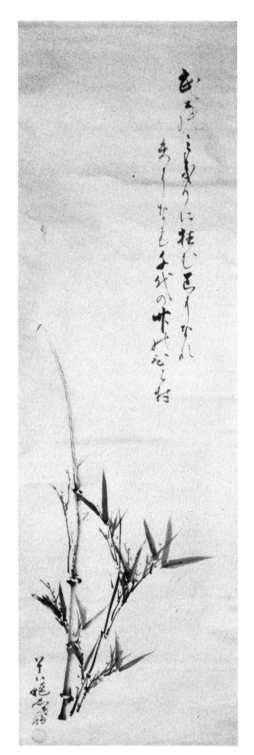

68. Takabatake Shikibu

Bamboo
Hanging scroll, ink on paper, 125 x 30 cm.
Signature: Hachijūhachi ō Shikibu
Seal: undecipherable
Mubōan Collection

The subject Shikibu most often painted was bamboo, usually confining it to the lower part of the composition as seen here. Although simply rendered, her unique combination of dry and wet brushstrokes imbues this plant with a tangible quality. Since bamboo connotes longevity and endurance, it was especially suitable for an artist to brush in his or her later years; above her signature, Shikibu recorded that she was eighty-eight years old.

The accompanying *waka* alludes to the symbolism of bamboo. Shikibu has written out the verse in two columns of characters, beautifully positioned so that they are evenly balanced with the bamboo. The long vertical thrusts of the strings of calligraphy are echoed by the stalk of bamboo at the left. Her writing has a rough vigor, displaying irregular rhythms created through alternating heavily inked characters with drier, more slender linework. The poem reads:

Mononofu no	Let us plant [bamboo]
Migiri ni uemu	in a warrior's garden.
Yumi ni nare	May you become bows,
Ya ni nare chiyo no	May you become arrrows–
Take no hitomura	Clumps of bamboo of ten thousand years.

69. Ōtagaki Rengetsu (1791-1875)

Spring Moon Over the River
Hanging scroll, ink on paper; 30.5 x 33 cm.
Signature: Rengetsu
Private collection

By the time she reached her late forties, Rengetsu had deeply immersed herself in the study of *waka*; upon request she would write out verses in gossamer calligraphy. At some point she also began to do paintings to accompany her poems, with image and text complementing one another. For the subject matter and style of her paintings, Rengetsu drew upon the Shijō tradition first developed by Goshun (1752-1811). Sources differ as to whether she studied with Nakajima Raishō (1796-1871) or Matsumura Keibun (1779-1843),[33] both well-known masters of this school. The Shijō style is characterized by soft washes of ink and pastel colors, combined with gently applied lyrical brushwork. Favored subjects were figures, birds and flowers, and rural Japanese landscapes. This tradition struck a responsive chord in the hearts of Kyoto's middle class, and remained popular throughout the nineteenth century.

Spring Moon Over the River is one of Rengetsu's earliest poem-paintings. It is not dated,[34] but the style of writing suggests that it may have been done during her late forties or fifties.[35] At this stage, Rengetsu's mature calligraphy style was not yet fully developed. Compared with the exhilarating freedom and openness of her later work, the characters are more tightly composed, with very little empty space between the lines forming them or between individual characters.

Rengetsu divided the lines of the poem (three on the right and two on the left) in order to leave space for the moon which rises up between them. The round shape of the full moon is formed by the white paper left after Rengetsu defined its outer rim with a curving band of ink wash.[36] The painting is so simple that it is easy to ignore the skillful manner in which Rengetsu brushed on more washes to partly obscure the lower half of the moon, giving the effect of vaporous clouds. This eloquent image is enhanced by the accompanying *waka* originally composed while making the journey by boat down the Yodo River to Naniwa (Osaka).[37]

Naniwa e ya	Naniwa Bay–
Kasumi mo nami no	As the night is deepening,
Sokohakato	Through the mist and waves,
Waka de fuke yuku	Not clearly distinguishable
Oboro yo no tsuki	The hazy evening moon.

"Sending a Congratulatory Bamboo" and reads:

Kono kimi wa	This gentleman
Medetaki fushi o	Continually putting forth
Kasanetsutsu	Auspicious new growth
Sue no yo no nagaki	Forms a model for
Tameshi narikeri	Longevity far into the future.

Many of the words have double meanings, referring to both the bamboo and the recipient. For example *Kono kimi* can be "this gentleman"[38] or the bamboo, as well as "you" or the person to whom the poem-painting was sent. Additionally, *fushi* can refer to the joints or nodes of the bamboo or good luck. Thus the bamboo continually putting forth new shoots alludes to a person "piling up" good fortune. Rengetsu expresses the wish that the scroll's recipient be blessed with a long and productive life.

Rengetsu's poetic inscription, written at age seventy-six, represents the mature style of calligraphy formulated in her sixties. In comparison with Cat. 69, the characters are simplified with larger open spaces within them. Written with a horizontal emphasis, fewer characters are linked together, making the poem easier to read. In general the lines are even in width, exhibiting only a very subtle thickening and thinning. Although delicate and restrained, Rengetsu's brushwork is packed with inner tension, often described as resembling a coiled spring.

Rengetsu did several paintings of bamboo, usually inscribed with the same poem.[39] The method and style of brushing the leaves and culms in the Burke painting is consistent with all of the other examples. Since the majority of Rengetsu's works are on paper, the fact that she utilized silk here may indicate that *Bamboo* was a special commission. Silk absorbs the ink differently from paper, resulting in less crisp lines and fuzzing along the edges of brushstrokes. Rengetsu has utilized this effect to create a soft, misty atmosphere.

Poem and painting are masterfully balanced. The vertical movement of the bamboo stalks springing up along the lefthand side of the picture plane is stabilized by the horizontal extension of some of the smaller stems and leaves. The longest stem curving inward to the right, rendered with fuzzy gray ink tones, defines an empty space perfect in size for Rengetsu's poem. As always, she kept in mind the overall compositional design when adding an inscription, here deliberately arranging the beginning characters of each line so that they form a gentle diagonal, continuing the circular movement begun by the stalk of bamboo reaching inward.

70. Ōtagaki Rengetsu

Bamboo
Hanging scroll, ink on silk, 88.9 x 49.9 cm.
Signature: Rengetsu nanajūrokusai
The Mary and Jackson Burke Foundation
Published: Tokyo National Museum, *A Selection of Japanese Art from the Mary and Jackson Burke Collection* (Tokyo: 1985), no. 79.

A large number of the subjects which Rengetsu painted have auspicious meanings, indicating that they were done as gifts; *Bamboo* was probably presented to a friend in celebration of the new year. The *waka* appears in her anthology of poetry *Ama no karumo* with the title

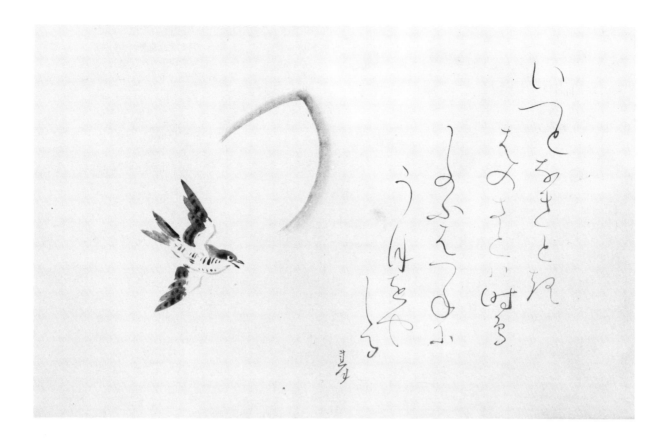

71. Ōtagaki Rengetsu

Cuckoo
Hanging scroll, ink and light colors on paper,
31.2 x 49.5 cm.
Signature: Rengetsu
Private collection
Published: Fister, "Ōtagaki Rengetsu," *Calligraphy Idea Exchange*, fig. 6; Tokuda, *Ōtagaki Rengetsu*, no. 58.

The cuckoo is one of the rare birds that sings as it flies. Here one can almost hear the cuckoo's melodious cry as it passes by a partially clouded moon. Rengetsu's *waka* inscription evokes the eternal quality of rural Japan's villages, punctuated only by the cycle of the seasons.[40]

Itsu to naki	In the timelessness
Tokiwa no sato wa	Of my unchanging native village,
Hototogisu	The faintly heard cry
Shinobu hatsune ni	Of the cuckoo
Uzuki o ya shiru	Tells us that summer is here.

Rengetsu displays her innate sense of design in the arrangement of the poem, cuckoo, and moon in this work. Although she has written the poem out in five columns, they do not reflect the *waka* format of 5-7-5-7-7 syllables. Instead, she has made the columns conform to her own compositional scheme, staggering the beginning characters in order to create a triangular shape. The bottom left tip of the triangle is formed by her signature. This diagonal is echoed in the shape of the moon and counterbalanced by the placement of the bird, whose outspread wings transform it into a miniature triangle. Thus movement is implied from both directions, with the calligraphy flowing down from the right corner and the cuckoo swooping down from the left. Rengetsu has strategically employed empty space so that image and text balance but do not collide with one another.

The ink washes describing the bird and moon display Rengetsu's knowledge of Shijō school techniques. Over the light gray washes she has sparingly applied dark ink to define the cuckoo's head and feathers, and added a barely perceptible yellow wash to color its beak and legs. The resulting image is imbued with the same simplicity, yet subtle richness of imagery that one finds in her poetry.

Rengetsu's calligraphy in this work represents her mature style, and judging from the signature it may have been done when she was around the age of seventy. In analyzing Rengetsu's unique manner of writing, there is no question that the spirit of the artist is communicated through the traces of the brush. Her tensile lines are freely flowing, yet firmly controlled, delicate, yet indomitable. Despite the fact that the line width remains relatively consistent, Rengetsu has infused her characters with sprightly movement and dancelike rhythms. She merges a sophisticated sense of elegance with a childlike simplicity. The result is pure and refreshing.

72. Ōtagaki Rengetsu

Kyūsu (Small teapot)
Pottery, 5.7 cm.
Signature: Rengetsu (outer box signed "Rakutō Rengetsu")
Private collection
Published: Fister, "Ōtagaki Rengetsu," *Calligraphy Idea Exchange*, fig. 2; Tokuda, *Ōtagaki Rengetsu*, no. 149.

After moving to Okazaki, Rengetsu began to make pottery in order to support herself. Her hermetic character may have led her to adopt this trade because it was something which she could do in privacy. Although an amateur, she acquired enough skill to create small vessels by hand and to glaze them. Rengetsu drew upon the resources of ceramic workshops in the Awata district in eastern Kyoto, both for raw materials and for firing her finished pieces.[41] The fact that she took advantage of the facilities offered by major workshops (huge wood-fired kilns as well as clay and glaze processors and supplies) was not uncommon; Rengetsu belongs to a long line of amateur potters who relied on the technical assistance of professional pottery workshops.[42]

More than half of the ceramics Rengetsu made were for use in drinking the steeped tea known as *sencha*.[43] This form of tea became extremely popular in Japan during the eighteenth and nineteenth centuries after being introduced from China.[44] Since the drinking of *sencha* was one of many literati pursuits in China, it came to be appreciated by Japanese *bunjin* who identified it with Chinese learning and arts.

The method of presentation of *sencha* is distinctly different from the classical Japanese tea ceremony (*cha-no-yu*) which utilizes a powdered green tea called *matcha*. Instead, *sencha* is made from dried tea leaves which are steeped in boiled water. In Rengetsu's day the ceremony was usually an informal one, often held in a garden or natural setting. Rather than ritualized movements and gestures, a relaxed atmosphere prevailed. The tea cups and serving vessels were small in comparison to those used in *cha-no-yu*. To use the teapot by Rengetsu illustrated here for *sencha*, tea leaves were placed inside, boiled water poured over them, and the leaves steeped for the appropriate amount of time.

During the early stages of its introduction to Japan, *sencha* enthusiasts often utilized imported Chinese wares. In time, ceramics of local manufacture were commissioned, and since Kyoto was the center of the *sencha* cult, Kyoto kilns came to furnish the wares. Aoki Mokubei (1767-1833) was famous for producing ceramics in the Chinese style, but *sencha* utensils made by amateurs like Rengetsu were also admired for their simple, rustic character. Rengetsu added a further personal touch to her pottery by inscribing or incising her *waka*, and the resulting union of poetry, calligraphy, and pottery made her wares especially appealing to scholars active in *sencha* circles.[45]

The teapot (*kyūsu*) illustrated here is exemplary of Rengetsu's *sencha* wares. In terms of materials her pieces are typical of many Awata (or other Kyoto) wares; Rengetsu's originality lies in her sense of hand-modeled form and her use of poetic inscriptions. She created this small pot using the coil method, and one can still feel the impressions that Rengetsu's fingers made on the thin inner and outer walls as she smoothed out the surface of the clay. Both the inner and outer surfaces were covered with a clear glaze and fired to a warm, earthy tan color. Light crackling in the glaze is evident, creating a delicately textured background for the calligraphy and painting. For decoration, Rengetsu painted a few cherry blossoms with iron pigment near the pouring spout and one petal on the lid; she then inscribed a *waka* which became one of her most famous:

Yado kasanu	Refused at the inn–
Hito no tsurasa o	But I took this unkindness
Nasake nite	As a gracious act;
Oborozuki yo no	Under the hazy evening moon
Hana no shita bushi[46]	I slept beneath blossoms.

Her calligraphy wraps comfortably around the vessel, taking up most of the available space. Because the surface was limited, Rengetsu began new lines after writing only two or three characters. Rengetsu's calligraphy style seems to have been influenced by the short, broad ceramic surfaces she frequently wrote upon. Not only did her individual characters gradually assume horizontal shapes, but even when writing on paper or adding inscriptions to paintings she regularly arranged the lines of her poems so that they spread laterally. Judging from her signature and writing style, this teapot was created when she was around the age of seventy.

73. Ōtagaki Rengetsu

Five Sencha Cups
Pottery, each 4.1 x 6.5 cm.
Signatures: Rengetsu
The Mary and Jackson Burke Collection

Sets of cups and dishes in Japan usually comprise five pieces, showing the culture's preference for irregular numbers. The Burke set exhibits a motif appearing in many of Rengetsu's ceramics, that of the lotus leaf wrapped around individual cups. Upon examining the bottom of the cups, it appears that she used molds to stamp portions of this design. The lotus was appropriate for Rengetsu because of its importance as a Buddhist symbol[47] as well as its connection to her name, meaning "lotus moon." Most scholars believe this lotus motif was developed for Rengetsu by her friend and helper, Kuroda Kōryō.[48]

It is not clear as to exactly when Rengetsu teamed up with Kuroda, but certainly by the time she was in her late sixties. They may have met while both were living near the Kumano Shrine.[49] Kuroda began as a pupil of Rengetsu, but eventually he surpassed his teacher's skills in pottery and created more sophisticated and complex wares. Numerous letters remain from Rengetsu to Kuroda proving that he assisted her in meeting the large demand for her pottery.[50] Sometimes he made the pots and Rengetsu would incise or inscribe her *waka*, but at other times she asked Kuroda to add the poems as well.[51] This presents grave problems in terms of establishing the authenticity of Rengetsu's works, for Kuroda imitated Rengetsu's style of writing so well that his works are virtually indistinguishable from hers.[52] He eventually succeeded

Rengetsu and with her permission adopted the title Rengetsu II.

The *waka* on the Burke cups were incised with a sharp bamboo tool. The clay exposed by the incised lines took on a slightly darker color when fired, causing the poems to stand out from the milky glazed background. Rengetsu may have started to incise her poems because the clay surface absorbed water so quickly that writing with a brush was sometimes difficult. Among her extant ceramics, those with incised poems outnumber those with inscribed ones. This set of cups is remarkable for the graceful way in which the calligraphy interplays with the veins of the lotus leaf motifs. The five *waka* are as follows:[53]

Yo no naka ni	Out into the world
Natsu wa nagarete	The summer has already flowed–
Ide tsuramu	Solitary and cool
Hitori suzushiki	Is the water running
Yama no shita mizu	At the foot of the mountain.
Chidori naku	Plovers cry out
Kamogawa tsutsumi	From the banks of the Kamo River.
Tsuki fukete	While the moon waxes
Sode ni oboyuru	I feel the first frost of the night
Yowa no hatsushimo	Dampening my sleeves.
Yo no naka ni	In this world
Mi no nariidete	There are certain forms
Omou koto	Which bring [welcome] thoughts to mind.
Nasu wa medetaki	The eggplant serves as
Tameshi narikeri	A symbol of happiness.
Ukarekite	Fluttering merrily and
Hana no tsuyu ni	Sleeping amidst the
Neburu nari	Dew on the flowers-
Kohata ga yume no	Might it be the butterfly of
Kochō naruran	Chuang Tzu's dream?
Tazunekite	More unkind than the
Mishi hana yori mo	[Evanescent] blossoms which
Tsurenaki wa	I had searched out to see
Haru no shiori no	Is the sign that spring has passed–
Yama hototogisu	The mountain cuckoo.

74. Ōtagaki Rengetsu

Lotus Cup
Pottery, 9.2 cm.
Signature: Rengetsu
Shōka Collection

75. Ōtagaki Rengetsu

Mizusashi (Water jar)
Pottery, 17.4 x 11 cm.
Signature: Rengetsu
Yanagi Takashi Collection
Published: Fister, "Ōtagaki Rengetsu," *Calligraphy Idea Exchange*, fig. 3; Koresawa, et al., *Rengetsu*, no. 5.

This cup bears a lotus leaf design similar to the set of *sencha* cups in Cat. 73. However, in addition to being taller, its foot has been designed to simulate the stem of a lotus plant. The function of this cup is not clear; it might have been used for serving a special type of food. It merits special attention because of the artful way the lotus leaf motif is employed in the overall design, with veins extending up the sides of the cup, and also for the marvelous glaze melting from a creamy gray into a light shade of salmon. Its surface is smooth and glossy, broken only by the veins of the leaves which are palpable to the touch. The surface is further enriched by Rengetsu's threadlike calligraphy written with iron pigment directly on the clay surface. The slightly misshapen form embodies the Japanese aesthetic of the imperfect, admired because its individual character communicates the spirit of the artist. Rengetsu has amplified the sense of intimacy by inscribing a *waka* entitled "Yearning for Autumn."[54]

Uchitokete	Even for lovers,
Itsuka wa hito o	Just as for the cedar trees
Miwa no yama	On Mount Miwa,
Shirushi no sugi mo	The autumn wind
Akikaze zo fuku	Will someday blow cold.

This type of jar is used for storing fresh, cool water; during the traditional Japanese tea ceremony (*cha-no-yu*) a host ladles water from a *mizusashi* into a kettle for boiling. Displaying a majestic robust shape, this *mizusashi* was made with Shigaraki[55] clay fired to a lustrous, burnished rust color. Although the upper surface is covered with tiny flecks of natural ash glaze, allover glazing was avoided in order to reveal the rich color of the clay.

The profile of the pot is greatly enhanced by the addition of lotus motifs. The lid was made in the shape of a lotus leaf, and around the shoulder of the jar, lotus stems were appended which ingeniously form two handles.[56] The flowing movement of the long stems which encircle the jar conforms beautifully to the shape of the vessel. Rengetsu echoed this rising and falling rhythm when she incised the following *waka*.

Tsumagoto no	Like a zither, plucked
Richi no shirabe ni	To create rhythms and melodies–
Kayo hikite	At the eaves of my house
Koe omoshiroki	The evocative voice of the wind
Noki no matsukaze[57]	Sings in the pines.

76. Ōtagaki Rengetsu

Chashaku (Tea scoop)
Bamboo, 17.7 cm.
Signature (on box): Rengetsu nanajūnana
Private collection
Published: Kyoto Furitsu Sōgō Shiryōkan, *Ōtagaki
Rengetsu: Bakumatsu joryū kajin no shoga to tōgei*,
no. 130.

This *chashaku* was crafted from bamboo by Rengetsu
to be used during the tea ceremony to transfer small
amounts of powdered tea from a small jar into the tea
bowl.[58] It is common for tea enthusiasts to name utensils
which they especially prized: Rengetsu gave this *chashaku*
the auspicious name of *Matsu* (Pine), inscribing the
character on the wooden cylinder which serves as its
box.[59] The pine motif is further developed in the poem she
added to lid of the larger container in which the *chashaku*
is stored.

Harugoto ni	Each spring,
Midori sohitsuhitsu	Putting forth new greenery
Iku chiyo ka	For many thousand years-
Yo ni suminoe no	In this world, Sumiyoshi
Matsu zo hishiki	Pines have long endured.

This *waka* appears in the *Ama no karumo* with the title
"Seventy-seventh Spring," indicating that it was written by
Rengetsu at that advanced age. The box containing the
"Pine" *chashaku* was also inscribed in that year. The poem
implies a connection between the enduring pines at
Sumiyoshi and Rengetsu's own longevity; she was perhaps
marveling at her ability to have withstood so many cold
winters.

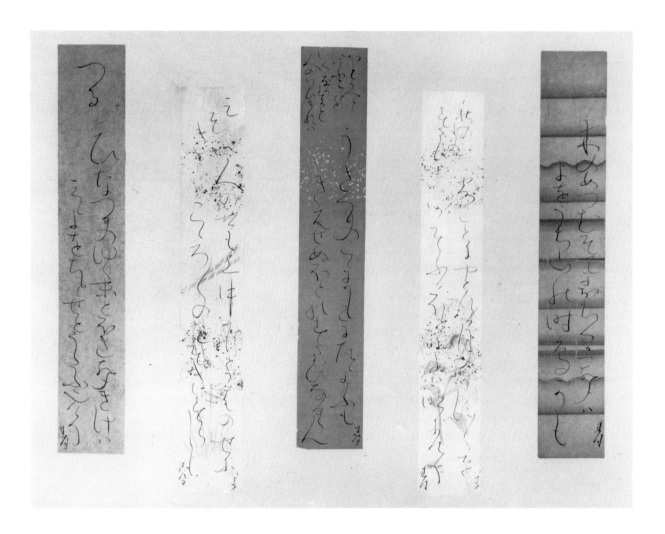

77. Ōtagaki Rengetsu

Five Tanzaku (Poem sheets)
Ink on paper, each about 35 x 6.2 cm.
Signatures: Rengetsu, Hachijūsai Rengetsu
Private collection

Rengetsu's mature calligraphy style is well-represented in this set of five *tanzaku*, two of which were inscribed at age eighty. The tall, thin format of this type of poem sheet was favored by the Japanese for writing out the short verse forms of *waka* or haiku. *Tanzaku* paper was often dyed beautiful colors and/or decorated with gold and silver designs like the examples here. Rengetsu probably wrote out poems on more than one thousand *tanzaku*, giving them away to friends as well as receiving orders from the *tanzaku* shop owner Emi Kohei and the paper shop owner Tanaka Soshin.[60]

Since the style of writing that Rengetsu developed is unique, it is difficult to pinpoint her sources. She undoubtedly studied calligraphy along with other arts while serving at Kameoka Castle as a youth. However, no examples of her early works have been preserved, and if they were, one probably would not be able to recognize them as by Rengetsu. The standard model for women's calligraphy books in the first half of the nineteenth century was the O'ie tradition,[61] featuring long flowing lines with dramatic variations in width. Traces of the O'ie style are apparent in the earliest known examples of Rengetsu's calligraphy, *tanzaku* thought to date from her forties.[62] Her writing at this stage exhibits continuous variation in line thickness, little empty space within and between characters, and long strings of characters linked together.[63] This is distinctly different from Rengetsu's mature style exemplified in these five *tanzaku*.

Japanese scholars often reiterate that Rengetsu was influenced by Heian calligraphy, especially that of the poetess Kodai Kimi (active early eleventh century). Rengetsu is also said to have followed the calligraphy style of Reizei (Okada) Tamechika (1823-1864).[64] However, a comparison of Rengetsu's writing with examples by Kodai Kimi and Reizei Tamechika reveals very little in common. Furthermore, Rengetsu did not follow current fashions, such as the style of the poet Katō Chikage (1735-1808) which was particularly in vogue. Rengetsu was not so much affected by the calligraphy of those around her as by her own personality and aesthetic sensibility.

A more plausible theory accounting for the development of Rengetsu's mature calligraphy style, maintained by several Japanese scholars, is that her brushwork was influenced by her incising of poetry into pottery. Certain changes that took place in her brushwork, all leading toward a simpler style and form, can be explained by technical considerations she developed from incising. For example, Rengetsu began to omit Chinese characters in favor of *kana* because the simpler *kana* syllabary were easier to incise, and created less excess clay which had to be cleaned away. In order to make her poems easier to incise (and read), Rengetsu chose to write characters individually, leaving generous amounts of space around the lines; unlike many calligraphers, it is rare to find her linking more than two or three characters together in her mature work. Also significant is the relatively consistent line width employed by Rengetsu in her later years, which resembles the line quality of her incised poems. She deliberately moved away from fluctuations in line thickness, perhaps because she liked the sharp, crisp lines she achieved through incising. In order to duplicate this effect in brushwork, Rengetsu used a long brush made of stiff hair (perhaps from a deer).[65]

While many calligraphers struggled to be inventive, Rengetsu repeatedly used similar *kana* forms, making her poems easy to read. In many respects Rengetsu was more a poet than a calligrapher; just as she led a simple life, so she did not need an ornate style of writing. Her calligraphy has an understated elegance and simplicity which people find attractive. Yet it is full of inner tension and strength that come from her personal character which withstood the tragedies of her early life.

From right to left, the *waka* illustrated here are as follows:[66]

Kono me tsumu	While the young leaves are being
Nobe ni ochikuru	harvested,
Hito koe wa	A single voice
Yo o Ujiyama no	Descends over the fields–
Hototogisu kana	It is the cuckoo
	Of the Uji mountains.

Pleasures of an Autumn Night

Tsuyugoto ni	While I count
Yadoreru tsuki no	The moons
Kazukazu o	Reflected in
Kazouru hodo ni	Each dewdrop,
Yo wa ake ni keri	The dawn is breaking.

As people laugh about my constantly changing dwellings …

Ukikumo no	Floating clouds,
Koko ni kashiko ni	Drifting through the sky
Tadayou no	Here and there–
Kiesenu hodo no	Until they disappear
Susabi narikeri	They seem to be enjoying themselves.

Misogi (Ablutions)

Hito no yo mo	In this world,
Ue naka shita to	People from all walks of life
Kawa no se ni	Go to the shallows of a stream
Kokoro kokoro no	And perform ablutions
Misogi surashimo	To purify their minds.

Tsuru (Crane)

Hina tsuru no	As I listen to the fledgling crane
Yuku sue to hoki	With its long future,
Koe kikeba	It sings
Miyo o chitose to	"The reign of the emperor
Utau narikeri	Will last forever."

Notes

1. Mori Keizō, "Tokugawa jidai no joryū kajin," in Miwata Gendō, ed., *Nihon josei bunka shi*, vol. 2, 565.
2. Kiyone was a retainer to the Chigusa family. Like many acupuncturists, he was blind.
3. According to Ichikawa Tarō's *Kinsei joryū shodō meika shi den*, Kiyone was a pupil of Shibayama Mochitoyo (1741-1815); however, other sources say that his teacher was a famous poet of the Chigusa family, perhaps Chigusa Arikoto. See Aida Hanji, *Kinsei joryū bunjin den*, 207 and Mori Keizō, *Kinsei joryū kajin no kenkyū*, 243.
4. Shikibu studied painting with Uragami Shunkin, calligraphy with a courtier named Niwata, the *biwa* with Ayanokōji Arinaga, and the *shō* with Hayashi Kōsai. Ichikawa, *Kinsei joryū shodō meika shi den*, 123.
5. Mori Senzō, *Kinsei jinmei roku shūsei*, vol. 3, 249.
6. The three books are *Mugi no sha shū* (1868) with over 500 *waka*; *Rengetsu Shikibu nijo waka shū* (1868) with forty-nine *waka* by Rengetsu and fifty-six by Shikibu; and *Katami no warabi* (1897). For further descriptions, see Joshi Gakushūin, *Joryū chosaku kaidai*, 24, 58, and 67.
7. The primary sources of information on Rengetsu's life are her own autobiography recorded in a letter to Tomioka Tessai at age eighty-four, other letters, Kuroda Kōryō's *Ōtagaki Rengetsu rirekisho*, and Murakami Sodō's *Rengetsu-ni zenshū*. Murakami actually knew Rengetsu when she was in her eighties while he was serving as a novice at Jinkōin. Other important publications are Koresawa, et al., *Rengetsu*; Maeda Toshiko, *Rengetsu*; Sugimoto Hidetarō, *Ōtagaki Rengetsu*; and Tokuda Kōen's two books, *Rengetsu-ni no shin kenkyū* and *Ōtagaki Rengetsu*. Sugimoto's research has shed light on some of the hazy areas of Rengetsu's background. Tokuda is presently the abbot of Jinkōin, the temple where Rengetsu spent the last ten years of her life. He has done extensive research on both Rengetsu's life and art, and his temple owns an impressive collection of Rengetsu's artworks.
8. Named Ōtagaki Hanzaemon Teruhisa.
9. Although Murakami wrote that Rengetsu's father was probably Tōdō Kinshichirō, lord of Ueno Castle in Iga (according to the recollections of a Kyoto woman whose mother had served the Ōtagaki family as Rengetsu's wet nurse), recent investigations by Sugimoto Hidetarō indicate that her father was Tōdō Shinshichirō Yoshikiyo (1767-1798), warden at Ueno Castle. See Sugimoto, *Ōtagaki Rengetsu*, 32. Rengetsu herself never wrote about her father, but there is evidence that she was aware of his identity. Sugimoto discovered that Rengetsu visited Yoshikiyo's grave in Ueno several times between 1848 and 1861, and that she entrusted a local merchant with arranging Buddhist services at the New Year and during the midsummer Bon festival for the dead. Sugimoto, 37-44.
10. According to Kuroda's biography, her mother later married a samurai in Kameoka fief in Tanba. If this is true, then it is unlikely that she was a courtesan.
11. According to some sources, Kameoka Castle is where her mother had gone to live, but it is unclear if Rengetsu had any contact with her or not.
12. There are several anecdotes regarding Rengetsu's mastery of the art of self-defense. Once when she and another girl were accosted by a group of drunken men while taking a walk, Rengetsu reportedly singlehandedly threw one of them to the ground. Sugimoto, *Ōtagaki Rengetsu*, 55.
13. Originally named Tenzō, the fourth son of Oka (Tainoshō) Ginzaemon from Hyōgo prefecture. Upon adoption into the Ōtagaki family his name was changed to Mochihisa.
14. Rengetsu may have had another son named Saiji who went to live with her husband's family after they separated. Some scholars theorize that upon Mochihisa's death, Saiji was adopted by his uncle Tenmin. When divorces occurred, it was common for eldest sons to go live with their father's family, and for girls to stay with their mothers. See Murai Yasuhiko, "Rengetsu-ni," in Koresawa, et al., *Rengetsu*, 158-159.
15. Some sources recount that Mochihisa was a playboy, and that he beat Rengetsu and did not heed his father-in-law's warnings to mend his ways. However, extant letters from Rengetsu to her brother-in-law after Mochihisa's death show her fondness for this first husband, suggesting that their separation may have been due more to conflict with her stepfather than conjugal problems. See Maeda, *Rengetsu*, 58.
16. This second husband, from Hikone, was originally named Ishikawa Chōjirō. Upon adoption he was given the name Hisatoshi.
17. Rengetsu may have been pregnant at the time of her second husband's death, giving birth to a son who died five years later. Maeda, *Rengetsu*, 61. There is a great deal of confusion as to how many children Rengetsu actually bore. According to Tomioka Tessai and Rengetsu's brother-in-law Tenmin, she had six children, all of whom died at a young age. Other records indicate that she had four children (three by her first husband, and

one by her second), three of which were girls and one was a boy. However, Rengetsu wrote in a letter to a nun friend that she had borne three children, two girls and one boy. See Tokuda, *Rengetsu-ni no shin kenkyū*, 34-35.
18. Rengetsu may have been able to rely on her adopted stepbrother Hisaatsu and his wife for support, but she probably did not feel comfortable depending upon them. Nevertheless, after she left Chion'in, she kept in close touch with them.
19. Murakami, *Rengetsu-ni zenshū*, part 2, 31.
20. Born the youngest son of a low-ranking samurai, Roan went to Kyoto at a young age and in 1753 became a pupil of Reizei Tamemura. Roan later established his own school, emphasizing the direct and honest expression of personal feeling.
21. In 1851 she spent the summer residing at the temple Hōkōji where she was able to study directly Roan's poetry collection entitled the *Rakujō eisō* in manuscript form. Later, she went to live at the temple Shinseiji near the cemetery where Roan is buried. Most scholars feel that he was the single most influential figure in the development of her *waka* style.
22. Rengetsu once moved thirteen times in one year. There are many anecdotes describing the methods she used to discourage visitors: one was to hang a card outside saying "Rengetsu rusu" (Rengetsu is out). Another ploy was to have the neighborhood children tell people that she was not at home. Tokuda, *Rengetsu-ni no shin kenkyū*, 186.
23. Letter of 14 November, 1986.
24. After her death, these were succeeded by the *Zōho Rengetsu waka shū* (1897), *Rengetsu-ni waka shū* (1918), *Rengetsu-ni no hito to waka* (1926), and *Rengetsu-ni waka shūi* (1927). For descriptions of all of these books, see Joshi Gakushūin, *Joryū chosaku kaidai*, 16, 67-68. For the text of *Ama no karumo*, see Nagasawa Mitsu, ed., *Nyonin waka taikei*, 498-517.
25. In addition, she was listed in the 1847 *Kōto shoga jinmei roku* as a poet, calligrapher, and painter. See Mori Senzō, vol. 4, 424.
26. Mori Keizō, "Tokugawa jidai no joryū kajin," 587.
27. For illustrations of two collaborative works, see Kyoto Furitsu Sōgō Shiryōkan, *Ōtagaki Rengetsu: Bakumatsu joryū kajin no shoga to tōgei*, nos. 69 and 70.
28. Tessai once drew a map showing where various artists and poets lived; Shikibu lived near Kumano Shrine on Marutamachi street. Tokuda, *Rengetsu-ni no shin kenkyū*, 81.
29. The present-day Tomioka family still has paper with inscriptions by Rengetsu which were apparently waiting for Tessai to add paintings. Tokuda Kōen, "Rengetsu no tōkoku no shofū," *Ōtagaki Rengetsu*, 236.
30. Tokuda, *Rengetsu-ni no shin kenkyū*, 164.
31. In 1866 she collaborated with Wada Gōzan to raise money to feed people during a famine. Together they created one thousand works (paintings by Gōzan with poetic inscriptions by Rengetsu) which were then sold by the famous paper shop Kyūkyodō. Sugimoto, *Ōtagaki Rengetsu*, 225. The owner of Kyūkyodō, Kumagai Naotaka, was one of the most important art patrons of the day. He also supported her friend Tessai and the woman poet-painter Chō Kōran (see chapter seven).
32. Melinda Takeuchi, *Poem Paintings* (London, 1977), 22.
33. Keibun was the younger brother of Goshun, founder of the Shijō school. Tessai's grandson reported Tessai as saying that Rengetsu studied painting with Keibun, and that they fell in love and lived together. Tokuda Kōen, "Bannen shokan ni miru Rengetsu," *Rengetsu*, 197.
34. Rengetsu did not begin to add her age to her signature until she was seventy-two.
35. The signature is comparable to two other early ones in the chart in Tokuda, *Ōtagaki Rengetsu*, 237 and Koresawa, et al., *Rengetsu*, 218. Like other early signatures, the grass radical of the character *ren* is quite distinct, and the character for moon (*getsu*) is elongated. The general calligraphy style of the *waka* resembles several *tanzaku* believed to date from Rengetsu's forties or fifties. See Tokuda, *Ōtagaki Rengetsu*, 214 and 223; Koresawa, *Rengetsu*, 218; Maeda, *Rengetsu*, nos. 41-45. Most scholars believe that Rengetsu did not begin painting until her sixties, but *Spring Moon* seems to indicate otherwise.
36. For another moon painting by Rengetsu, see Tokuda, *Ōtagaki Rengetsu*, no. 197.
37. This verse is included in a collection of Rengetsu's poems entitled *Shūi*.
38. Bamboo was designated as a "gentleman" because certain qualities it embodied such as endurance (staying green all winter along) and flexibility (bending with the wind but not breaking) were likened to those admired in venerable scholars. The "four gentlemen" of East Asian art are bamboo, plum, orchid, and chrysanthemum.
39. For illustrations, see Tokuda, *Ōtagaki Rengetsu*, no. 196; Koresawa, et al., *Rengetsu*, nos. 43, 117, and 145.

40. This poem is included in the *Ama no karumo*.
41. The districts of Awata, Awataguchi, Kiyomizuzaka, and Gojōzaka were major pottery centers in Rengetsu's day. According to Kuroda's biography, Rengetsu took her pottery to the kilns of Sanjō Taizan Yohei, Gojō Kiyomizu Rokubei, and later Shimo Kawabara Kuroda. From her letters we know that she also used the kilns of Kinkōzan and Hōzan, being especially fond of Kinkōzan. See Tokuda, *Ōtagaki Rengetsu*, 217.
42. Beginning perhaps with Hon'ami Kōetsu (1558-1637) and his connection to Raku Dōnyū (1599-1656).
43. Rengetsu may have first been introduced to *sencha* by Ueda Akinari, one of the leaders of the *sencha* movement in Japan who published several books on the subject.
44. For a general overview of the history of *sencha* in Japan, see Patricia J. Graham, "Sencha (Steeped Tea) and Its Contribution to the Spread of Chinese Literati Culture in Edo Period Japan," *Oriental Art*, vol. 31, no. 2 (Summer 1985), 186-195.
45. Rengetsu was not the first to inscribe poems on her pottery. She may well have been inspired by the work of Kyoto potters such as Ogata Kenzan (1663-1743) and Aoki Mokubei.
46. This *waka* appears in the *Ama no karumo* with the title "A Flower-Viewing Excursion." It was clearly one of her favorite poems, as she inscribed the same verse on other teapots and on paintings of cherry blossoms. See Tokuda, *Ōtagaki Rengetsu*, nos. 45, 48, 93, 123, 192, and 193.
47. Because it grows up from the mud at the bottom of ponds and opens into a beautiful flower, in Buddhism the lotus came to symbolize the struggle of mankind striving for enlightenment. Buddhist deities are often shown holding lotus flowers or seated on pedestals formed by lotus petals.
48. Mitsuoka Tadanari, "Rengetsu-ni no tōgei," in Koresawa, et al., *Rengetsu*, 202. Present-day descendants of Kuroda living at Jōrakuji in Kyoto still own molds with lotus designs which they believe were used by Kuroda. This information came from Karen Gerhart who visited them in March 1986.
49. Tokuda, *Ōtagaki Rengetsu*, 218. Kuroda was originally from Ōmi province and came to Kyoto around 1858.
50. The letters frequently include a list of the types and quantity of wares Rengetsu was requesting him to make for her. Murai Yasuhiko, "Rengetsu-ni," in Koresawa, et al., *Rengetsu*, 170-171. Another person who helped Rengetsu to fill pottery orders in her late years was Yoshida Yasu, the wife of a Kyoto farmer.
51. A letter exists from Rengetsu to Kuroda asking him to incise the poems for her on a particular batch of pottery. Tokuda, *Ōtagaki Rengetsu*, 219, and Mitsuoka Tadanari, "Rengetsu-ni no tōgei," 210.
52. In some cases it is clear that Kuroda made the pottery because he impressed his seal; however, the question remains as to who added the poetic inscriptions signed "Rengetsu." For examples of Kuroda's pottery and calligraphy, see Tokuda, *Ōtagaki Rengetsu*, 218-219. Rengetsu's style of pottery became so famous that unauthorized imitations appeared as early as 1860. Anecdotes relate that some copyists even brought their pots to Rengetsu to inscribe because they were unable to reproduce her calligraphy successfully. Because she felt sorry for these people who were struggling to make a living Rengetsu would oblige. Tokuda, *Rengetsu-ni no shin kenkyū*, 59.
53. The first poem appears in *Shūi* and the following four in *Ama no karumo*.
54. Included in the *Ama no karumo*.
55. Louise Cort has noted that it may be the Shigaraki-type clay which was widely used in Kyoto workshops to achieve certain effects.
56. The conception and execution of this *mizusashi* is so sophisticated that it seems likely that it was made by Kuroda, even though he did not impress his seal.
57. This *waka* is included in Rengetsu's *Ama no karumo*, and is entitled "Wind Passes Through the Pines and Enters the Blinds."
58. There is a long tradition in Japan of tea practitioners carving their own *chashaku*. Although there are professional *chashaku* craftsmen, those made by tea people are especially prized.
59. Rengetsu is also believed to have made this wooden container.
60. Murai Yasuhiko, "Rengetsu-ni," in Koresawa, et al., *Rengetsu*, 171.
61. Also known as the Shōren'in school, founded by Prince Son'en (1298-1356) in Kyoto.
62. See Koresawa, et al., *Rengetsu*, 218 and Tokuda, *Ōtagaki Rengetsu*, no. 252.
63. Rengetsu also utilized many *hentaigana* in her earliest known calligraphy. Japanese scholars divide the evolution of Rengetsu's calligraphy style into three stages, with the work of her forties representing the first (*urana jidai*). At this time she always added her signature on the verso of the *tanzaku*. During the second stage (*omotena jidai*) which lasted from her fifties to her seventies, she began to sign her name on the front of *tanzaku*, and gradually formulated the gossamer style for which she is celebrated. The third and final stage (*saishomei jidai*) is represented by works dated from the age of seventy-four.
64. Koresawa Kyōzō, "Rengetsu-ni no sho," *Rengetsu*, 220.
65. Maeda Toshiko, "Rengetsu-ni," *Nihon bijutsu kōgei*, no. 399, 65.
66. The first, fourth and fifth *waka* can be found in the *Ama no karumo*, while the third appears in *Shūi*.

Chapter Ten: Early Meiji-period *Bunjin*

The late nineteenth century witnessed Japan's dramatic metamorphosis from a semi-feudal to a modern state, generating changes in the art world and in the status of women artists. Following the political revolution culminating in the Meiji Restoration (named after the Emperor Meiji who ascended the throne in 1868), the feudal system was abolished, resulting in the dissolution of the samurai class and the establishment of basic legal equalities for all people. A large number of artists employed by samurai and noble families suddenly found themselves without stipends, and many were forced into other occupations. The Kano and Tosa schools suffered the most from the elimination of the old class system, and there are many tragic stories about the destitute lives that talented artists were forced to lead. One of the few painting traditions that continued to flourish in the early years of the Restoration, however, was *bunjinga*.

The primary reason for the endurance of literati painting was that it was favored by many of the leaders of the new Meiji government, the majority of whom had classical Chinese educations. They had consequently developed an appreciation for *bunjinga* and the philosophy that underlay it. In the Edo period, *bunjin* artists had come to depend upon a broader base of patronage than the official Kano and Tosa schools, encompassing people from all classes. The *bunjin*/patron relationship was frequently a very personal one, and therefore when the class system was abandoned, associations between artist and patron were unaffected.

In time, however, the transformation taking place in the art world began to affect the popularity of *bunjinga*. Seeking to modernize Japan, the Meiji government encouraged the importation of Western technology and culture, resulting in the introduction of Western art techniques and designs which captured the interest of forward-looking artists. The growing fascination with Western oil painting subsequently stimulated a reactionary movement led by the American Ernest Fenollosa (1853-1908). A Harvard graduate who was invited to Japan in 1879 to teach Western philosophy and economics at Tokyo University, he was distressed at the Japanese' infatuation with Western art. Fenollosa lectured passionately on the importance and beauty of traditional Japanese art, trying to open the Japanese' eyes to the necessity of preserving their heritage. He even went so far as to argue the superiority of Japanese painting over Western oil painting, imploring artists not to abandon native ideals by adopting Western art methods and aesthetics. Fenollosa wielded so much influence that at first Western-style painting seemed to be in jeopardy. He encouraged artists to develop a style representing modern Japan (which came to be called *nihonga*), blending stylistic elements from traditional schools. Fenollosa had strong prejudices for the kinds of Japanese art to be emulated; he was openly critical of *bunjinga* because of its Chinese origins and Sinophile form of expression. By the end of the nineteenth century, Western oil painting and *nihonga* had emerged as the two most viable pictorial arts. Interest in *bunjinga* consequently began to wane during the late 1880s as young artists adopted one or the other of the "modern" styles of painting. The reputations of well-established *bunjin* artists remained intact, but their paintings were now considered conservative and old-fashioned.

Although support for literati painting gradually declined during the late nineteenth century, the status of women was rising. Among the avid supporters of women's rights in the early Meiji period were the education minister Mori Arinori and the famous educator Fukuzawa Yūkichi. Through their writings and activities, educational opportunities for women expanded. A law making compulsory elementary education apply to both sexes was put into effect in 1872, and the government also established several girls' schools devoted to secondary education.[1] At the instigation of Mori, the Japanese government sent five girls to the United States in 1871 to study; Mori promoted the need to educate women in order to make the best use of their talents in the challenge of the new age. Two years after the compulsory education system was instituted, the Tokyo Normal School for Women was established with the purpose of training girls as teachers. The number of schools for the training of women teachers steadily increased, providing females with opportunities to enter a profession that had an acknowledged intellectual and social standing. Women moved into other professions more slowly: in 1900, a female doctor named Yoshioka Yayoi opened the first Japanese medical school for women, and in the following year, Japan's first college for women was founded.

Better educational opportunities gave rise to a new age in women's literature, the most famous Meiji female writer being Higuchi Ichiyō (1872-1896).[2] By the middle of the Meiji period, women's magazines such as the *Jogaku zasshi* (Magazine for Women's Learning)[3] were coming into existence. As time went by, some women writers began to express strong social concerns.

A few Japanese had absorbed liberal ideals from the West and campaigned for women's suffrage and other rights in the early Meiji period. However, the securing of equal rights for women in areas outside of public education proceeded slowly. Around the start of the Taishō period (1912-1926), the stirrings of feminist thought had begun among a small circle of women intellectuals; the earliest feminist group was the Seitōsha (Bluestocking Society) which was established in 1911. Most progressive women were products of the higher education for women that had begun at the turn of the century.

Two women, Okuhara Seiko and Noguchi Shōhin, lived into the Meiji era and ranked among the most celebrated *bunjinga* artists of their time. Neither had husbands nor fathers who were painters, indicating that the art world had more fully opened its doors to women. Painting was recognized as their profession, not just a female pastime. These two artists were fortunate to have had enlightened parents who encouraged their daughters' artistic talents and helped them to develop careers. They both received the patronage and support of one of the leading spokesmen for the new Meiji government, Kido Takayoshi (1833-1877). Judging from Kido's diary, he treated Seiko and Shōhin with the same respect and cordiality that he extended to his male friends. Both artists participated in domestic exhibitions, and Shōhin also submitted paintings to World Expositions, a practice that was clearly borrowed from the West. Although the two women still concentrated on landscapes and the plant subjects which had traditionally formed the literati repertoire, they experimented tentatively with Western pictorial techniques. As a result, many of their paintings have a more naturalistic quality than earlier *bunjinga*. How each artist handled life in Meiji Japan is quite interesting: women of opposite temperaments and characters, the careers of Seiko and Shōhin overlapped, but they eventually chose to go in very different directions.

Okuhara Seiko (1837-1913)

Photographs of Seiko (Figure 16) reveal her masculine character and robust figure. She wore men's clothing, and had her hair cropped in a manly style. The tough image that Seiko projected has led to speculation that she was homosexual. While this may be true, her masculine traits may also have been a vehicle which she employed in order to fit more comfortably into a world still dominated by men.

Seiko's personality and life are equally fascinating.[4] She was born in the domain of Koga (Ibaragi prefecture), the fourth daughter of Ikeda Han'uemon Masaaki, a high-ranking samurai serving the Koga daimyo. From her youth, Seiko (then called Setsuko) was interested in scholarship, painting, and the martial arts. Her first painting teacher was Hirata Suiseki (1801-1868), an artist who had studied under Tani Bunchō while living in Edo.[5] From Suiseki, Seiko learned to paint bamboo and landscapes in an eclectic Chinese manner. However, she deepened her knowledge of Chinese art by studying woodblock-printed manuals and by making copies of paintings in local collections. Many of her early sketchbooks still remain in the Ikeda family collection in Koga. They include copies of paintings with signatures of such Chinese artists as Mu Ch'i, Su Shih, Wu Chen, Li Shih-ta, Hsia Ch'ang, Shen Chou, Hsieh Shih-ch'en, Chang Jui-t'u, Wen Cheng-ming, Wang Yüan-ch'i, and Shen Nan-p'in.[6] In addition, Seiko also made copies of Japanese *bunjinga* that she saw; her sketches remain of paintings by Nakabayashi Chikutō, Tani Bunchō, and

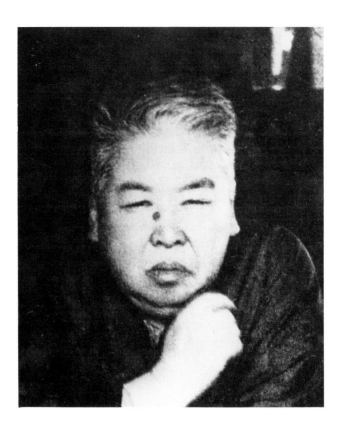

16. *Okuhara Seiko*
Courtesy of the Ibaragi
Kenritsu Rekishikan

Watanabe Kazan among others. Although she supposedly remained Suiseki's pupil for
close to twenty years,[7] it is obvious that she learned a great deal from her independent
study of Chinese and Japanese painting (perhaps encouraged by Suiseki). The
individualistic style she eventually developed was the outcome of her eclectic training.

Seiko received the standard samurai education, becoming well-versed in Chinese
literature and philosophy. One might imagine that a provincial domain such as Koga was
culturally barren, but in fact the opposite was true. Besides Suiseki, there were a number of
distinguished *bunjin* active who were influential on Seiko in one way or another. She
studied Chinese poetry with Ōnuma Chinzan (1818-1891), mastering Chinese verse so
thoroughly that she frequently added her own poems to her paintings. Her early calligraphy
style was influenced by two Koga calligraphers, Koyama Kagai and his son Gooka. Seiko
also studied under Kayane Ichiō who excelled in Chinese-style poetry as well as *waka* and
the tea ceremony; furthermore, she occasionally visited Takami Senseki (1785-1858), a
well-known scholar of Dutch studies.[8] Seiko's education was exceptionally well-rounded
for a male or female; her intelligence and wide range of interests later led her to become
one of the most sought-after figures at scholarly gatherings.

In time Seiko yearned to go to Edo to study, but official regulations in the late Edo
period forbade women from leaving the domain of Koga. However, she cleverly managed to
circumvent the law; Seiko's parents arranged for her to be adopted by an aunt[9] who resided
in the neighboring fief of Sekiyado. In the spring of 1865 Seiko boarded a palanquin, and
accompanied by her younger brother and others, set out for Sekiyado. Her maid servant,
Oden, was sent ahead to Edo along with Seiko's luggage to arrange for her living quarters.
After staying three days at the residence of her new parents, Seiko was able to set out for
Edo, for Sekiyado laws did not prevent women from leaving.

In Edo, Seiko moved into a house which she named Bokutoen'unrō (Ink Disgorging
Smoke Cloud Mansion) in the area of Shitaya in Ueno. Her Chinese poetry teacher Ōnuma
Chinzan maintained his Edo residence in Shitaya, and there were a number of other *bunjin*
artists living nearby.[10] During these years, *bunjinga* was at the height of its popularity, and
Shitaya was a famous gathering place. With Seiko's gregarious personality and budding

artistic talent, it did not take long for her to make a name in Edo. In the twelfth month of 1865 (the year she moved to Edo), she held a party for fellow artists at a restaurant on the island Bentenjima at Shinobaza Pond in Ueno.[11] At such gatherings, participants would eat and drink, have lively discussions on art and poetry, and frequently band together to produce impromptu paintings like the later example in Cat. 88. This social event firmly established Seiko's acceptance into the milieu of the Edo *bunjin*. It was around this time that she adopted the name Seiko.[12] As Seiko's fame increased, she began to receive requests to accept students, among whom was the young woman Seisui (1852-1921) who came to study with Seiko in 1866 at the age of fifteen.

Seiko's new life in Edo was temporarily interrupted at the time of the Meiji Restoration. Because of the agitated political situation and outbreaks of violence, she and her pupil Seisui left Edo in the second month of 1868 and went to Kumagaya (Saitama prefecture). Seiko returned to Edo briefly, but found the city in such turmoil that she decided to wait in Kumagaya. She was an ardent supporter of the movement to restore rule to the imperial house, and showed her patriotism at this time by signing her paintings "Nihon (Japan) Seiko" and "Ajia (Asia) Seiko," as well as by inscribing the year using a number system based on the founding of the imperial line.

Once the Restoration had been carried out and Japan was once again at peace, Seiko's life in Edo (now Tokyo) returned to normal. After 1871 she must have cut an even more mannish figure than before, for she responded to the government edict that topknots be shorn off by cropping her own hair.[13] She continued to flourish as an artist and teacher, and opened a school at her residence in 1871. A year later she built a boarding house which she called Shunchōgakusha. Her female students were permitted to live there, but males were required to commute. At one point Seiko's students were said to number around three hundred.[14] One of her most famous pupils was Okakura Kakuzō (Tenshin, 1862-1913), who went on to become a leading promoter of *nihonga*.[15]

Seiko's name became more and more celebrated due to her friendship with two distinguished political figures, Yamanouchi Yōdō (1827-1872) and Kido Takayoshi. They were both cultivated men who enjoyed associating with *bunjin* artists, and they held gatherings to which Seiko was invited. Kido frequently visited Seiko at her home, which had become a favorite meeting place for artists. Kido was so fond of her that in addition to inviting Seiko to accompany him to various places, he arranged for her to have an audience with the empress in 1872.[16] Seiko was the first woman artist to be honored in that way.

Because of her financial success, Seiko lived extravagantly. She continually renovated and expanded her residence so that it increased in grandeur over the years. It is said that she enjoyed hearing the sounds of carpenters in the morning and evening. Her fondness for fine food led her to become quite heavy in her later years; she not only indulged herself but entertained her guests in high style.

Although Seiko concentrated on Chinese-style painting and Chinese-style poetry, her broad interests led her to participate in other activities. In addition to writing haiku, she wrote the preface to a biography of George Washington (called *Tsuzoku Washinton den*) that was published in 1873. The latter contribution indicates that she did not completely reject Western culture as is sometimes believed.

Around 1874 Seiko with several friends[17] formed a small artistic society called the Hankansha. Seiko was described as being so skillful in the art of conversation that she was always in control of the discussions. Once she was securely established as a successful artist, she stopped going to large *bunjin* gatherings. Such social events were a means through which artists made themselves known, and Seiko no longer needed to promote herself. Juried exhibitions were now frequent occurrences in Tokyo, but Seiko rarely entered her works because she disliked competition. However she did attend them, and her pupils entered their works. There is an amusing anecdote regarding Seiko's attendance at an exhibition opening. One of the guests got drunk and began to get rowdy. Saying that he wanted to find out if Seiko was truly a woman, he reached out from behind her and tried to grab her breast. Turning red with anger, Seiko seized him around the waist and threw him over the tray set before her.

In 1878 Seiko set off on her first journey to the Kansai (Kyoto-Osaka) area, the trip

17. Seiran, *Seiko's Hokuetsu Journey* (detail), 1896 Hasegawa Yoshikazu Collection

lasting six months. After passing through Nagoya, she went to Tsukigase to view the beautiful groves of plum trees. She then traveled to Nara, Osaka, and Kyoto, staying for several months and associating with well-known *bunjin*.[18] This trip strengthened Seiko's reputation in central Japan, although she was most honored in Tokyo. Her fame in the capital was such that her works could be found in the homes of many middle-class people, and it was fashionable for teahouses and restaurants to have a scroll by her. This stimulated the production of forgeries, most of which imitate the bold, cursory style which Seiko practiced in the 1870s.

The Tokyo art world began to undergo some changes in the 1880s, with the increasing interest in Western oil painting and the influence of Fenollosa. New art schools and societies were formed, and painters debated ideas and formal issues with one another. A close friend of Seiko's, Kawakami Tōgai, became one of the pioneers of Western oil painting in Japan. Seiko herself supposedly collected oil paintings,[19] but it was not a direction she chose to pursue in her own art. Nevertheless, some of her work does show the influence of Western perspective and coloring. While those around her were renouncing *bunjinga* in favor of the more "modern styles," Seiko resolutely clung to her own preferences. She worried about the future of her pupils, however, and recommended that they study Western-style painting instead of following her.

In 1889, Seiko was forced to move because her home was in the path of the construction of a railroad. After having resided there for more than twenty years, she reluctantly sold her studio and relocated elsewhere in Shitaya. She was not completely satisfied with her new residence, however, and in 1891 she left Tokyo and retired to Kumagaya. Although perhaps prompted by her unhappiness with her new home, the primary reason underlying her permanent departure from Tokyo seems to have been the transformation taking place in the art world. Seiko was well aware of the criticism *bunjinga* was receiving and the heightened interest in Western oil painting and *nihonga*. Her major spokesman, Kido Takayoshi, had died in 1877. A whole new generation of artists had emerged, and Seiko now felt out of place. Determined to proceed with her own art form, she decided to withdraw from Tokyo. She chose to go to the village of Kamikawakami in the northern part of Kumagaya because she had close family friends there. She was accompanied by her faithful pupil Seiran who acted as companion and secretary until the end of Seiko's life.

After living so many years in the city, Seiko found the village to which she had moved a bit provincial. However, she had her home rebuilt to suit her taste, and had a beautiful garden constructed.[20] Seiko's move to Kumagaya seems to have triggered a change in her artistic style. She gradually shifted away from her early free and uninhibited style to one featuring more detailed brushwork, richer color, and more thorough modeling of forms. She continued to paint primarily landscape and bird-and-flower subjects, rarely doing figures. Her works at this time exhibit a harmony between realistic depiction and idealization.

In 1896, Seiko made a four-month trip with her pupil Seiran to the Hokuetsu region. Seiran painted an amusing handscroll of one segment of this journey, with a scene of Seiko about to be carried by palanquin (Figure 17). Seiko continued to make several treks in the following years, visiting Kyoto again in 1898. She rarely executed paintings on these trips, but took delight in traveling, seeing art, and talking with people. If she received requests for paintings she would usually wait until she returned home to fulfill them.

The paintings Seiko created after her retirement to Kumagaya are considered to represent the pinnacle of her artistry. By removing herself from the capital, Seiko was little affected by the rapid modernization of Japan and the Russo-Japanese War. In the peace and quiet of her country home, she concentrated solely on her art. Despite the fact that she was no longer a visible figure in Tokyo, her patrons did not forget her and there continued to be a demand for her works.

Seiko usually painted at night, first placing a rug in the room, then arranging candles at the four corners; she would paint as many as thirty works at one sitting. One of her pupils would be responsible for grinding the ink and keeping her inkstone full. Seiko paid particular attention to her brushes, inkstones, and pigments, using only those of the highest quality. Afterwards, she would take some tobacco out of a pouch, put it in a long stemmed pipe and puff away, blowing out rings of smoke.

Seiko's health began to fail in 1912, and she hung a plaque on her gate saying that she would no longer be taking orders. She never fully recovered and died one year later at the age of seventy-seven.

Noguchi Shōhin (1847-1917)

Shōhin was ten years younger than Seiko and came from a different part of Japan, but she, too, was drawn to the art scene in Tokyo, and eventually the two women met and became colleagues. Born in Osaka, Shōhin was the only child of the doctor Matsumura Shuntai.[21] She was considered a prodigy, and like Seiko showed an amazing aptitude for literature and art. By the age of five Shōhin began to read and write, first trying to copy the Chinese characters on the medicine labels in her father's pharmacy. She soon began to study *waka*, memorizing the poems in the *Hyakunin isshu* and learning to compose her own as well. Her father did not send her to a *terakoya* because he felt that the teachers were not very good; instead he preferred to educate Shōhin himself at home. Shōhin was not like other children who liked to play outdoors; she would linger inside when her father and his friends discussed poetry, and her parents would find her practicing reading and writing late at night. She began to show an interest in painting from the age of four, and was enrolled as a pupil of Ishigaki Tōhei (1806-1876)[22] at the age of eight. Although Shōhin also had lessons in playing the *koto*, sewing, and archery, she was excited most by painting and began to funnel her energies primarily into that art.

In 1860, when she was fourteen, Shōhin's father sold their house in Osaka and took the family on an extended tour of northern Honshū. They ended up in Nagoya, but her father became ill and died early in 1862. Shōhin was only sixteen at the time; she remained with her mother in Nagoya and sold her paintings in order to support them.[23] Prior to this time, she had led a sheltered life, and never had to concern herself with finances. Fortunately she was able to attract some patrons. She was befriended by a feudal lord in Owari who invited her to poetry and painting gatherings. One night at the home of a neighboring doctor, she responded to a dare to do one thousand paintings in twenty-four hours. Shōhin did a

18. Shōhin, *Bunjin Gathering*
(detail), 1862
Noguchi Chūzō Collection

painting memoralizing this event, depicting herself brushing a design upon a fan (Figure 18).

Shōhin and her mother left Nagoya in 1865, traveled to Ise, Matsuzaka, Yamada, Tsu,[24] and Ōmi Hachiman before reaching Kyoto around 1867. There she became a pupil of the *bunjinga* master Hine Taizan (1813-1869);[25] it was around this time that she started using the name Shōhin. She was greatly influenced by her teacher, her early works showing a careful structuring of traditional forms combined with a certain freedom of brushwork. She concentrated on landscapes as well as flower and plant subjects, occasionally doing figure paintings. Shōhin soon became an active member in the Kyoto *bunjin* world, and by 1868 had become so friendly with Kido Takayoshi that she was invited to join the Kido family to celebrate the enthronement of the Emperor Meiji on 12 October, 1868.[26] Taizan died in 1869, followed shortly by Shōhin's mother in 1870. Now fully independent, Shōhin tried to expunge her sorrow by pouring herself into her art. The fact that she had been forced to support herself and her mother from the age of sixteen, and that eight years later she was parentless, acted as a catalyst in activating her painting career.

In 1871, one year after her mother's death, Shōhin moved to Tokyo. Thinking it unwise to room by herself, she rented a place with two servant girls. Probably around this time Shōhin became acquainted with Okuhara Seiko. There is no evidence that they became close friends, but they had many mutual acquaintances including Kido Takayoshi, and consequently attended some of the same social gatherings. Shōhin's reputation as an artist was gradually established, and two years later she was invited to paint the sliding door panels surrounding the sleeping quarters of the empress. Shōhin became somewhat of a traveling artist, moving to those areas where she was offered work; in 1875 she went to Kōfu in Yamanashi prefecture. She became such a prominent figure that one year later the Kōfu newspaper included a short article about her. There she met her future husband, Noguchi Masaakira (1849-1922), the eldest son of a family of *sake* brewers. They were married in 1877, but not without some resistance from the Noguchi family who felt that an itinerant painter would not be a suitable wife for their son. However, in the end, they accepted Shōhin into the family. Professionally, the marriage may have worked in her favor. Her husband and his family supported her work, and she was allowed to devote her time to painting. Her father-in-law had been a patron of Hine Taizan, and may have helped by recommending new sponsors to Shōhin.

At first the newly married couple lived with the Noguchi family in Shiga prefecture; a daughter was born to Shōhin and Masaakira in early 1878. The following year, they returned to Kōfu where Masaakira was put in charge of a branch of the family business. Shōhin did very few paintings in the early years of her marriage, probably because of the demands of raising a child. However, there exist examples of beer labels that she designed for the Noguchi family. Unfortunately her husband did not succeed in managing the family business there, and was dismissed by his father. The couple thereupon left Kōfu and went to Tokyo in 1882.

From this point on, Shōhin was the breadwinner, and for awhile they struggled to make ends meet. At times she had to accept jobs in other prefectures in order to help with the family finances. For example, in the summer of 1884 Shōhin traveled north to Sendai, and in the following year, she went to Maebashi (Gumma prefecture). In time, however, Shōhin's talents came to be publicly recognized in Tokyo. Other artists and intellectuals began to seek her out, and the number of her pupils increased. Official acknowledgement came in 1889 when she was appointed Professor of Painting at the Peers' Girls School. In the same year she entered one of her works in the Paris Exposition, and another in the Nihon Bijutsu Kyōkai (Japan Art Association) exhibition where it received an honorable mention. Four years later, in 1893, she had a landscape exhibited in the Chicago World Exposition where it received a prize. Judging from the large number of her extant works, she painted incessantly. Shōhin herself said that excepting days when she was sick, a day did not pass during which she did not pick up a brush.[27]

Shōhin resigned from her position at the Peers' Girls School in 1893 because of illness. Nevertheless, she continued to enter her works in national exhibitions where they regularly received prizes. She achieved such renown that in 1899 she was appointed painting instructor for the Higashi Fushimi princess. She continued to receive the favor of the imperial family; in 1901 she was asked to paint sliding door panels for the palace, and in the following year she became instructor to Empress Manko of the Kitashirakawa palace. Her ultimate recognition came when she was appointed official artist of the Imperial Household in 1904. Her duties included teaching members of the imperial family and painting works for the palace.

Perhaps as a result of such lofty recognition, Shōhin became more of a presence in the exhibition world, serving as a judge for many of the national exhibitions. Not wishing to retire, she remained active until late 1916 when she became seriously ill. Shōhin died in the second month of 1917 at the age of seventy-one. A photograph of her in her later years shows that she was physically quite the opposite of Seiko—a small-framed woman—yet nurtured a similarly intense spirit (Figure 19). Shōhin's daughter wrote that her mother was very modest and reserved, and that she did not like voicing her opinions to reporters.[28] Although Shōhin supported the family, she never boasted about her role. Wives who were painters were still rare, and Shōhin often exclaimed to her daughter how fortunate she was, humbly saying that she had not achieved this position through any power of her own. Lest someone criticize Shōhin for indulging herself in her art and ignoring her family, Shōhin's daughter firmly stated that she had been a good wife and mother. Yet despite all of this emphasis on virtuousness and modesty, one cannot ignore the fact that Shōhin went against the norm and chose to devote her entire life to painting. Shōhin spoke of her philosophy of life in the following passage:[29]

> Once deciding to pursue something, one must have strong determination to the death. No matter what art is pursued, the path will not be easy. One must fight against difficulties. An old proverb says that when grief comes, it doubles courage. If one gives up halfway, one should never have started. Unless one is superhuman or has outstanding character, it is not good to be too wealthy, nor to be too poor. Worrying about food and clothing, one cannot devote oneself to being a good painter. On the other hand, acquiring too much wealth can make one too relaxed, and this obstructs mastery of an art.

Upon reading Shōhin's description of the inner strength necessary to become successful as an artist, it is clear that this psychology was most crucial for women. Although society was changing its attitudes, a woman still needed more than just talent to succeed. Seiko and Shōhin both possessed the necessary ingredients of ambition, family support, and patrons that allowed them to fulfill their dreams. In the end, Seiko found herself unable to

19. *Noguchi Shōhin*
    Courtesy of the Yamanashi
    Kenritsu Bijutsukan

cope with modern Tokyo and obstinately withdrew from the public art world. Shōhin found
it easier to adapt to the changing times. Instead of rejecting modern Japan, she took an
active role in artistic organizations and the growing numbers of exhibitions, both domestic
and foreign. Although practicing what had become, by the twentieth century, an outmoded
style, Shōhin was able to withstand the pressures and ultimately found a comfortable niche
for herself.

Neither Seiko nor Shōhin had much impact upon the next generation of artists.
Although Seiko had many pupils at one time in her life, only her closest followers such as
Seiran continued to paint in her manner. Shōhin's best pupil was her daughter, Iku
(Shōkei), who continued to produce fine works following the style of her mother. Seiko and
Shōhin were among the last flashes of brilliance within the *bunjinga* tradition before the
tide fully turned toward more modern styles of painting.

78. Okuhara Seiko (1837-1913)

Orchids, 1870
Folding fan, ink on mica paper, 14.1 x 49.9 cm.
Signature: Seiko kyōjin
Seals: undecipherable
Shōka Collection
Published: Stephen Addiss, "Japanese Literati Artists of the
Meiji Period," *Essays on Japanese Art Presented to Jack
Hillier* (London: Robert G. Sawers Publishing, 1982), fig. 9.

This fan is dated 1870, five years after Seiko had
moved to Tokyo, and was inscribed as having been painted
at her Bokutoen'unrō studio. It represents the bold and
dashing brushwork she practiced in the 1870s and 1880s,
loosely modeled upon the brush manner of the Chinese
artist Cheng Hsieh (Cheng Pan-ch'iao, 1693-1765). Cheng
was a noted master of bamboo and orchids, his style
celebrated for its freedom of expression. Seiko is
supposed to have owned an album by Cheng, and she was
influenced by his brushwork in her painting and even more
in her calligraphy.

Seiko has centered the cluster of orchids which sprout
leftward from the crevices of a rock. She loosely defined
the rock edges with moist gray ink which puddled in areas
due to the hard mica surface. A similar gray was used to
form the orchid flowers; for contrast, she brushed the
leaves in rich black. To the left she has inscribed the date
and place of execution, and at the right the following
Chinese-style poem:

> Amidst the mountains, the orchids aspire to grow as freely as
> weeds;
> Leaves warm themselves, flowers flutter, saturated with the
> spirit of the season.
> The orchid sends forth its fragrance; although not extending
> too far,
> It wafts past the dirt and dust of the everyday world.

Poem and painting are composed with similar
brushstrokes, the calligraphy relating naturally to the
painted orchids. It is said that when Cheng Hsieh painted
these flowers, they were like calligraphy, and when he
wrote out the character for orchids, it resembled flowers.
The same applies to Seiko, her brushwork throughout
exhibiting an uninhibited freedom balanced by a masterful
control of the brush. The shiny mica surface imbues the
poem and image with a soft glow appropriate to this
modest literati subject.

79. Okuhara Seiko

Summer Mountains, 1883
Hanging scroll, ink and light colors on satin,
46.8 x 57.4 cm.
Signature: Tōkai Seiko shiga
Seals: Seiko; Seiko na Seikan azana etsu Seiko
Otaka Fukutarō Collection

Throughout her life Seiko occasionally painted landscapes following the tradition of the Chinese scholar-painter Mi Fu (1051-1107), composed of layers of repeated horizontal strokes in varying tones of ink. The so-called Mi style was favored by literati painters in both China and Japan, particularly when they wanted to portray lush summer scenery (see Cat. 49). Seiko's landscape is imbued with a deep, resonant misty quality, evoking the seasonal rains that come to southern China and Japan in early summer.

The mountainous scene is bathed in mist, with only the uppermost peaks exposed. Two scholars sit in a pavilion overlooking a wide expanse of lake, listening to the waves lap quietly at the shore. The empty areas of mist and lake are crucial to the compositional design, balancing and intensifying the richly painted trees and land forms. Seiko's composition represents an unusual variation on the standard design of Mi-style landscapes, which usually depict a series of rounded mountain peaks centered on a vertical axis. Instead she has placed two large mountain forms slightly off-center; the upper one is leveled off and the lower slightly pointed, establishing an interesting dialogue.

Seiko's choice of the shimmering satin surface augments the damp, foggy atmospheric quality. Although the landscape appears to be rendered entirely in ink, on closer inspection one discovers light touches of a peach color applied sparingly for accent. Seiko's Chinese-style poem reads:

Enclosed by fresh greenery in my mountain dwelling,
Seaside friends come by to discuss poetry.
Amidst the rain—the voice of the cuckoo at the eaves—
The mountain colors interspersed with mist are wondrous.

80. Okuhara Seiko

River Village in Spring, 1896
Hanging scroll, ink and colors on silk, 128 x 52.5 cm.
Signature: Seiko shi ga
Seals: Seiko; Tōkai Seikan; Shōbokusō
Hasegawa Yoshikazu Collection
Published: Saitama Kenritsu Hakubutsukan, *Tokubetsu ten:
Okuhara Seiko ten zuroku*, pl. 101; Fujijake, *Okuhara Seiko
gashū*, pl. 39.

This scroll was painted five years after Seiko retired to
Kumagaya, at the request of Hasegawa Ichirō (died 1897),
her friend and patron living in Tsukayama of Niigata
prefecture. An upper-class samurai, Hasegawa presided
over a small domain. Seiko and her pupil Seiran were
frequent guests at his mansion, staying for up to a month at
a time. In return for being entertained at the Hasegawa
home, Seiko created what are now recognized as some of
her masterpieces. Many of the works were painted during
her sojourns; the Hasegawa family's hospitality and
harmonious surroundings appear to have suited Seiko well.
After Hasegawa Ichirō's untimely death, Seiko continued
to visit his mother, indicative of her close friendship with
the family.

Seiko recorded that this scroll was painted in the fourth
month of 1896.[30] It depicts a wide river winding through
mountainous countryside, not unlike the scenery near the
Hasegawa home in Tsukayama. Spring has arrived, and
the banks are flush with willows and blossoming peach
trees. While fishermen ply their oars, other people wile
away the time rambling through the hills or sitting in the
pavilions dotting the shore, as though intoxicated by the
verdant surroundings. Seiko emphasized the lush scenery
by employing a range of greens and blue color washes.
The lavish spectrum and reliance on fine, delicate
brushstrokes illustrate the stylistic changes that took place
after she moved to Kumagaya. Seiko's poem reads:

Willows bend delicately, creating many gestures;
The peach blossoms are radiant in appearance.
Lakes and mountains winding for thirty *li–*
This beautiful view inspires good poetry.

81. Okuhara Seiko

Cranes, 1905
Pair of hanging scrolls, ink and colors on silk,
each 135 x 71.5 cm.
Signatures: Seiko chō; Seiko utsusu
Seals: Seiko; Seifu taitsu; Seiko
The Museum of Modern Art, Saitama, Japan
Published: Saitama Kenritsu Hakubutsukan, *Tokubetsu ten:
Okuhara Seiko ten zuroku*, pl. 63; Iizuka, *Nihonga taisei*,
vol. 24, pls. 94-95; Fujikake, *Okuhara Seiko gashū*, pls.
76-77.

Like the previous landscape, this monumental pair of
scrolls was painted for the Hasegawa family in Niigata.
They bear celebratory inscriptions saying "Great and
boundless joy to your descendants" and "May the pleasure
of your descendants be doubled by wealth, honor,
prosperity, and harmony." The compositions are bursting
with symbols of longevity, suggesting that the scrolls may
have been painted for a felicitous occasion such as the new
year or a birthday. Each painting contains a group of six
large white cranes, believed to be the vehicles of
immortals; thus cranes came to be associated with long
life. In the right scroll, the cranes are standing beneath a
peach tree laden with fruit, another symbol of immortality.
The cranes in the left scroll are shielded by a twisted pine
tree, around which grows blossoming plum. Pine and
plum are two of the "Friends of Winter," representing
endurance and rejuvenation because of their ability to
withstand cold, harsh weather.

The full and complexly organized compositions,
combined with brilliant coloring and descriptive
brushwork, recall the style introduced to Japan by the
Chinese artist Shen Nan-p'in, which came to be known as
the Nagasaki tradition (see Cat. 33). By Seiko's time,
knowledge of Nagasaki school painting was widespread.
She is known to have copied at least one painting by Shen
in her formative years; it is interesting that the Nagasaki
style did not seem to influence Seiko until her move to
Kumagaya. Seiko found herself moving away from an
impressionistic brush manner towards more descriptive
methods of texturing, perhaps being influenced by the
experimentation with Western realism taking place around
her. She did not abandon her Chinese heritage, but when
painting bird-and-flower subjects, she shifted away from
pure *bunjinga* prototypes to the semi-naturalistic Nagasaki
style.

Seiko's use of rich colors such as malachite green,
combined with bold compositional designs, imbue her
subjects with life and vigor. In general she defined the
forms with a combination of broken lines and dotting,
applying color washes or scores of small brushstrokes
within. The vegetation is especially vividly described with
meticulous texture strokes, and exhibits a full range of
greens. Seiko brushed gold lines for veins on some of the
larger leaves, increasing the painting's luminosity. In
contrast, portions of the cranes' bodies were left unpainted,
allowing the cream-colored silk to function as feathers.
White highlights were applied to some of the feathers,
intensifying the purity of these "birds of the immortals."
Painted for one of her most important patrons, this pair of
scrolls shows the radiant beauty of Seiko's late style.

82. Noguchi Shōhin (1847-1917)

Woman Bunjin Preparing Sencha
Folding fan mounted as a hanging scroll,
ink and colors on paper, 15 x 46.1 cm.
Signature: Shōhin Joshi Chika utsusu
Seal: Shōhin
Private collection

The subject of this fan is highly unusual: a lady *bunjin* preparing Chinese steeped tea known as *sencha*.[31] Holding the *kyūsu* (teapot) in her right hand, she is about to pour tea into the small cups arranged on the banana leaf before her. To her right are a brazier used to heat the water and a basket of charcoal topped by a feather used to fan the coals. The other items represent the various accouterments and favored objects of scholars: books, scrolls, pine branches, orchids, and a basket of fruit.

Japanese *bunjin* active in the nineteenth century were enamored of the *sencha* ceremony, and they frequently depicted men enjoying *sencha* in their paintings. To see a woman in this role, however, is rare if not unique to Shōhin. That she would paint this scene explicitly shows her personal identification with the *bunjin* lifestyle, and it may be a kind of self-portrait.

The style of painting suggests that this fan may be an early work by Shōhin, perhaps done in the 1870s.[32] The figure of the woman is based on an ukiyo-e prototype; however, the brushwork features the broken linework associated with *bunjinga* rather than the smooth lineament of ukiyo-e. Shōhin's brushwork has a relaxed and casual quality, creating a lively yet delicate rhythm. The ink and pale colors blurred slightly when her brush was wet, the resulting uneven lines adding to the subtle charm of this *bunjin* painting.

83. Noguchi Shōhin

Women Practicing Arts in a Garden, 1872
Hanging scroll, ink and colors on silk, 111.5 x 37 cm.
Seals: Matsumura-shi, Shōhin
Noguchi Chūzō Collection
Published: Yamanashi Kenritsu Bijutsukan, *Noguchi Shōhin ten zuroku*, fig. 6; Moriya, "Noguchi Shōhin kenkyū," *Yamanashi Kenritsu Bijutsukan kenkyū kiyō*, no. 3, fig. 3; Noguchi, ed., *Shōhin iboku shū*, vol. 1.

This painting celebrates the artistry of women. From the top of the scroll to the bottom, Shōhin has represented women playing music (both lute and flute), listening to music, reading books, painting, and practicing *sencha*. The subject matter recalls scenes of Chinese scholars amusing themselves in garden settings, particularly with the addition of the banana trees. Shōhin has created a playful variation upon this theme by depicting Japanese women instead of men; she may have wanted to express her feelings that females could be just as talented and intellectually oriented as male counterparts.

Shōhin painted this work one year after moving to Tokyo. The scroll bears a hidden signature and the date 1872, written in tiny script on the scroll of peonies hanging just to the right of the woman playing the lute. Shōhin also added a box inscription thirty-nine years later, relating that it was painted for Tani Tesshin, a samurai from Hikone who became famous for his poetry and calligraphy.

The delicate brushwork and color sensibility combine here to produce a work of extraordinarily refined beauty. Shōhin created the surrounding garden landscape by blending ink and pale green washes, establishing an appropriately quiet setting for the kinds of activities taking place. The figures were drawn with fine, threadlike lines. Their garments are surprisingly understated in both coloring and design, with bamboo and orchids figuring prominently in the textile patterns, alluding to Shōhin's own literati interests. Because of the emphasis on ink tonalities and pale colors, the bold red accents appearing in the architecture and in some of the fabrics add a note of contrast that enlivens the total composition.

84. Noguchi Shōhin

Two Bijin
Hanging scroll, ink and colors on silk, 104.6 x 34 cm.
Signature: Shōhin utsusu
Seals: Matsumura-shi, Shōhin
Mizutani Ishinosuke Collection

Shōhin obviously enjoyed painting beautiful women engaged in artistic activities; here she has depicted two Japanese courtesans. The figure at the right stands majestically, her robes flowing around her feet like water. She glances downward as though to converse with her kneeling friend, who looks up from the book she has been reading. Two decorated *tanzaku* (poem sheets) lay on the floor in front of them, waiting to be inscribed with poems.

This scroll differs from standard courtesan paintings by the inclusion of several objects alluding to the artistic and scholarly interests of these women. In addition to the books and *tanzaku*, on the table sit three containers containing plants identified with literati: orchid, bamboo, and plum. The setting is stark, with most of the surrounding objects rendered in monochrome ink. Ink was also used to render portions of the textiles; subtle shading, particularly around the folds, is evident. Like in Cat. 83, Shōhin has employed a brilliant red for contrast. Her brushlines defining the forms are precise, but never hard. Although she modeled her women upon ukiyo-e figure types, Shōhin's brushwork is more refined and delicate, exhibiting features of classical Chinese painting.

85. Noguchi Shōhin

Autumn Flowers and Grasses, 1888
Hanging scroll, ink and colors on silk, 143.5 x 49.5 cm.
Signature: Shōhin Joshi Noguchi Chika
Seals: Noguchi Chika no in; Shōhin Joshi;
Kyū shū ran i i hai
Nakagami Ryōta Collection

Among Shōhin's most popular works were her
paintings of seasonal flowers and grasses. This example
represents a real tour de force in that genre; Shōhin has
almost completely filled the composition, lavishing a great
deal of attention on accurately representing many species
of plants. She firmly grounded the design by painting in
monochrome ink the large rock at the left and another
section of foreground in the lower right. Plant forms
encircle the rock, rise above it, and shield it like an
umbrella.

The flora and fauna depicted include hibiscus,
begonia, chrysanthemum, pinks, amaranth, and
dayflowers. Because of the plethora of foliage, an
extraordinary range of green coloring dominates,
intensifying by contrast the red and yellow autumnal
blossoms. In representing the leaves and flowers, Shōhin
has used a brush method referred to as *mokkotsu* or
"boneless." Instead of outlining each of the leaves and
then adding colors within, she has freely brushed on the
areas of color without boundary lines. Afterwards, she
added slender strokes to represent the veins of the leaves.
Shōhin was skillful at manipulating the wet brush to create
the effect of light and shade, a practice learned from her
study of Chinese painting; she perhaps was also influenced
by the growing public interest in Western empiricism.

86. Noguchi Shōhin

Lotus, 1905
Hanging scroll, ink and gold on silk, 116 x 41 cm.
Signature: Shōhin Chika utsusu
Seals: No Chika no in; No-shi Seien
Noguchi Chūzō Collection
Published: Yamanashi Kenritsu Bijutsukan, *Noguchi Shōhin
ten zuroku*, fig. 31; Moriya, "Noguchi Shōhin kenkyū,"
Yamanashi Kenritsu Bijutsukan kenkyū kiyō, no. 3, fig. 12.

Rendered solely with monochrome ink and gold, this
work has a stark elegance causing it to stand out among
Shōhin's works in the plant genre. The subject is the lotus,
a plant heavily laden with Buddhist symbolism. Because it
grows up from the mud at the bottom of ponds and
blossoms into a beautiful flower upon reaching the surface,
the lotus came to be used as a metaphor for enlightenment.
Shōhin referred to the special meaning of the lotus in her
short inscription: "Beyond comparison, it ranks highest
among the immortals."

It may seem surprising that a freely rendered ink
painting could be so naturalistic, but obviously, Shōhin has
carefully observed the way a lotus grows and bends.
Flowers are shown at various stages of blossoming, and the
leaves are also depicted in different positions. Shōhin's
manipulation of the wetly inked brush and the "boneless"
technique here are masterful. The varied tonalities of ink
truly give the impression of three-dimensionality, as well
as being satisfying as an abstract play of light areas
contrasting with dark. Shōhin brushed lines of black ink
on the leaves for veins, and then sparingly overlaid them
with gold. Gold lines have also been used to show
striations within the flower petals, and a light gold wash
was brushed over the surrounding empty silk, enhancing
the subtleties of the ink brushwork.

87. Noguchi Shōhin

Mountains in Autumn, 1910
Hanging scroll, ink and colors on silk, 204.5 x 86.4 cm.
Signature: Shōhin Joshi Chika
Seals: Chōsei kakei; Noguchi Chika in; Shōhin Joshi; Shunjū
ta kahi
Philadelphia Museum of Art: Gift of Ralph E. Balestrieri
Published: Frederick Baekeland, *Imperial Japan: The Art of
the Meiji Era* (Ithaca, New York: Herbert F. Johnson
Museum of Art, Cornell University, 1980), no. 32.

Painted ten years before her death, *Mountains in
Autumn* represents the height of Shōhin's achievements in
the realm of landscape. The composition is rich in detail,
featuring refined brushwork and a sophisticated design.
Although she seems to have studied with Hine Taizan for
only two years, the brush methods Shōhin utilized forty
years later still show traces of his influence. In particular,
she learned from Taizan a system of texturing by
methodically building up areas of repeated small
brushstrokes to recreate rock surfaces, mountain foliage,
and trees. Shōhin composed this landscape almost entirely
of ink, using light washes of green and red color for the
pine trees and foliage.

Shōhin was especially fond of representing a group of
venerable pine trees in the foreground, above which rise
majestic mountains. This landscape is made even more
interesting by the unusual rock formation dominating the
center of the composition. Shōhin occasionally painted
actual views, but most of her landscapes are idealized
mountainscapes like this, culled from her imagination.
Frequently there is a reference to the scholarly lifestyle;
looking inside the hut in the lower foreground we can see
books and a scroll lying on the table. No figures are
present, but one suspects they are sitting in some secluded
spot, imbibing tea and absorbing the natural beauty of the
surroundings. Shōhin's poem further describes the scene:

A waterfall flows in amongst the trees
    and gushes forth again,
The cliffs and rocks have a lingering purity.
With maple leaves as vivid as brocade,
The autumn mountains return to their bright luster.

88. Noguchi Shōhin, Okuhara Seiko, and others

Collaboration of Paintings and Poems, 1896-1902
Hanging scroll, ink and colors on silk, 129.5 x 37.2 cm.
Private collection

Collaborative works like this scroll were common in the late Edo and Meiji periods, often the creative outcome of *bunjin* gatherings. This example features contributions by twenty-three different artists. Although some joint endeavors were produced at one sitting, this example seems to have been done over a period of several years for a Mr. Ryūtei.[33] The irregularly shaped sections were marked off ahead of time, and selected artists and poets requested to paint or write something within. The alternation between calligraphy and painting and the asymmetrical layout of the individual sections result in an aesthetically pleasing abstract design.

The title "Good Taste" was inscribed in the upper right-hand corner. Of special interest are the contributions of three women artists, including Shōhin and Seiko. Seiko painted two Chinese-looking sages (Cat. 88a), and above them added the following couplet:

> Eyes open wide to the colors of the tall mountains,
> Ears listen to the sound of the flowing waters.

Shōhin brushed a clump of lilac blossoms (Cat. 88b), also adding a couplet in Chinese:

> Concentrated dew opens the young stamens,
> Wind gently scatters their subtle fragrance.

A third female artist, Nakabayashi Seishuku (died 1912), painted the branch of plum blossoms extending leftward near the middle of the composition. The daughter of the famous *bunjinga* artist Nakabayashi Chikutō, Seishuku never achieved the fame of Shōhin and Seiko, but was still highly regarded as a painter of plum blossoms. The fact that three women artists were invited to contribute to this collaboration is proof that they were fully integrated into the art world of their time.

a.

b.

Notes

1. By 1897 the rate of elementary school attendance was more than fifty percent for girls and more than eighty percent for boys; by the end of the Meiji era in 1912 the rate was ninety-eight percent for girls and ninety-nine percent for boys. See Robins-Mowry, *The Hidden Sun: Women of Modern Japan*, 40.

2. For further information on Higuchi Ichiyō's life and work, see Robert Lyons Danly, *In the Shade of Spring Leaves* (New Haven, Conn.: Yale University Press, 1981).

3. Founded by Iwamoto Zenji. The name was later changed to *Bungakkai* (Literary World).

4. The most comprehensive book regarding Seiko's life is Fujikake Shizuya's *Okuhara Seiko gashū*. Unless otherwise noted, the biographical information in this chapter was drawn from this source.

5. Suiseki originally lived and worked in Edo, but he eventually moved to the domain of Koga where he had many friends and patrons.

6. For illustrations of some of Seiko's copies of Chinese paintings, see Yamanouchi Chōzō, "Okuhara Seiko no gagyō to funpon," *Nihon nanga shi*, 400-401.

7. After Seiko left Koga, she seems to have severed ties with Suiseki. It is believed that as Seiko matured into a young woman, Suiseki became infatuated and confessed his feelings to her. When Seiko ignored him, Suiseki supposedly got bolder–in anger she pushed him off the second floor of his studio, after which she fled, never to see him again.

8. The stature of some of these men attracted other *bunjin* to visit Koga, including Ōtsuki Bankei (1801-1878), Fukuda Hankō (1804-1864), and Okamoto Shūki (1807?-1862).

9. The younger sister of Seiko's father, wife of the samurai Okuhara Genzaemon.

10. These included Seki Sekkō (1827-1877), Fukushima Ryūho (1820-1889), Inose Tōnei (1829-1910), and Suzuki Gako (1816-1870), who were referred to collectively as the "Shitaya literati."

11. Those in attendance were Ōnuma Chinzan, Suzuki Shōtō (1823-1898), Seki Sekkō, Uemura Roshū (1830-1885), Takasai Tanzan (died 1890), Yamanouchi Kōkei (1843-?), Matsuoka Kansui (1830-1887), Suzuki Gako, Sakada Ōkaku (d. circa 1881), Fukushima Ryūho, and Hattori Hanzan (1827-1894).

12. There are two theories regarding the adoption of this name. One is that she borrowed the characters from the name of the visiting Chinese artist Fei Ch'ing-hu (J: Hi Seiko, d. circa 1793). The other is that in her youth, although her name was officially Setsuko, she was nicknamed Seiko.

13. The government seems to have anguished over whether or not to put a stop to women cutting their hair.

14. Her two most famous pupils were women, Seisui (mentioned earlier) and Watanabe Seiran (1855-1918), the latter of whom began to study around 1870. Among Seiko's pupils were also geisha.

15. Although Tenshin turned away from *bunjinga*, he remained friends with Seiko throughout her life, writing her letters and poems.

16. Not having the appropriate formal wear, she bought a new kimono for the event. It was a rainy day and Seiko was not used to wearing formal kimono. She found it very awkward and slipped while walking in the imperial garden, falling into the mud. The attendant asked if someone should be sent to her residence to fetch another robe, but Seiko replied that she did not have another. She then removed her wet clothes, which were washed and dried in time for her to meet the empress.

17. Washizu Kidō (1825-1882), Konagai Shoshū (1829-1888), Ichikawa Ban'an (1807-1877), and Kawakami Tōgai (1827-1881).

18. Maeda Handen (1817-1878), Tani Tesshin (1820-1905), Okamoto Kōseki (1811-1898), Yamanaka Shinten'ō (1823-1885), Itakura Kaidō (died 1879), Nakanishi Kōseki (1813-1884), Murata Kōkoku (1830-1912), and Tomioka Tessai (1836-1924).

19. Saitama Kenritsu Hakubutsukan, *Tokubetsu ten: Okuhara Seiko ten zuroku*, 90.

20. She named her new residence Shūbutsusōdō, but later changed the name to Shūsuisōdō after she had a tributary of running water created to run through her compound.

21. The best sources of information on Shōhin's life are the articles by Moriya Masahiko and the exhibition catalogue, *Noguchi Shōhin ten zuroku* published by the Yamanashi Kenritsu Bijutsukan. Shōhin's daughter, Noguchi Iku (Shōkei), wrote two essays about her mother, and also collected articles from a number of people who had known Shōhin which she had privately published under the title *Watashi no haha*.

22. An artist of the Shijō school, also known by the names of Tsunuga and Higashiyama.

23. Shōhin's circumstances are similar to those experienced by the Meiji woman writer, Higuchi Ichiyō. Because her father died when she was seventeen, Ichiyō was expected to support her mother and younger sister. At that point she considered writing fiction and selling it, and went on to become a well-known novelist.

24. While in Tsu, she became an artist-in-residence for the feudal lord Tōdō. See *Noguchi Shōhin nenpu*, 27.

25. There is some confusion as to exactly when she began to study with Taizan. See Moriya, "Noguchi Shōhin kenkyū," 2-3.

26. Brown and Hirota, *Diary of Kido Takayoshi*, vol. 1, li. Shōhin is mentioned frequently in Kido's diaries.

27. "Gajin no shōgai wa ita no ma no rakusho yori hajimaru," *Noguchi Shōhin ten zuroku*.

28. Noguchi Shōkei, *Watashi no haha*, 19.

29. Quoted in Japanese in Noguchi, *Watashi no haha*, 17-18.

30. In that same month, Seiran painted a handscroll depicting Seiko's long journey to the Hasegawa home, a section of which appears in Figure 17.

31. For background on *sencha*, see Cat. 72.

32. The brushwork is similar to a *bijin* painting in the Noguchi Collection that is recorded as having been done at the age of eighteen or nineteen.

33. Several of the paintings and poems are dated, the years ranging from 1896-1902.

Conclusion

Two controversial issues inevitably arise in any discussion of Japanese women artists. First, was there a "women's style?" Japanese scholars are fond of saying that art by women has a peculiarly effeminate quality, using such descriptive terms as *joseiteki* (feminine) or *josei rashii* (womanlike). However, I believe that these terms are inaccurate, and would argue that stylistically, artworks by Japanese women are essentially no different than those by Japanese men working in the same school in the same era. This is not surprising since in almost all cases, women artists studied with men. Following Japanese tradition, all students learned and mastered the style of their teachers, gradually evolving their own personal characteristics. Works by Japanese women can frequently be identified because the characters equivalent to Miss or Mrs. appear in their signatures. If one were to cover up the signatures, however, in most cases I do not believe that one could determine whether the artist was male or female. Furthermore, the tremendous range of creativity seen in the works presented here should negate any notions of a "women's style."

With regard to subject matter, women generally painted the same subjects as did men, following the school or tradition with which they were affiliated. However, there is evidence that some women were attracted to certain subjects because of their feminine sensibilities. For example, Kiyohara Yukinobu painted a larger percentage of female figural subjects than did male Kano school artists. It is not clear if this was due to Yukinobu's personal choice; she may have been responding to the wishes of patrons who enjoyed the novelty of having a female subject painted by a woman. One of the rare works in the exhibition which depicts a subject unlikely to have been painted by a man is Cat. 82. The artist, Noguchi Shōhin, painted a female in a setting that would traditionally have included a male *bunjin*. It may in fact be a kind of self-portrait, although it is not inscribed as such.

A second issue concerns the contribution of women to the history of Japanese art. If their work was as significant as that by contemporary males, why haven't women been integrated more than occasionally into exhibitions and literature on art? The answer involves social rather than art history. Until the late nineteenth century, Japanese women were generally discouraged from assuming leadership roles; cautioned not to make outward displays of their talents, they were held back from doing anything radically new or creating works that would challenge the artistic norms. These societal pressures can be sensed in traditional Japanese biographies of women artists, which stress the gentle, virtuous nature of their subjects. If women were married, authors were quick to point out their faithfulness as wives, and if unmarried or widowed, their modesty. These commentaries were obviously colored by descriptions of the "proper" female in moral instruction books like the *Onna daigaku*. Lest readers think that by being artists these women were frivolously indulging themselves, biographers justified their status by emphasizing their virtuous conduct and industriousness, obscuring their contributions to art history.

Because of the persisting Confucian image of women in secondary roles, female artists have continued to be neglected by most Japanese. Traditionally, women were not thought of as individuals, but in terms of their relationships (wife, sister, daughter) to men. The Japanese woman artist who is most well-known today, Ike Gyokuran, achieved recognition in large part because she was the wife of a famous painter. In both China and Japan, art appreciation has often been connected to the status of the individual and not based on the quality of the art itself. There are other women artists whose works are equal in quality to Gyokuran's, but they are still virtually unknown.

Although their names are rarely included in modern art historical texts, there is evidence that in their own day women artists were recognized and to some extent integrated into the artistic world in Japan. In Edo- and Meiji-period Who's Who types of publications and biographical dictionaries of artists, women were usually listed alongside men.[1] We have seen that many women earned the plaudits of their peers and became important figures in both literary and artistic circles. One of the justifications for this exhibition is that women have been overlooked by later scholars, and consequently there is very little understanding of how they fit into the history of Japanese art. A few women artists have been studied as individuals in recent years, but as a group they have not yet been a subject of focused inquiry either in Japan or the West. No one denies the importance of women in Japanese literature, but until now there has not been a corresponding appreciation of women in the visual arts.

Having surveyed nearly one hundred artworks by selected Japanese women, we have seen a more rich and complex world emerge than might have been imagined. In the designated three-hundred-year period, women artists came from diverse segments of society, worked in many different schools and traditions, and created artworks displaying a wide range of styles. The sheer number of women who actively produced art is impressive, even though they represent a very small fraction of the artists active during this period.[2] It is unrealistic to expect that they would generate as many major masters as male artists who numbered in the thousands. Yet women explored fully whatever creative outlets were open to them, making imaginative, individual contributions within established traditions. Ranging from the elegant *waka* of Ono Ozū to the "wild cursive" script of the prodigy Okon, from the dramatic prints of Kakuju-jo to the sensitive pottery of Rengetsu, and from the evocative *haiga* of Chiyo to the vibrant literati landscapes of Seiko, the ultimate significance of women artists lies in the richness and diversity they added to Japanese art. By omitting them, the total is diminished. It is hoped that this exhibition and catalogue will help to rectify an incomplete view of Japanese art history.

Notes
1. A few books, like the *Gajō yōryaku*, list women in a special category of female artists.
2. For example, Ichikawa's dictionary of Edo-period female calligraphers, *Kinsei joryū shodō meika shi den*, contains biographies of 264 women.

Bibliography

General

Ackroyd, Joyce. "Women in Feudal Japan." *Transactions of the Asiatic Society of Japan*, Third Series, vol. 7 (1959): 31-68.

Aida Hanji. *Kinsei joryū bunjin den*. Tokyo: Meiji Shoin, 1960.

Akagi Shizuko. *Nihon shi sho hyakka*. Vol. 2, *Josei*. Tokyo: Kondō Shuppansha, 1977.

Akai Tatsurō, ed. *Nikuhitsu ukiyo-e*, vols. 2, 7, 9. Tokyo: Shūeisha, 1982-1983.

Akamatsu Bunjirō, ed. *Unge Shōnin ikō*. Nakatsu: Gochōkaku, 1933.

Asaoka Okisada. *Koga bikō*. 16 vols. Tokyo: Kōbunkan, 1904.

Ban Kōkei. *Kinsei kijin den*. Kyoto: 1790. Reprint. Vol. 202 of *Tōyō bunko* series. Tokyo: Heibonsha, 1940.

Beard, Mary R. *The Force of Women in Japanese History*. Washington, D.C.: Public Affairs Press, 1953.

Beasley, W. G. *The Modern History of Japan*. New York: Frederick A. Praeger, 1963.

Blacker, Carmen. *The Japanese Enlightenment: A Study of the Writings of Fukuzawa Yukichi*. Cambridge, Mass.: Cambridge University Press, 1964.

Brown, Sidney Devere and Akiko Hirota, trans. *The Diary of Kido Takayoshi*. 3 vols. Tokyo: University of Tokyo Press, 1983-1985.

Conroy, Hilary, Sandra T.W. Davis, and Wayne Patterson, eds. *Japan in Transition: Thought and Action in the Meiji Era, 1868-1912*. London and Toronto: Associated University Presses, 1984.

Dalby, Liza. *Geisha*. Berkeley: University of California Press, 1983.

Deutsch, Sanna Saks and Howard A. Link. *The Feminine Image: Women of Japan*. Honolulu: Honolulu Academy of Arts, 1985.

Dore, R.P. *Education in Tokugawa Japan*. Berkeley: University of California Press, 1965.

Earl, David Magarey. *Emperor and Nation in Japan*. Seattle: University of Washington Press, 1964.

Enchi Fumiko. *Jinbutsu Nihon no josei shi*. Vol. 10, *Edoki josei no ikikata*. Tokyo: Shūeisha, 1977.

Enchi Fumiko. *Nihon josei shi jiten*. Tokyo: Sanseidō, 1984.

Fister, Patricia. "Women Artists in Traditional Japan." In *Women in the History of Chinese and Japanese Painting*, edited by Marsha Weidner. Honolulu: University of Hawaii Press. Forthcoming.

Funatsu Katsuo. "Kinsei ni okeru jukyōteki josei ron no tenkai to seikaku." *Aiizumi Joshi Tanki Daigaku kiyō*, no. 10 (1975): 1-23.

Furuya Tsunatake. "Meiji Women: Landmarks They Have Left." *Japan Quarterly*, no. 14 (July-September 1967): 318-325.

Hanasaki Kazuo, ed. *Zue Edo onna hyaku sugata*. Tokyo: Miki Shobō, 1976.

Huber, Thomas M. *The Revolutionary Origins of Modern Japan*. Stanford: Stanford University Press, 1981.

Ichikawa Genzō (vols. 1 and 3) and Miwata Gendō (vol. 2), eds. *Nihon josei bunka shi*. 3 vols. Tokyo: Zenkoku Kōtō Gakkō Chō Kyōkai, 1938-1939.

Iizuka Beiu. *Nihonga taisei*. 36 vols. Tokyo: Tōhō Shoin, 1931-1934.

Ikeda Tsunetaro. *Nihon shoga kotto daijiten*. Tokyo: Seikōkan, 1929.

Inoue Kazuo, ed. *Ukiyo-e shi den*. Tokyo: Watanabe Hangaten, 1931.

Irokawa Daikichi. *The Culture of the Meiji Period*. Translation edited by Marius B. Jansen. Princeton: Princeton University Press, 1985.

Ishikawa Matsutarō. *Onna daigaku shū*. Vol. 302 of *Tōyō bunko* series. Tokyo: Heibonsha, 1977.

Itabashi Kuritsu Bijutsukan. *Josei gaka: Onna no shiki utau*. Tokyo: Itabashi Kuritsu Bijutsukan, 1986.

Japanese Women's Commission for the World's Columbia Exposition. *Japanese Women*. Chicago: A.C. McClurg and Co., 1893.

Josei Shi Sōgō Kenkyū Kai. *Nihon josei shi*. Vol. 3, *Kinsei*. Tokyo: Tokyo Daigaku Shuppan Kai, 1982.

Josei Shi Sōgō Kenkyū Kai. *Nihon josei shi kenkyū bunken mokuroku*. Tokyo: Tokyo Daigaku Shuppan Kai, 1983. (A comprehensive bibliography of materials related to women's studies in Japan)

Kodama Naganari, ed. *Teisō setsugi kokin meifu hyakushu*. Tokyo: 1881.

Koh Hesung Chun, ed. *Korean and Japanese Women: An Analytic Bibliographical Guide*. Westport, Conn.: Greenwood Press, 1982.

Kōsaka Masaaki, ed. *Japanese Thought in the Meiji Era*. Translated and adapted by David Abosch. Tokyo: Pan-Pacific Press, 1958.

Koyama, Takashi. *The Changing Social Position of Women in Japan*. Paris: United Nations Educational, Scientific and Cultural Organization, 1961.

Kyoto Shinbunsha. *Miyako ni moeta onna*. Kyoto: Kyoto Shinbunsha, 1974.

Lebra, Joyce, Joy Paulson, and Elizabeth Powers, eds. *Women in Changing Japan*. Boulder: Westview Press, 1976.

Madden, Maude Whitmore. *Women of the Meiji Era*. New York: Fleming H. Revell, 1919.

Mainichi Shinbunsha. *Josei no shoga meisaku ten*. No. 46 of *Nihon bijutsu* series. Tokyo: Mainichi Shinbunsha, 1964.

Mikuma Katen and Ban Kōkei. *Zoku kinsei kijin den*. Kyoto: 1798. Reprint. Vol. 202 of *Tōyō bunko* series. Tokyo: Heibonsha, 1940.

Mizue Renko. *Kinsei shi no naka no onnatachi*. Tokyo: Nihon Hōsō Shuppan Kyōkai, 1983.

Mori Senzō, ed. *Kinsei jinmei roku shūsei*. 5 vols. Tokyo: Benseisha, 1978.

Mori Senzō. *Mori Senzō chosaku shū*. 13 vols. Tokyo: Chūōkōronsha, 1971.

Morosawa Yōko. *Onna no rekishi*. 2 vols. Tokyo: Matsuraisha, 1970.

Nagoya Jōhakukaisai Iinkai. *Tokubetsu ten: Edo jidai no onnatachi*. Nagoya: Nagoya Jōhakukaisai Iinkai, 1984.

Naruse Jinzō. "The Education of Japanese Women." In *Fifty Years of New Japan*, edited by Ōkuma Shigenobu, vol. 2. London: Smith, Elder, and Co., 1909.

Nihon Ukiyo-e Kyōkai. *Genshoku ukiyo-e dai hyakka jiten*. Tokyo: Daishukkan Shoten, 1982.

Okamoto Ryōichi and Kinoshita Masao. *Nyonin shofu*. Tokyo: Shinshindō, 1983.

Passin, Herbert. *Society and Education in Japan*. New York: Columbia University Press, 1965.

Paul, Diana Y. *Women in Buddhism*. Berkeley: University of California Press, 1985.

Robins-Mowry, Dorothy. *The Hidden Sun: Women of Modern Japan*. Boulder: Westview Press, 1983.

Rubinger, Richard. *Private Academies of Tokugawa Japan*. Princeton: Princeton University Press, 1982.

Ruiju denki dai Nihon shi. Vol. 15, *Josei hen*. Tokyo: Yūzankaku Shuppan Kabushiki-gaisha, 1981.

Sawada Fujiko. *Hana kagari*. Tokyo: Jitsugyō no Nihonsha, 1985.

Seki Tamiko. *Edo kōki no joseitachi*. Tokyo: Tsuki Shobō, 1980.

Shiga Tadashi. "Historical View of the Education of Women Before the Time of Meiji." *Education in Japan: Journal for Overseas* (International Educational Research Institute, Hiroshima University), vol. 6 (1971): 1-14.

Shirai Kayō. *Gajō yōryaku*. 2 vols. Naniwa (Osaka): 1831.

Sōga Tetsufu, ed. *Zusetsu jinbutsu Nihon no josei shi*. Vol. 7, *Edoki josei no bi to gei* and vol. 8, *Hōken josei no aikan*. Tokyo: Shōgakukan, 1980.

Tai Yūkiko. *Nihon no josei shi*. Vol. 5, *Edo jo hyakkabu*. Tokyo: Kaishobō, 1980.

Takaishi Shingoro. *Women and Wisdom of Japan*. London: John Murray, 1905. (Contains translation of the *Onna daigaku* by Kaibara Ekken)

Takamure Itsue. *Dai Nihon josei jinmei jisho*. Tokyo: Kōseikaku, 1942. Reprint. Tokyo: Shinjinbutsu Ōraisha, 1980.

Toda Kenji. *Descriptive Catalogue of Japanese and Chinese Illustrated Books in the Ryerson Library of the Art Institute of Chicago*. Chicago: 1931.

Tsubota Itsuo, ed. *Nihon josei no rekishi*, nos. 1, 2, 4, and 6. Tokyo: Gyō Kyōiku Tosho Kabushiki-gaisha, 1982.

Ukiyo-e taisei. 12 vols. Tokyo: Tōhō Shoin, 1930-1931.

Umezawa Seiichi. "Keishū sakka." In *Nihon nanga shi*, 880-893. Tokyo: Nanyōdō, 1919.

Yoshida Teruji. *Ukiyo-e jiten*. 3 vols. Tokyo: Gabundō, 1965-1971.

Calligraphy

Hanawa Taneko. "Josei to shodō bunka: Edo jidai." *Sho no tomo*, no. 6:13: 14-19.

Ichikawa Tarō. *Kinsei joryū shodō meika shi den*. Tokyo: Kyōiku Shuppansha, 1935.

Kabushiki-gaisha Daiichi Shuppan Center. *Nihon shodō taikei*. Vol. 7, *Edo/Meiji/Taishō*. Tokyo: Kōdansha, 1972.

Komatsu Shigemi. *Nihon shoryū zenshi*. 2 vols. Tokyo: Kōdansha, 1970.

Komatsu Shigemi, ed. *Nihon shoseki taikan*. 25 vols. Tokyo: Kōdansha, 1978-1980.

Maeda Toshiko. "Josei no sho." *Sho no Nihon shi*. Vol. 6, *Edo*, 77-84. Tokyo: Heibonsha, 1975.

Maeda Toshiko. *Nyonin no sho*. Tokyo: Kōdansha, 1974.

Women and Literature

Fukui Kyūzō. *Kinsei waka shi*. Tokyo: Seibidō Shoten, 1930.

Furutani Chishin, ed. *Edo jidai joryū bungaku zenshū*. 4 vols. Tokyo: Nihon Tosho Center, 1979.

Furutani Chishin, ed. *Joryū bungaku zenshū*. 4 vols. Tokyo: Bungei Shoin, 1918.

Imai Kuniko, ed. *Nihon joryū bungaku hyōron*. Tokyo: Echigoya Shobō, 1943.

Inoguchi Atsushi. *Josei to kanshi: Wakan joryū shishi*. Tokyo: Kasama Shoin, 1978.

Joshi Gakushūin. *Joryū chosaku kaidai*. Tokyo: Nihon Tosho Center, 1978.

Kamitsuki Otohiko. "Genroku no yon haijo." In *Nihon josei no rekishi*, edited by Tsubota Itsuo. Vol. 1, *Edo to Kamigata no onna*, 62-65. Tokyo: Gyō Kyōiku Tosho Kabushiki-gaisha, 1982.

Katsumine Shinpū. *Keishū haika zenshū*. Tokyo: Shūeikaku, 1922.

Kawashima Tsuyu. *Joryū haijin*. Tokyo: Meiji Shoin, 1957.

Kikuchi Gozan. *Gozandō shiwa*. Edo (Tokyo): 1807.

Mori Keizō. *Kinsei joryū kajin no kenkyū*. Tokyo: Shirōtosha Shoya, 1935.

Mori Keizō. "Tokugawa jidai no joryū kajin." In *Nihon josei bunka shi*, edited by Miwata Gendō, vol. 2, 565-607. Tokyo: Zenkoku Kōtō Gakkō Chō Kyōkai, 1938-1939.

Nagasawa Mitsu, ed. *Nyonin waka taikei*. Tokyo: Kazama Shobō, 1968.

Nakamura Shinichirō. *Edo kanshi*. Tokyo: Iwanami Shoten, 1985.

Yamamoto Zentarō. "Tokugawa jidai no joryū haijin." In *Nihon josei bunka shi*, edited by Miwata Gendō, vol. 2, 611-659. Tokyo: Zenkoku Kōtō Gakkō Chō Kyōkai, 1938-1939.

Yokoyama Seiga, ed. *Josei haika shi*. Tokyo: Tōei Shobō, 1972.

Yoshida Seiichi, ed. *Nihon joryū bungaku shi*. Tokyo: Dōbun Shoin, 1969.

Women and Zen

Mori Ōkyō. *Kinko zenrin sōdan*. Tokyo: Zōkyō Shoin, 1919. Reprint. Kyoto: Zen Bunka Kenkyūjo, 1986.

Shimizu (Fueoka) Hōgan. *Bijin Zen*. Tokyo: Uchiushi Shuppansha, 1915. Reprint. Vol. 20, *Josei to Zen* of Zen series. Tokyo: Kokusho Kankō Kai, 1978.

Chiyo

Fudeuchi Yukiko. *Kaga no Chiyo*. Kanazawa: Hokkoku Shuppansha.

Maeda Toshiko. "Kaga no Chiyo." *Nihon bijutsu kōgei*, no. 417 (1973.6): 46-49.

Maeda Toshiko. "Kaga no Chiyo." In *Nyonin no sho*, 168-174. Tokyo: Kōdansha, 1974.

Maruyama Kazuhiko. "Kaga no Chiyo." In *Nihon joryū bungaku shi*, edited by Yoshida Seiichi, 90-104. Tokyo: Dōbun Shoin, 1969.

Matsutō Shi Chūō Toshokan. *Kaga no Chiyo sankō bunken shū*. Matsutō: 1985. (Contains a comprehensive bibliography of books and articles on Chiyo)

Murakami Genzō. "Kaga no Chiyo." In *Zusetsu jinbutsu Nihon no josei shi*, edited by Sōga Tetsufu. Vol. 7, *Edoki josei no bi to gei*, 53-68. Tokyo: Shōgakukan, 1980.

Nakamoto Jodō. *Chiyo-ni no issei*. Matsutō: Hakuzan Gansha, 1932.

Nakamoto Jodō. *Kaga no Chiyo kenkyū*. Kanazawa: Hokkoku Shuppansha, 1972.

Nakamoto Jodō. *Kaga no Chiyo shinseki shū*. Kanazawa: Hokkoku Shuppansha, 1966.

Nakamoto Jodō. *Kaga no Chiyo zenshū*. Kanazawa: Kaga no Chiyō Zenshū Kankō Kai, 1955.

Nakano Itsuki. *Chiyo-ni ihō*. Kanazawa: 1929.

Nakano Tōyū. *Kaga no Chiyo: Sono fukō to robanashi*. Kanazawa: Hokkoku Shuppansha, 1974.

Ogawa Ryōryō. *Chiyo-ni den*. Kanazawa: Ishikawa Ken Toshokan Kyōkai, 1956.

Sōma Gyofū. *Teishin to Chiyo to Rengetsu*. Tokyo: Shunshūsha, 1930.

Yamamoto Shihō. *Chiyo-ni nenpu*. Matsutō: 1959.

Yamanaka Rokuhiko. *Chiyo-jo to Kikusha-ni*. Kyoto: Jinbun Shoin, 1942.

Gion, Three Women of

Addiss, Stephen. "The Three Women of Gion." In *Women in the History of Chinese and Japanese Painting*, edited by Marsha Weidner. Honolulu: University of Hawaii Press. Forthcoming.

Fujita Tokutarō. "Gion no sansai jo." In *Nihon joryū bungaku hyōron*, edited by Imai Kuniko, 225-231. Tokyo: Echigoya Shobō, 1943.

Mori Senzō. "Taiga to Yuri." *Nanga kenkyū*, vol. 2, no. 9: 12-13.

Nonomura Katsuhide. "Gion no sansai jo." In *Nihon joryū bungaku shi*, edited by Yoshida Seiichi, 55-75. Tokyo: Dōbun Shoin, 1969.

Tadamura Hatsu, ed. *Gion sanjo waka shū*. Kyoto: Gion Furyū, 1910.

Watson, Burton, trans. "The Biography of Yuri" by Rai San'yō. In *Japanese Literature in Chinese*, vol. 2, 162-167. New York: Columbia University Press, 1976.

Gyokuran

Akatsuka Matajirō. "Gyokuran Joshi." *Shoga kottō zasshi*, no. 128: 4-6.

Hitomi Shōka. "Gyokuran." *Nanga kenkyū*, vol. 2, no. 9: 10-11.

Hitomi Shōka. "Taigadō fujin Gyokuran Joshi." *Tōei*, vol. 12, no. 3 (1936): 12-18.

Hitomi Shōka. "Taigadō o chūshin ni." *Ike Taiga kenkyū happyō*, no. 2 (1938): 12-27.

"Ike Gyokuran hitsu: Kikka zu." *Kokka*, no. 649 (April 1946): 329-331.

Maeda Toshiko. "Gyokuran: Keishū gajin no kakō." In *Nyonin no sho*, 175-180. Tokyo: Kōdansha, 1974.

Maeda Toshiko. "Ike Gyokuran: Keishū no gajin." *Nihon bijutsu kōgei*, no. 396: 58-61.

Matsushita Hidemaro. "Tokuyama Gyokuran." In *Ike Taiga*, 233-241. Tokyo: Shunshūsha, 1967.

Mizuo Hiroshi. "Ike Gyokuran hitsu: Kakei sansui zu." *Kokka*, no. 779 (February 1957): 65 and 70.

Narazaki Muneshige. "Gyokuran hitsu: Shiki sansui zu." *Kokka*, no. 758 (May 1955): 124-125 and 127.

Shimizu (Fueoka) Hōgan. "Gashu Zenshu: Ike no Gyokuran." In *Bijin Zen*, 112-118. Tokyo: Uchiushi Shuppansha, 1915.

Soeda Tatsumine. "Taigadō to Gyokuran Joshi." *Gajin kawa* (1928): 51-63.

Suzuki Susumu. "Taiga to Gyokuran." *Kobijutsu*, no. 44 (April 1974): 37-48.

Udaka Ōba. "Ike Taiga to Gyokuran." *Fude no tomo*, no. 249: 3-9.

Yoshizawa Chū. "Ike Gyokuran hitsu: Fūrin teisha zu." *Kokka*, no. 885 (December 1965): 20-21.

Kankan

"Bunchō, Kankan, Shun'ei kaku hitsu sanpukutsui sansui zu." *Kokka*, no. 644 (July 1944): 193-200.

Satake Eiryō. "Bunchō fujin Kankan Joshi." *Tōei*, vol. 12, no. 3 (1936): 19-20.

Kikusha

Kawada Jun, ed. *Kikusha-ni haiku zenshū*. Tokyo: Sara Shoten, 1937.

Yamanaka Rokuhiko. *Chiyo-jo to Kikusha-ni*. Kyoto: Jinbun Shoin, 1952.

Yamanaka Rokuhiko. "Kikusha-ni." In *Nihon josei bunka shi*, edited by Miwata Gendō, vol. 2, 663-691. Tokyo: Zenkoku Kōtō Gakkō Chō Kyōkai, 1938-1939.

Kōran

Fister, Patricia. "The Life and Art of Chō Kōran." In *Women in the History of Chinese and Japanese Painting*, edited by Marsha Weidner. Honolulu: University of Hawaii Press. Forthcoming.

Itō Shin. *Saikō to Kōran*. Gifu: Yabase Ryūkichi, 1969.

Itō Shin, ed. *Seigan zenshū*, vol. 5. Gifu: Yanagawa Seigan Zenshū Kankō Kai, 1958.

Itō Shin. *Yanagawa Seigan Ō*. Gifu: Yanagawa Seigan Ō Itoku Kenshō Kai, 1925.

Maeda Toshiko. "Yanagawa Kōran." *Nihon bijutsu kōgei*, no. 398 (1971.11): 46-49.

Matsushita Hidemaru. "Mino no futa meika." *Tōhō bungei*, no. 14 (1955): 9-10.

Nakamura Yōko. "Shijin Yanagawa Seigan to sono fujin Kōran." *Nihon bijutsu kōgei*, no. 254 (1959): 20-25.

Nanjō Norio. "Yanagawa Kōran." In *Zusetsu jinbutsu Nihon no josei shi*, edited by Sōga Tetsufu. Vol. 8, *Hōken josei no aikan*, 93-108. Tokyo: Shōgakukan, 1980.

Naramoto Tatsuya. "Kōran to Saikō." In *Nihon josei no rekishi*, edited by Tsubota Itsuo. No. 6, *Bakumatsu ishin no josei*, 50-52. Tokyo: Gyō Kyōiku Tosho Kabushiki-gaisha, 1982.

Naramoto Tatsuya, ed. "Yanagawa Kōran." In *Nihon shi no jinbutsu zō*, vol. 10, 234-252. Tokyo: Chikuma Shobō, 1967.

Ninchōji Seison. "Kōran mibōjin no shokan." *Kamigata*, no. 111 (1940): 138-141.

Ōgaki Shi Bunka Kaikan. *Ishin kaiten no senku ningen: Seigan--sono kiseki*. Ōgaki: Ōgaki Shi Bunka Kaikan, 1978.

Ōhara Tomie. *Nihon no tabibito*. Vol. 12, *Yanagawa Seigan/Kōran*. Kyoto: Tankōsha, 1973.

Reizan Kenshō Kai. *Ishin no michi: Gifu*, no. 2 (1984.3).

Soeda Tatsumine. "Ema Saikō to Yanagawa Kōran." *Tōei*, vol. 12, no. 3 (1936): 21-24.

Soeda Tatsumine. "Yanagawa Seigan to Kōran Joshi." *Gajin kawa* (1928): 149-162.

Tōkari Soshinan. "Seigan fusai no tegami." *Atorie*, vol. 15, no. 5 (1938): 24-27.

Tominaga Chōjo. *Mino Ōgaki no senken*, 36-68. Ōgaki: 1979.

Tominaga Chōjo. *Seigan zenshū*, vol. 4. Gifu: 1958.

Ōhashi

Shimizu (Fueoka) Hōgan. "Daishi ichiban daikatsu gensei: Yūjo Ōhashi." In *Bijin Zen*, 172-185. Tokyo: Uchiushi Shuppansha, 1915.

Ōi

Edo Tatsuo. "Katsushika Ōi no seishi ni tsuite." *Ukiyo-e geijutsu*, no. 47 (1976): 33-34.

Hayashi Yoshikazu. *Enpon kenkyū: Oei to Eisen*. Tokyo: Arimitsu Shobō, 1967.

Iijima Hanjūrō. *Katsushika Hokusai den*, vol. 2, 61-65. Tokyo: Kobayashi Bunshichi, 1893.

Sekine Shisei. *Ukiyo-e hyakka den*, 110-112. Tokyo: 1925.

Yamaguchi Genshu. "Katsushika Ei-jo." *Tōei*, vol. 12, no. 5 (1936): 33-36.

Yasuda Gōzō. "Hokusai no musume: Oiei-jo." *Ukiyo-e*, no. 86 (1981): 32-44.

Okon

Fister, Patricia. "Tōkai Okon." *Calligraphy Idea Exchange*, vol. 3, no. 4 (Summer 1986): 26-33.

Mimura Seizaburō. "Tōkai Kon-jo." *Sho no tomo*, vol. 8, no. 1: 29-31.

Ozū (Otsū)

Iwahashi Koiyata. "Ono Otsū shū den." *Rekishi chiri*, no. 37:1-4 (1921): 67-74.

Komatsu Shigemi, ed. "Ono Ozū." In *Nihon shoseki taikan*, vol. 13, no. 34, pls. 105-109. Tokyo: Kōdansha, 1979.

Komatsu Shigemi. *Nihon shoryū zenshi*, vol. 1, 722-726; vol. 2, pls. 591-597. Tokyo: Kōdansha, 1970.

Maeda Toshiko. "Ono Otsū." *Nihon bijutsu kōgei*, no. 389 (1971): 42-45.

Maeda Toshiko. "Ono Otsū." In *Nyonin no sho*, 96-103. Tokyo: Kōdansha, 1974.

Soda Kōichi. "Ono Otsū to Jōruri monogatari." In *Nihon josei no rekishi*, edited by Tsubota Itsuo. No. 4, *Sengoku jidai no josei*, 104-106. Tokyo: Gyō Kyōiku Tosho Kabushiki-gaisha, 1982.

Sudō Motome. *Ono Otsū*. Tokyo: 1917. This book was reprinted as an article in *Teikoku bungaku*, vol. 12:12 (1906): 3-21.

Yanagida Kunio. "Ono Otsū." *Bungaku*, vol. 7, no. 5 (1939): 583-604.

Raikin

Aimi Kōu. "Kō Fuyō to Raikin." *Nanga kenkyū*, no. 2:8-10.

Rengetsu

Akai Tatsurō. "Ōtagaki Rengetsu." In *Nihon bunka*. Vol. 3, *Kinsei no gaka*. Tokyo: Kadokawa Shoten, 1976.

Bi to kōgei, no. 160. Kyoto: Kyoto Shoin, 1970.

Bokubi, no. 103 (1961.1).

Fister, Patricia. "Ōtagaki Rengetsu." *Calligraphy Idea Exchange*, vol. 4, no. 4 (Summer 1987): 15-21.

Iwahashi Kunie. "Ōtagaki Rengetsu." In *Zusetsu jinbutsu Nihon no josei shi*, edited by Sōga Tetsufu. Vol. 7, *Edoki josei no bi to gei*, 109-124. Tokyo: Shōgakukan, 1980.

Katagiri Akinori. "Ōtagaki Rengetsu." In *Nihon joryū bungaku shi*, edited by Yoshida Seiichi, 123-137. Tokyo: Dōbun Shoin, 1969.

Koresawa Kyōzō, Tanaka Junji, Tokuda Kōen, Mitsuoka Tadanari, and Murai Yasuhiko. *Rengetsu*. Tokyo: Kōdansha, 1971.

Kuroda Ryōji. "Rengetsu o kataru." *Tosetsu*, no. 9 (1961): 28-39.

Kyoto Furitsu Sōgō Shiryōkan. *Ōtagaki Rengetsu: Bakumatsu joryū kajin no shoga to tōgei*. Kyoto: Kyoto Furitsu Sōgō Shiryōkan, 1984.

Maeda Toshiko. *Bunjin shofu*. Vol. 11, *Rengetsu*. Kyoto: Tankōsha, 1979.

Maeda Toshiko. "Rengetsu-ni." *Nihon bijutsu kōgei*, no. 399 (1971.12): 64-67.

Maeda Toshiko. "Rengetsu-ni." In *Nyonin no sho*, 190-196. Tokyo: Kōdansha, 1974.

Murakami Sodō, ed. *Rengetsu-ni zenshū*. Kyoto: 1927. Reprint. Kyoto: Shibunkaku, 1980.

Sayama Susumu. "Ōtagaki Rengetsu no uta." In *Nihon joryū bungaku hyōron*, edited by Imai Kuniko, 301-308. Tokyo: Echigoya Shobō, 1943.

Shimizu (Fueoka) Hōgan. "Shinshin datsuraku." In *Bijin Zen*, 258-264. Tokyo: Uchiushi Shuppansha, 1915.

Sōma Gyofū. *Teishin to Chiyo to Rengetsu*. Tokyo: Shunshūsha, 1930.

Sugimoto Hidetarō. *Ōtagaki Rengetsu*. Kyoto: Tankōsha, 1976.

Sumi, vol. 44 (September 1983). Tokyo: Geijutsu Shinbunsha.

Tokuda Kōen. *Rengetsu-ni no shin kenkyū*. Kyoto: Sanmitsudō Shoten, 1958.

Tokuda Kōen. *Ōtagaki Rengetsu*. Tokyo: Kōdansha, 1982. (Contains a comprehensive bibliography of books and articles on Rengetsu)

Ubukata Tatsue. "Ōtagaki Rengetsu." In *Jinbutsu Nihon no josei shi*, edited by Enchi Fumiko, vol. 10, 73-96. Tokyo: Shūeisha, 1977.

Ubukata Tatsue. "Rengetsu-ni to Bōtō-ni." In *Nihon josei no rekishi*, edited by Tsubota Itsue. No. 6, *Bakumatsu ishin no josei*, 42-47. Tokyo: Gyō Kyōiku Tosho Kabushiki-gaisha, 1982.

Ryōnen

Addiss, Stephen. "The Zen Nun Ryonen Gensho (1646-1711)." *Spring Wind*, vol. 6, nos. 1, 2 and 3 (1986): 180-187.

Daishishi Kurin. "Ni Ryōnen." *Kansō*, vol. 22 (1924): 9-18.

Hasegawa Shigure. "Ryōnen-ni." *Denki*, 2/1 (1935): 52-57.

Komatsu Shigemi. *Nihon shoseki taikan*, vol. 20, no. 84. Tokyo: Kōdansha, 1979.

Mori Ōkyō. *Kinko zenrin sōdan*, 267-269. Tokyo: Zōkyō Shoin, 1919.

Mori Senzō. "Ryōnen-ni." In *Mori Senzō chosaku shū*, vol. 9, 217-238. Tokyo: Chūōkōronsha, 1971.

Nagata Tairyō. *Ōbaku Ryōnen-ni monogatari*. Kyoto: Wakō Insatsu Kabushiki-gaisha, 1984.

Nagata Tairyō, ed. *Shijitsu Ryōnen-ni*. Kyoto: Wakō Insatsu Kabushiki-gaisha, 1984.

Shimizu (Fueoka) Hōgan. "Shosan fūgai no koe: Ryōnen-ni." In *Bijin Zen*, 51-58. Tokyo: Uchiushi Shuppansha, 1915.

Ryū-jo

Ushiyama Mitsuru. "Yamazaki Ryū-jo kō." *Fusui bunko*, no. 6 (May 1933): 1-18.

Saikō

Ema Saikō. *Shōmu ikō*. Tokyo: 1872. Reprint. Ōgaki: Ōgaki Shi Bunka Zairyoku Kai, 1960.

Fujimori Seikichi. "Ema Saiko." In *Shirarezaru kisai tensai*, 249-276. Tokyo: Shunshūsha, 1965.

Fujimoto Giichi. "Ema Saikō." In *Zusetsu jinbutsu Nihon no josei shi*, edited by Sōga Tetsufu. Vol. 7, *Edoki josei no bi to gei*, 69-84. Tokyo: Shōgakukan, 1980.

Gifu Ken Rekishi Kyōiku Kenkyū Kai. "Kanbungaku no joryū shijin: Ema Saikō." In *Nōhi jinbutsu shi*. Gifu: 1985.

Hiroshima Kenritsu Bijutsukan. *Rai San'yō o chūshin to shita nanga ten*. Hiroshima: Hiroshima Kenritsu Bijutsukan, 1984.

Itō Shin. "Rai San'yō to Saikō Joshi." *Tōyō bunka*, nos. 30-34 (1926-1927).

Itō Shin. *Saikō to Kōran*. Gifu: Yabase Ryūkichi, 1969.

Kado Reiko. *Ema Saikō*. Tokyo: BOC Shuppanbu, 1979.

Kasugai Ryūdō. "Saikō Joshi to San'yō Sensei." *Fude no tomo*, no. 254: 1-3.

Konishi Shirō and Naramoto Tatsuya, eds. *Rai San'yō ten*. Tokyo: Ōtsuka Kōgeisha, 1982.

Matsui Yukiko. "Saikō to Kōran." In *Nishi Mino waga machi*, no. 52 (1981.9): 10-15.

Matsushita Hidemaro. "Mino no futa meika." *Tōhō bungei*, no. 14 (1955): 9-10.

Naramoto Tatsuya. "Kōran to Saikō." In *Nihon josei no rekishi*, edited by Tsubota Itsuo. No. 6, *Bakumatsu ishin no josei*, 50-52. Tokyo: Gyō Kyōiku Tosho Kabushiki-gaisha, 1982.

Ōgaki Shi Bunka Kaikan. *Ōgaki no senken ten: Ransai to Saikō*. Ōgaki: Ōgaki Shi Bunka Kaikan, 1979.

Soeda Tatsumine. "Ema Saikō to Yanagawa Kōran." *Tōei*, vol. 12, no. 3 (1936): 21-24.

Soeda Tatsumine. "San'yō to Saikō Joshi." *Gajin kawa* (1928): 115-132.

Tominaga Chōjo. *Mino Ōgaki no senken*, 70-94. Ōgaki: 1979.

Seiko

Fujikake Shizuya. "Meiji gadan no joketsu Okuhara Seiko." *Tōei*, vol. 12, no. 3 (1936): 29-31.

Fujikake Shizuya, ed. *Okuhara Seiko gashū*. Tokyo: Kōgeisha, 1933.

Fussa Shi Kyōdo Shiryōshitsu. *Keishū gaka: Okuhara Seiko*. Fussa: Fussa Shi Kyōiku Iinkai, 1985.

Inamura Ryōhei, ed. *Okuhara Seiko*. Tokyo: Seiko Shuppanbu, 1929.

Ishii Hakutei. "Okuhara Seiko." *Chūō bijutsu*, vol. 3, no. 7 (July 1917): 142-171.

Katsura Hidezumi. *Joketsu gaka: Okuhara Seiko*. Saitama Ginkō Kōhōbu Kōhō Tantō G.

Kawashima Junji. *Okuhara Seiko*. Tsuchiura: Chikunami Shorin, 1985.

Muramatsu Shōfu. "Okuhara Seiko." In *Honchō gajin den*, vol. 2, 369-413. Tokyo: Chūōkōronsha, 1941.

Saitama Kenritsu Hakubutsukan. *Tokubetsu ten: Okuhara Seiko ten zuroku*. Ōmiya: Saitama Kenritsu Hakubutsukan, 1978. (Contains a comprehensive bibliography of books and articles on Seiko)

Takami Yasusaburō. "Shūyō jidai no Okuhara Seiko." *Denki*, vol. 2, no. 6 (1935): 10-19.

Yamanouchi Chōzō. "Okuhara Seiko: Kanojo no ikikata to sakuhin." *Sansai*, no. 351 (November 1976): 44-57.

Yamanouchi Chōzō. "Okuhara Seiko no gagyō to funpon." In *Nihon nanga shi*, 395-408. Tokyo: Riru Shobō, 1981.

Shōgen

Komatsu Shigemi, ed. "Sasaki Shōgen." In *Nihon shoseki taikan*, vol. 19, no. 46. Tokyo: Kōdansha, 1979.

Komatsu Shigemi. "Shizuma ryū." In *Nihon shoryū zenshi*, vol. 1, 676-682. Tokyo: Kōdansha, 1970.

Yoneda Yatarō. "Shizuma ryū to karayō ni tsuite." *Shoron*, no. 11 (Autumn 1977): 137-158.

Shōhin

Atomi Gyokushi. "Shōhin-san no omoide." *Chūō bijutsu*, no. 3:4 (April 1917): 25-29.

Harada Heisaku. "Noguchi Shōhin." In *Bakumatsu Meiji kyōraku no gajintachi*, 179-188. Kyoto: Kyoto Shinbunsha, 1985.

Kosaka Shibata. "Noguchi Shōhin Joshi no geijutsu." *Chūō bijutsu*, no. 3:4 (April 1917): 23-25.

Moriya Masahiko. "Noguchi Shōhin kenkyū." *Yamanashi Kenritsu Bijutsukan kenkyū kiyō*, no. 3 (1981): 1-50.

Moriya Masahiko. "Noguchi Shōhin no inpu ho i." *Yamanashi Kenritsu Bijutsukan kenkyū kiyō*, no. 4 (1982): 60-68.

Noguchi Iku, ed. *Shōhin iboku shū*. 2 vols. Tokyo: Tokyo Bijutsu Kurabu, 1929.

Noguchi Iku. "Watashi no haha Noguchi Shōhin." *Tōei*, vol. 12, no. 3 (1936): 32-36.

"Noguchi Shōhin nenpu." *Chūō bijutsu*, no. 3:4 (April 1917): 27-29.

Noguchi Shōkei. *Watashi no haha*. 1929.

Yamanashi Kenritsu Bijutsukan. *Noguchi Shōhin ten zuroku*. Kōfu: Yamanashi Kenritsu Bijutsukan, 1982. (Contains a comprehensive bibliography of books and articles on Shōhin)

Shunsa

Ibaragi Kenritsu Rekishikan. *Mito no nanga*. Mito: Ibaragi Kenritsu Rekishikan, 1978.

Ogawa Tomoji. "Hayashi Jikkō-Tachihara Kyōsho to sono sakuhin." *Kobijutsu*, no. 61 (January 1982): 61-83.

Ōhashi Bishō. "Geien zatsuwa." *Kaiga sōshi*, no. 224 (1905): 15-16.

Saitō Ryūzō. "Mito no shi gajin." *Gasetsu*, no. 4: 53-62.

"Tachihara Shunsa hitsu kiku seki zu kai." *Kokka*, no. 588 (November 1939): 349-350 and 353.

Tobita Shūzan. "Tachihara Shunsa Joshi." *Tōei*, vol. 12, no. 3 (1936): 25-26.

Yukinobu

"Kiyohara Yukinobu hitsu naka, Sei Shōnagon, sayū uzura zu." *Kokka*, no. 605 (April 1941): 116-121.

"Kiyohara Yukinobu hitsu O Shō-kimi zu." *Kokka*, no. 597 (August 1940): 239.

Narazaki Muneshige. "Kiyohara Yukinobu hitsu nyōbo sanjūrokkasen zu." *Kokka*, no. 712 (July 1951): 253 and 255-256.

Narazaki Muneshige. "Yukinobu hitsu Yō Ki-hi zu." *Kokka*, no. 829 (April 1961): 144-146.

Soeda Tatsumine. "Onna Yukinobu no hanashi." *Tōei*, vol. 12, no. 3 (1936): 9-11.

"Yukinobu." *Kokka*, no. 63 (December 1894): 281.

Index

Lenders to the Exhibition

Asian Art Museum of San Francisco, The Avery Brundage Collection
Mary Baskett Gallery
Mr. and Mrs. Peter Brest
Mrs. Mary Griggs Burke
The Mary and Jackson Burke Foundation
Dr. and Mrs. George A. Colom
Ema Shōjirō
Hakutakuan Collection
Harvard University Art Museums (Arthur M. Sackler Museum)
Hasegawa Yoshikazu
Hirose Chōji
Ibaragi Kenritsu Rekishikan
Idemitsu Art Museum
Kato Shōshun
Estate of Louis Vernon Ledoux
Mr. and Mrs. Leighton R. Longhi
Los Angeles County Museum of Art
Marui Kenzaburō
Mizutani Ishinosuke
Mubōan Collection
Museum of Fine Arts, Boston
Museum of Fine Arts, Springfield, Massachusetts
Museum of Modern Art, Saitama, Japan
Nagoya City Museum
Nakagami Ryōta
Noguchi Chūzō
Otaka Fukutarō
Philadelphia Museum of Art
Private collections (The Hague, Japan, and the United States)
Prof. Dr. Med. Gerhard Pulverer
Robert Ravicz
Mr. and Mrs. William J. Rushton
The Shin'enkan Collection
Shōka Collection
Spencer Museum of Art
Tokuriki Collection
Yanagi Takashi

Photographs courtesy of respective lenders except Cat. Nos. 2, 10-11, 21-22, 25-29, 36, 38, 40-41, 44-45, 47, 49-57, 61, 69, 72, 74, 77-78, 82, 88 by Jon Blumb; Nos. 5, 31-32, 70, 73 by Otto E. Nelson; No. 12 by Isaäc Brussee; and Nos. 4, 7, 13 by Pollitzer, Strong & Meyer.